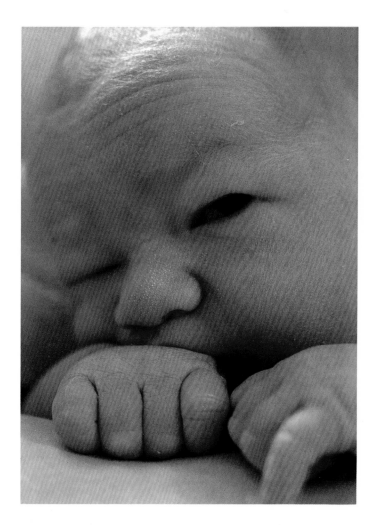

USA.
FRED WARD/
BLACK STAR

Children—

new generations—

are the best barometers

of the economic

and social conditions

on a continent.

WODAABE WOMAN
AND CHILD, NIGER.
CAROL BECKWITH,
FROM *NOMADS OF
NIGER*, PUBLISHED
BY HARRY N.
ABRAMS, INC., 1983

KUNA MOTHER AND
CHILD, GULF OF
URABÁ, COLOMBIA.
DANNY LEHMAN

They are the first to die,

      the first to be neglected,

the first to recover

      if things happen.

DR. ARNFRIED A. KIELMANN

JAPANESE FATHER
AND FIRST-BORN
SON AT A KITE
FESTIVAL.
DAVID ALAN
HARVEY/WOODFIN
CAMP, INC.

USA.
ELLIOTT ERWITT/
MAGNUM

GENERATIONS

A UNIVERSAL FAMILY ALBUM

EDITED BY ANNA R. COHN AND LUCINDA A. LEACH

INTRODUCTIONS BY SHEILA KITZINGER

Pantheon Books
New York

Smithsonian Institution Traveling Exhibition Service
Washington

This book was published to accompany *Generations,* the exhibition inaugurating the Smithsonian's International Gallery, September 1987.

Library of Congress Cataloging-in-Publication Data
Generations: a universal family album.

Published on the occasion of the exhibition *Generations,* organized by the Smithsonian Institution Traveling Exhibition Service to inaugurate the Smithsonian's International Gallery in September 1987
    1. Birth customs.   2. Childbirth.   3.Children.
4. Infants (Newborn).   I. Cohn, Anna R., 1950-
II. Leach, Lucinda A., 1955-   III. Kitzinger, Sheila. IV. Smithsonian Institution. Traveling Exhibition Service.
GT2460.G46   1987   392'.12   87-22250
ISBN 0-394-56562-2
ISBN 0-394-75741-6 (pbk.)

Acknowledgments of permission to reprint copyrighted material appear on page 316.

Manufactured in the United States of America
First Edition

KOREAN BABY SHOES OFTEN WERE TOO LARGE FOR SMALL FEET IN ORDER TO SYMBOLIZE GROWTH AND LONG LIFE (cat. 181).

CONTENTS

CHINESE SHOES
ORNAMENTED WITH
TIGER IMAGERY
THOUGHT TO PROTECT
THE WEARER FROM
DEMONS (cat. 183).

CHILDREN FROM
WEALTHIER FAMILIES
SPENT MUCH OF THEIR
INFANCY IN LONG
PETTICOATS THAT
TRAILED WELL OVER
THEIR FEET, COVERING
SILK AND SATIN SHOES
LIKE THESE (cat 174).

WHEN THESE SHOES WERE MADE, CHILDREN OFTEN WORE GROWN-UP STYLES TO CREATE THE APPEARANCE OF ADULT MATURITY (cat. 176).

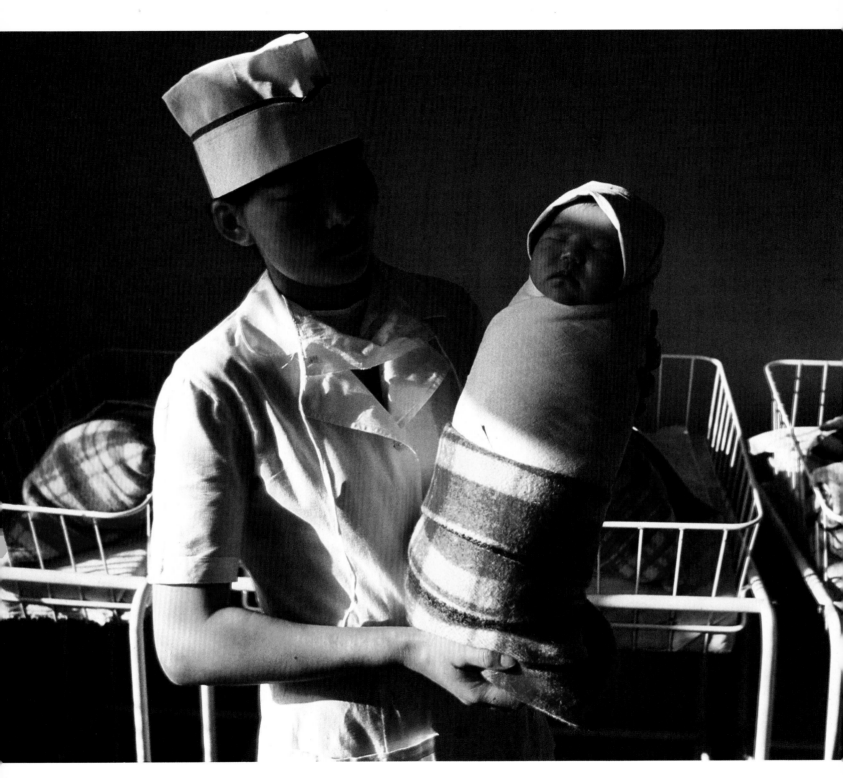

NURSERY, MONGOLIA. DEAN CONGER,

© 1986 NATIONAL GEOGRAPHIC SOCIETY

Aspirations may shape our vision of the future for new generations, but what realities will shape their lives? Prospects for the young vary widely in every corner of the world. Some will find privilege, while others will be born into environments with few opportunities. If we hope to prepare our children to meet the challenges of an ever-changing world, then we must show concern for their interaction with the natural, manmade, and family environment; their physical health and emotional well-being; their ability to survive a possible collapse of prevailing social or political systems; and their skills at meeting future needs and problems.

Generations is about the aspirations each of us holds for the young, the ways of life we hope they will continue, and the very real conditions they will inherit. We chose to explore these fundamental aspects of the human condition in the exhibition inaugurating the Smithsonian's International Gallery.

Generations is in keeping with a new commitment at the Smithsonian to utilize the Institution's international collections and curatorial expertise to communicate the interrelatedness of human societies. It is a unique, multidisciplinary investigation of the art and rituals associated with birth and cultural continuity. We hope it will foster a new generation of exhibition programs that will stimulate not only the eye and the mind, but also the conscience.

Robert McC. Adams
Secretary
Smithsonian Institution

GENERATIONS

AN EXHIBITION INAUGURATING THE SMITHSONIAN'S INTERNATIONAL GALLERY

EXHIBITION STAFF

Project Director
ANNA R. COHN

Exhibition Assistant
ELIZABETH S. PARKER

Curator of Collections
PRISCILLA RACHUN LINN

Curator of Ethnography
KRIS L. HARDIN

Curator of Photography and
Publication Coordinator
LUCINDA A. LEACH

Curator of Public Programs
CHERYL LaBERGE

Publications Director
ANDREA PRICE STEVENS

Text Editor
DAVID B. ANDREWS

AMERICANS WHO
COULD AFFORD THESE
ELABORATE SHOES FOR
THEIR CHILDREN TOOK
PRIDE IN BEING ABLE
TO KEEP UP WITH
EUROPEAN FASHION
(cat. 173).

CURATORIAL CONTENT GROUP

RICHARD E. AHLBORN, Curator
Division of Community Life, National Museum
of American History, Smithsonian Institution

MARY JO ARNOLDI, Curator
Department of Anthropology, National Museum
of Natural History, Smithsonian Institution

ANNA R. COHN, Project Director
Generations Exhibition

KRIS L. HARDIN, Assistant Professor
Department of Anthropology, University of
Pennsylvania

IVAN KARP, Curator
Department of Anthropology, National Museum
of Natural History, Smithsonian Institution

RICHARD KURIN, Deputy Director
Office of Folklife Programs, Smithsonian
Institution

CHERYL LaBERGE, Curator of Public Programs
Generations Exhibition

LUCINDA A. LEACH, Publication Coordinator
Generations Exhibition

PRISCILLA RACHUN LINN, Curator of
Collections, Generations Exhibition

BARBARA MELOSH, Curator
Division of Medical Sciences, National Museum
of American History, Smithsonian Institution

ELIZABETH S. PARKER, Assistant
Generations Exhibition

PAUL TAYLOR, Curator
Department of Anthropology, National Museum
of Natural History, Smithsonian Institution

CURATORIAL RESEARCH GROUP

LEONARD C. BRUNO, Senior Science Specialist
Library of Congress

ANNA R. COHN, Project Director
Generations Exhibition

RICHARD DANIEL De PUMA, Professor of Art
History, The University of Iowa

GRACE COHEN GROSSMAN, Curator of
Collections, Hebrew Union College Skirball
Museum

CHANG SU HOUCHINS, Curator of
Anthropology, National Museum of Natural
History, Smithsonian Institution

PRISCILLA RACHUN LINN, Curator of
Collections, Generations Exhibition

KRISTYNE S. LOUGHRAN, Graduate School of
Fine Arts and Art History
Indiana University

KATHLEEN T. MANG, Curator of the Lessing J.
Rosenwald Collection, Library of Congress

DARIELLE MASON, National Graduate Fellow
History of Art Department, University of
Pennsylvania

CHRISTOPHER ROY, Associate Professor of Art
History, The University of Iowa

SHEILA SALO, Research Collaborator
Smithsonian Institution

JANE ELLIOT SEWELL, Research Fellow
Institute of the History of Medicine, The Johns
Hopkins University

YEDIDA K. STILLMAN, Associate Professor of
Classical and Near Eastern Studies
The State University of New York at Binghamton

ROBERT WELLER, Assistant Professor of
Anthropology, Duke University

LENDERS TO THE EXHIBITION

American Museum of Natural History, New York
Department of Anthropology

The Nathan Aronson Collection

Asian Art Museum of San Francisco
The Avery Brundage Collection

Robert V. Berg

Rosalind Berman

B'nai B'rith Klutznick Museum, Washington, D.C.

The British Museum, London
Department of Greek and Roman Antiquities

Chang Suk-hwan Collection, Korea

Duke University Medical Center Library
Trent Collection in the History of Medicine

Joanne B. Eicher

The Harrison Eiteljorg Collection, Indianapolis, Indiana

Major General and Mrs. Robert George Fergusson

Hebrew Union College Skirball Museum
Los Angeles, California

The Marcia and Irwin Hersey Collection

Hirshhorn Museum and Sculpture Garden,
Smithsonian Institution

Horim Museum, Korea

Indiana University Art Museum, Bloomington

Library of Congress, Washington, D.C.
Rare Book and Special Collections Division

Priscilla Rachun Linn

Gordon E. Mestler
State University of New York, Health Sciences Center,
Brooklyn

Museum of Fine Arts, Boston, Department of Classical Art

Museum of International Folk Art
A Unit of the Museum of New Mexico, Santa Fe

Museum für Völkerkunde, Berlin
Staatliche Museen Preussischer Kulturbesitz

The National Library of Medicine
Bethesda, Maryland

National Museum of African Art, Smithsonian Institution

National Museum of American History, Smithsonian Institution
   Division of Community Life
   Division of Costume
   Division of Domestic Life
   Division of Medical Sciences

The National Museum of Korea, Seoul

National Museum of Natural History, Smithsonian Institution
Department of Anthropology

Pace Primitive, New York

Peabody Museum, Salem, Massachusetts

Philadelphia Museum of Art

The Pilgrim Society, Plymouth, Massachusetts

Princeton University Library
Garrett Collection of Arabic Manuscripts

The Science Museum, London
The Wellcome Museum for the History of Medicine

The David and Alfred Smart Gallery
The University of Chicago

Sŏk Chu-sŏn Memorial Museum of Ethnology, Korea

The Margaret Woodbury Strong Museum, Rochester, New York

The Textile Museum, Washington, D.C.

INDONESIAN FAMILY
SURROUNDS
NEWBORN
MOMENTS AFTER
BIRTH.

CO RENTMEESTER/
LIFE PICTURE
SERVICE

CURIOSITY AND MYSTERY

How did they explain where you came from?

Did they say the stork brought you?

Or that you were found in a cabbage patch?

Did they say you were the reincarnation

of someone who lived before,

perhaps an ancestor from generations ago?

Did they say you

emerged from a seed

that grew in the womb,

from a set of genes

shared by your father and mother?

Did they say your flesh

and spirit came to your mother

as she passed by a stream?

MOTHER AND
CHILD, NEPAL.
KEVIN BUBRISKI

A child is born! But by what long journey, mysterious alchemy that turned desire to flesh, did this child come to be, new life sprouting like a hidden seed in the swelling dark of a woman's body? Answers abound. God listened to her prayer. Heaven mingled with earth. The spirit of the man was strong. A woman slept and in a dream conception came. An ancestor—or the soul of a dead baby—rose up and slid into her body to be born again. The powers of the totem animal or bird were made manifest. A serpent coiled its smooth way into her womb and laid an egg.

We talk of hormonal cycles, ovulation; tell how sperm rush, cells fuse, segment, multiply, travel, embed themselves in the lining of the womb. Yet how did the union of this particular egg and sperm urge life forward to make this child and no other?

The more we learn, greater the wonder, more the mystery. ■

Sheila Kitzinger

ARISTOTLE'S THEORIES
OF FETAL DEVELOP-
MENT FORMED THE
BASIS OF MOST
THINKING ABOUT
EMBRYOS FOR 2,000
YEARS. HE DID NOT
BELIEVE THAT A FETUS
WAS PERFECTLY FORMED
FROM THE BEGINNING,
BUT HELD INSTEAD TO
THE THEORY OF
EPIGENESIS, SAYING
THAT IT BEGAN AS AN
UNDIFFERENTIATED
MASS AND WENT
THROUGH VARIOUS
DEVELOPMENTAL
STAGES OR STEPS.
THE FIRST STAGE
INVOLVED THE BLEND-
ING OF SEMEN AND
MENSTRUAL BLOOD IN
THE UTERUS. BY A LATER
STAGE, BLOOD VESSELS
WERE APPARENT. BY
THE LAST STAGE, THE
FULLY FORMED FETUS
SAT IN THE UTERUS, AS
WAS BELIEVED, WITH ITS
FACE TOWARD ITS
MOTHER'S BACK. JUST
BEFORE BIRTH, THE
FETUS SUPPOSEDLY
TURNED ITSELF TOWARD
ITS MOTHER'S NAVEL,
THUS ASSISTING IN ITS
OWN DELIVERY (cat. 7).

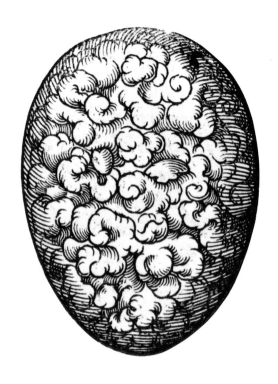
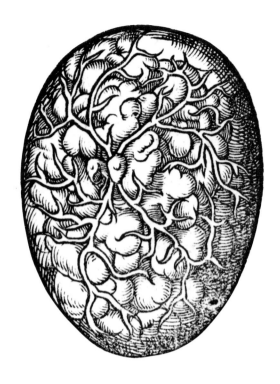

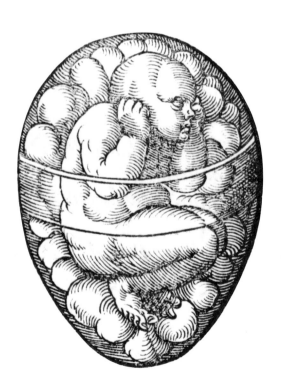

LYNN MORGAN   EXPLAINING THE MYSTERY OF
                  CONCEPTION

The mystery of human life begins with conception. How do babies begin? How are they connected to their families and their ancestors? Not surprisingly, cultures around the world have devised many diverse ways to explain conception, reflecting each society's beliefs about the power of men and women, where human beings come from, and how they are integrated into kin groups. Where the blood line is traced through men, theories often emphasize the father's spiritual and physical contribution to conception; where ancestry is traced through women, the mother's contribution is considered more important. In societies like the United States, where property can be inherited from both parents, people say that mothers and fathers contribute equally to forming their child.

All societies recognize that sexual intercourse is a necessary precursor to pregnancy, yet not all societies believe that it is sufficient. Each society has its own unique way of interpreting and imposing meaning on the natural world. Pregnancy may be attributed to natural or supernatural forces including fertility rites, magic, phases of the moon, the fusion of gametes, or the reincarnation of ancestral souls. Many beliefs allow humans a degree of control over the miraculous process of generating life; many emphasize the metaphysical as well as physical aspects of conception.

The Ashanti of West Africa believe that the child's body is formed entirely from the blood of the mother. This is consistent with their matrilineal social structure, which traces descent through the mother's blood line. Fathers give neither names nor property to their children; instead the mother's brother plays this role and is the most significant male in a child's life. Sexual intercourse is nonetheless necessary to give the child a soul, or *ntoro*, which is passed on by the father and creates a lifelong spiritual bond between father and child. Even though the father is not thought to have a role in forming his child's body, his contribution of spiritual substance is essential.

Matrilineal peoples on the Trobriand Islands in Melanesia hold similar beliefs about the father's role in conception. Virgins cannot become pregnant, but men are not thought to cause pregnancy directly. Their role is to have frequent sexual intercourse with their wives, thus "opening the path" for a spirit-child who will enter the woman's womb to create a pregnancy. Conception is a matter for the woman and her matrilineal ancestor spirits, with the father playing only an ancillary role.[1]

ACCORDING TO GREEK MYTHOLOGY, APHRODITE'S BIRTH OCCURRED WHEN THE GOD KRONOS CASTRATED HIS FATHER, URANOS. THE SEVERED ORGAN WAS THROWN INTO THE SEA, BUT THE FOAM ENGENDERED AS IT FLOATED IN THE WATER COALESCED INTO APHRODITE, THE GODDESS OF LOVE. BECAUSE SHE WAS BORN FROM THE SEA FOAM, DEPICTIONS OF APHRODITE'S BIRTH OFTEN SHOW HER RISING FROM AN OPEN SEASHELL. SOME DEPICTIONS, LIKE THIS ONE, ALSO INCLUDE FIGURES OF PAN, THE GOAT-HEADED GREEK DIVINITY ASSOCIATED WITH FERTILITY AND SEXUAL ENERGY (cat. 1).

In contrast, the people of rural Malaysia believe that a child begins in its father's brain, thought to be the locus of human rationality and self-control. From there the child drifts gradually lower in his body until it is finally thrust into its mother's womb, where it resides until birth.[2] Malaysia is a patrilineal society, where descent is traced through the male blood line and power is vested in men. Such societies commonly use a "seed" metaphor for conception: The father plants the seed that contains the essence of life, while the mother's body is a fertile field, a passive environment where the fetus grows. This metaphor is used in many parts of India, where a woman has no rights over the harvest, and where people say that her passive role in conception also precludes her from having custody rights over her children.[3]

Other theories of conception also accentuate the father's contribution to building the child. The male-dominated Mundurucu people of the Brazilian Amazon believe that children are formed from accumulated seminal fluid, thus many sexual encounters are necessary to produce a child.[4] Arapesh fathers in Papua New Guinea form their children by having intercourse with their pregnant wives every night for six weeks.[5] European scientists of the 17th and 18th centuries believed that a preformed person was encased in each sperm cell. This "homunculus," as the diminuitive person was known, needed its mother's womb only for nurturance.

The distinction between metaphysical and physical conception is blurred in societies where forming a spiritual being is just as important as forming a physical being. There, beliefs often refer to spirits that invade the mother's body, breathing life into shapeless blood and semen. People in rural Thailand believe that the *khwan* soul flies into the womb during sexual intercourse to create the fetus.[6] The Arunta aborigines of central Australia believe that a pregnancy begins at "quickening," when fetal movements indicate that a spirit-child has entered the woman's body.[7] In these societies, spirits must accompany sexual intercourse in order for conception to occur, otherwise the child would have a bodily existence but be spiritually bereft.

The relative weight of each parent's contribution to conception reveals an important aspect of social relations, but conception beliefs also reflect a society's beliefs about theology and metaphysics. Where ancestral spirits are thought responsible for life events, conception can occur only when supernatural forces intervene. Where science is invoked to explain existence, however, conception will occur only when the biological circumstances are optimal. Each society's beliefs about conception interpret nature in a way that is consonant with its overall social organization and worldview. ■

Dr. Lynn Morgan is assistant professor of anthropology at Mount Holyoke College.

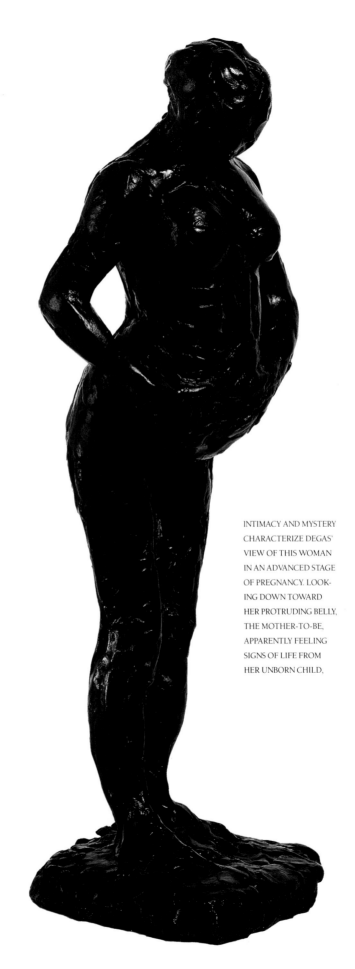

INTIMACY AND MYSTERY CHARACTERIZE DEGAS' VIEW OF THIS WOMAN IN AN ADVANCED STAGE OF PREGNANCY. LOOKING DOWN TOWARD HER PROTRUDING BELLY, THE MOTHER-TO-BE, APPARENTLY FEELING SIGNS OF LIFE FROM HER UNBORN CHILD, TOUCHES HER ABDOMEN. BIRTH SEEMS IMMINENT, FOR THE WOMAN BENDS HER KNEES SLIGHTLY TO RETAIN HER BALANCE AGAINST THE WEIGHT OF THE BABY, WHICH PULLS HER BODY FORWARD. A CAREFUL AND EXACTING OBSERVER, DEGAS COMBINED HIS SKILL AT ANATOMICAL RENDERINGS WITH AN UNDERSTANDING OF THE PSYCHOLOGICAL MOOD OF HIS SUBJECT TO ACHIEVE IN THIS FIGURE A TRUE-TO-LIFE YET UNIVERSAL IMAGE OF PREGNANCY (cat. 14).

ERIK ECKHOLM   SCIENCE SEARCHES FOR
                     THE ORIGIN OF LIFE

Secrets gleaned from rocks on land and vents on the ocean floor, from probes far into space and deep inside living cells are producing what researchers call an exciting and dynamic new phase in the search for the origin of life.

The 285 scientists from 22 countries who gathered in Berkeley, California, in July 1986 to discuss the origin of life may have been one of the few audiences anywhere that could listen without blinking as the speaker said, "The division between life and non-life is perhaps an artificial one."

These scientists speak of advanced chemistry and not of the religious fundamentalism of Creationists. Still, their discussions sometimes have an almost Biblical resonance. A theory that has intrigued a number of the experts, for example, holds that growing crystals of clay formed the first replicating, evolving systems and ushered in the age of organic cells. The notion that life sprang from clay evokes the creation myths of many cultures and the account in Genesis, which says the Lord formed man from the "dust of the ground."

The Berkeley conference was the eighth in a series that began in Moscow in 1957. The conference was dominated by the effort to make sense of important new findings flowing in from many directions rather than by any dramatic breakthroughs. No one expects to create a living cell in a test tube anytime soon, but enthusiasm was in the air nonetheless.

"This field has recently accumulated huge amounts of exciting data that we've hardly begun to digest," said Hyman Hartman, a biochemist from the Massachusetts Institute of Technology. Just in the last few years, rocks in Australia and South Africa were found to contain traces of bacteria that formed floating mats on shallow seas some 3.5 billion years ago, about a billion years after the earth congealed from a cloud of interstellar particles. The fossils show that life developed from inanimate chemicals much more quickly than many had assumed.

The story of life on earth, biologists observe, is overwhelmingly a story of bacteria, microscopic cells that lack nuclei. For two billion years, more than half the time there has been life on earth, the bacteria, or prokaryotes as non-nucleated cells are also called, had the planet to themselves. They altered the atmosphere and evolved "all of life's essential, miniaturized chemical systems—achievements that so far humanity has not approached," as Lynn Margulis, a biologist, and her co-author, Dorion Sagan, write in their new book *Microcosmos*.

Only one and a half billion years ago did eukaryotes, the first cells with a nucleus and other advanced internal structures, appear. Only in the last half-billion years have plants and animals lived on land.

In the effort to reconstruct the chemical evolution of life, accounting for the presence of organic building blocks was a crucial and historic step, but only a small one. Now many scientists are contemplating a giant leap—the explanation of how the building blocks became organized into the complex protein enzymes and genetic structures found inside the simplest of cells, and how these two types of molecules were enclosed in a membrane and began collaborating as an organism.

Because all known life carries the same genetic language and other identical traits, scientists believe that all life on earth, from bacteria to sequoia trees to humans, evolved from a single ancestral cell.

Thought on how the first cell formed has long been stymied by what has been called the ultimate chicken-and-egg conundrum: Which came first, the protein catalysts needed to spur reproduction by nucleic acids, or the nucleic acids, which carry the genetic blueprint and do the reproducing? But the discussion at the Berkeley meeting was animated by a recent report on newly discovered properties of RNA, one of the two types of nucleic acids that carry genetic messages. Thomas Cech and others at the University of Colorado showed that molecules of RNA can stimulate the rearrangement of other RNA molecules, a catalytic function formerly thought limited to proteins.

Hailing the report as "an enormously exciting development," Leslie Orgel, a bio-chemist with the Salk Institute, said the discovery meant that it was plausible that ancestral cells containing only RNA could have been able to duplicate themselves without the aid of proteins.

Other scientists, however, questioned whether even a billion years was long enough for something as complex as an RNA molecule to have been created through the chance reshuffling of chemicals.

Sidestepping some of the thorny issues of the evolution of organic chemicals, the clay theory proposes that the first duplicating systems had neither nucleic systems nor proteins but, rather, were made of inorganic minerals. This theory has generated one of the sharpest debates in this field, between what some call "mud versus soup" as the birthplace of life. The idea, proposed by A. Graham Cairns-Smith of Glasgow University, is that clay crystals forming and expanding in a repetitive manner were the first replicat-

ing, hence "genetic," organisms.

The theory has intrigued a number of researchers but is dismissed by many more. In a debate at the 1986 Berkeley conference, David H. White of Santa Clara University in California noted that no clay has yet been shown to reproduce with enough precision to qualify as a "genetic" replicator. And even if a replicating clay is found, he and others argued, it is unlikely to have been involved in producing organic life.

André Brack, a French chemist, said, "The general feeling still is that it all began in water."

Even as some researchers scour the earth for living clays, others are drawing up an agenda for research they hope to pursue on Mars, in other parts of the solar system, and in deep space. If space exploration does not produce direct signs of life elsewhere, they say, it will certainly disclose facts about the conditions of the early earth and the processes of chemical change that spawned life.

The crowning research effort, in the minds of many, is the hunt for signs of extraterrestrial intelligence, now pursued with radio antennas.

Some of the scientists investigating how life began are skeptical about the prospects of finding answers, stressing the extreme improbability of the sequence of events that produced bacteria, let alone humans, on earth. ■

Erik Eckholm is deputy science editor for the New York Times.

THIS IS HOW A 17th-
CENTURY ANATOMIST
DESCRIBED THE NEAR-
TERM FETUS *IN UTERO*.
ANATOMICALLY THE
DRAWING IS CORRECT,
SHOWING THE UMBILI-
CAL CORD AND PLA-
CENTA, AS WELL AS
A PROPERLY POSITIONED
FETUS. THESE DETAILS
ARE PRESENTED IN A
TASTEFULLY ARRANGED
SCENE THAT IMBUES
THE PREGNANT WOMAN
WITH AN AIR OF ROMAN-
TIC ELEGANCE EVEN AS
IT DISPLAYS ANATOMI-
CAL REALISM WITH A
HIGH DEGREE OF TECH-
NICAL SOPHISTICATION
(cat. 9).

BOYCE RENSBERGER ALL FAMILY TREES LEAD TO AN AFRICAN "EVE"

A STRANGE UNREALITY OFTEN DOMINATED 16th-CENTURY ANATOMICAL DESCRIPTIONS OF THE FETUS *IN UTERO*. THESE ILLUSTRATIONS SHOW THE FETUS AS A FULLY GROWN FIGURE WITH A HEAD OF HAIR, NO APPARENT UMBILICAL CONNECTION, AND AMPLE ROOM TO STRETCH OUT IN ACROBATIC POSITIONS WITHIN THE FLASK-SHAPED UTERUS (cat. 6).

About 200,000 years ago there lived one woman who was a maternal ancestor of every human being living today, a team of biologists has concluded after analyzing special genes in the cells of people from all the world's major racial and ethnic groups.

The scientists have taken to calling the woman "Eve" because she is thought to be the one maternal ancestor common to all the family trees of every member of the human race.

The name may be misleading, however, because she is not the sole maternal ancestor. The claim is not that every person is descended only from Eve, or that she was the only woman having children 200,000 years ago. She had many contemporaries who were each among the ancestors of many living today.

The claim is simpler: If each person could trace a family tree far enough back, everyone's ancestors doubling in number with each generation into the past, the tree would reach a time in which there were several thousand ancestors sharing one generation. Among each person's many ancestors living 200,000 years ago, the claim argues, the same woman would appear on all the charts.

The claim is likely to be controversial. But the scientists behind it, from the University of California at Berkeley, have considerable stature in the study of evolutionary relationships as they can be interpreted from genetic studies.

The claim does not contradict the general understanding of human evolution. It accepts the fossil evidence that the human lineage diverged from that of the apes a few million years ago into a species called *Australopithecus*, which evolved into *Homo habilis*, followed by *Homo erectus* and, about 400,000 years ago, by early forms of *Homo sapiens*.

The claim also generally agrees with the view widely shared among anthropologists that anatomically modern forms of *Homo sapiens*, the species to which all living people belong, arose more than 100,000 years ago and probably in Africa.

The findings suggest that while there were primitive forms of *Homo sapiens* living throughout Africa, Europe, and Asia, fully modern humans arose in only one small population in one place and their descendants eventually spread throughout the Old World, replacing the earlier population.

The genetic evidence cited by the Berkeley group also implies that all of today's racial differences evolved after descendants of Eve had grown quite numerous and migrated out of Africa into Eurasia. The differences arose after various populations of the descendants had become geographically separated and could no longer interbreed to any significant degree with other populations.

The claim is being advanced by Allan C. Wilson, Mark Stoneking, and Rebecca L. Cann. Wilson is a pioneer in the use of genetic differences among living organisms to study evolutionary relationships.

In making the interpretation about Eve, Wilson and his colleagues have examined a special set of genes possessed by all human cells but not carried in the nucleus, where the vast majority of every cell's genes reside. The special genes are carried in structures within cells, called mitochondria.

Mitochondria function as a cell's powerhouse, converting the chemical energy from food into a form that the cell can use. They are the only structures in cells that carry their own genes and which reproduce in the cell by splitting exactly as if they were bacteria inhabiting the cell. (Many biologists believe mitochondria originated as bacteria that became permanent symbiotic partners of cells.)

At conception, when a sperm, which lacks mitochondria, fertilizes an egg, which has many thousands, the resulting embryo inherits only its mother's mitrochondrial genes. At each subsequent cell division, the new cells acquire their mitochondria simply by apportioning the mother's mitochondria between them.

"It's this special kind of inheritance—we all get our mitochondria only from our mothers—that makes it possible to come to this kind of a conclusion," Stoneking said. "And, if you believe in evolution, it's not remarkable to say that we are all descended from a common ancestor. What we've done is find a way to estimate when the most recent common maternal ancestor lived."

The method involves comparing mitochondrial genes from a wide variety of humans to count the differences. From other evidence, Wilson, Stoneking, and Cann have concluded that in every million years there is about a 2 percent to 4 percent change in the mitochondrial genes.

Working backward from the amount of difference among all peoples today as sampled in 147 persons from all over the world, the group concluded that it would have taken 140,000 to 290,000 years for today's amount of difference to accumulate. The most probable number in the range is about 200,000 years.

The conclusion that Eve lived in Africa emerged from comparing the amount of difference between every possible pairing of individuals among the 147 tested. The researchers then drew a "family tree" linking all the individuals according to how closely their genes were related.

The diagram turned out to have two major branches, one including only certain Africans and all other groups.

The common ancestor of the two branches, the scientists concluded, must have been African.

The researchers emphasize that their claim covers only the ancestry of mitochondrial genes. It is virtually certain that the nuclear genes, the ones that control most of human heredity, were contributed by many mothers and fathers. ■

Boyce Rensberger writes for the Washington Post.

WODAABE CLAN GROUP AT ANNUAL GATHERING, NIGER. CAROL BECKWITH, FROM *NOMADS OF NIGER*, PUBLISHED BY HARRY N. ABRAMS, INC., 1983

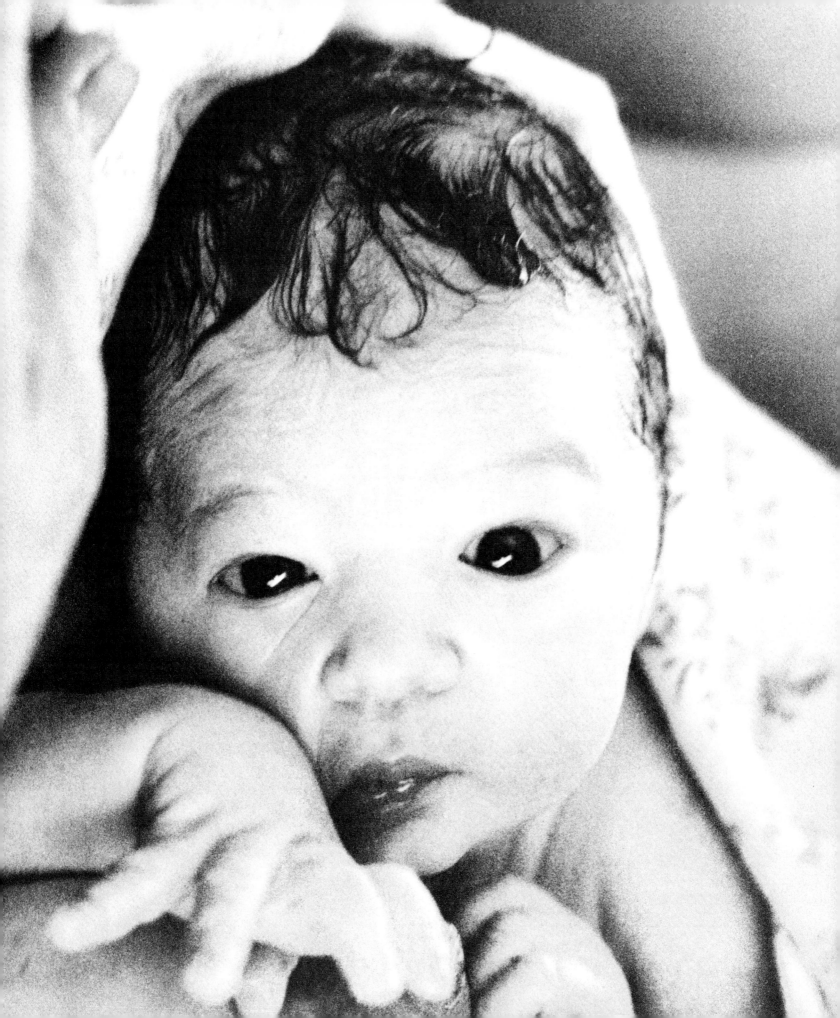

The procreative task of an Arapesh father is not finished with impregnation. The Arapesh have no idea that after the initial act which establishes physiological paternity, the father can go away and return nine months later to find his wife safely delivered of a child. Such a form of parenthood they would consider impossible, and furthermore, repellent. For the child is not the product of a moment's passion, but is made by both father and mother, carefully, over time. The Arapesh distinguish two kinds of sex activity, play, which is all sex activity that is not known to have induced the growth of a child, and work, purposive sex activity directed towards making a particular child, towards feeding it and shaping it during the first weeks in the mother's womb. Here the father's task is equal with the mother's; the child is the product of father's semen and mother's blood, combined in equal amounts at the start, to form a new human being. When the mother's breasts show the characteristic swelling and discoloration of pregnancy, then the child is said to be finished—a perfect egg, it will now rest in the mother's womb. From this time on, all intercourse is forbidden, for the child must sleep undisturbed, placidly absorbing food that is good for it. The need of a gentle environment is emphasized throughout. The woman who wishes to conceive must be as passive as possible. Now as the guardian of the growing child, she must observe certain precautions: She must not eat the bandicoot or she will die in hard labor, for the bandicoot burrows too far into the ground, nor the frog, or the child will be born too suddenly, nor the eel, or the child will be born too soon. She must not eat sago that comes from a *marsalai* place, nor coconuts from a tree that has been tabooed by the *tamberan*, the supernatural patron of the men's cult. If the woman wants the child to be male, other women will tell her never to cut anything in half, for this cutting will produce a female.

Morning sickness during pregnancy is unknown. During all the nine months, the unborn child sleeps. The child is said to grow like the chick in an egg; first there is just blood and semen, then the arms and legs emerge and finally the head. When the head is loosened, the child is born. No one recognizes that a child may show signs of life until just before birth, when the child turns over and so produces the first labor pain. ∎

Dr. Margaret Mead was a world-renowned anthropologist and curator of ethnology at the American Museum of Natural History. She conducted field research on the Arapesh people during a two-year expedition to New Guinea between 1931 and 1933. Dr. Mead died in 1978.

TWENTY-MINUTE-
OLD INFANT, BORN
IN A HOME WATER-
BIRTH, USA.
SUZANNE ARMS

PRIA DEVI AND RICHARD KURIN

CONCEPTION IN INDIA

The act of coupling to bear children is considered a major sacrament in the ancient codes for Hindu householders. The relationship between male and female reproductive roles is often linked to that between seed and field. According to Indian folk biology, male and female reproductive fluids are distillates or concentrations of blood and hence of the bodies of those who produce them. Male fluid, like the seed, is more formative, while female fluid, like the field, is more nurturing. Seeding the field is an act of transferring the power of life, and while to some extent considered a sacrifice, is nonetheless necessary for its perpetuation. When the life-empowering fluids of male and female meet, and if the gods sanction it, a child is conceived. This conception is taken as a sign that indeed the bride and groom, now husband and wife, were and are compatible, justifying the wisdom of the two families' match-making. For the husband, conception means his life and his name will continue. For the wife, expectant motherhood solidifies her standing in her husband's family home and indicates that her transformation to one of their own has been accomplished.

In western Rajasthan, the *pīdo*, a turmeric-colored veil with a tie-dyed red dot at its center, is traditionally worn by women who have recently borne a son. Making or asking for the *pīdo* is a way for a wife to communicate her pregnancy and her hope for the birth of a son to her husband, as illustrated by this traditional *pīdo* song of Rajasthan:[1]

The wife breaks the news to her husband:
Dear one, the time has come for you to bring me pīdos
The veils my little and elder sisters-in-law already wear.
Your beloved who was envious is now happy.
So glad am I, bring me not one pīdo, but six.
Joyfully drape the first one over my mother-in-law
For she gave life to you.
The second give to my sister-in-law
Who held you in her lap as a child.
The third give to my sister-in-law
Who gave us for a night our very first room of love
Where we played together, turning like the swastika, the traveling sun.
The fourth to my little sister-in-law
Who gave us the couch on which we rested that same night.
The fifth to the midwife
Who gives me courage to withstand the hour of labor.
And with this sixth pīdo, my husband,
Drape your tender wife who gives you now continuance of your family name.

■

Pria Devi is well known in India for her creative writing in English. Dr. Richard Kurin is an anthropologist who has conducted intensive field research in rural and urban India and Pakistan. He is deputy director of the Office of Folklife Programs of the Smithsonian Institution, and professorial lecturer at Johns Hopkins University School of Advanced International Studies. Dr. Kurin served on the curatorial committee for the Smithsonian's Generations exhibition.

INSPECTING HUMANITY FROM *TUSITA* (JOYFUL) HEAVEN, THE BODHI-SATTVA (BUDDHA-TO-BE) CHOSE MĀYĀ, PURE AND PEERLESS QUEEN OF KING ŚUDDHODANA, TO BEAR HIM IN HIS FINAL INCARNATION. MĀYĀ BEGGED HER HUSBAND TO ALLOW HER TO LEAD A CHASTE AND MORAL LIFE. ACCOMPANIED BY HER WOMAN, SHE LAY HERSELF ON A BED HIGH IN AN ISOLATED PALACE. BUDDHA THEN DESCENDED FROM HEAVEN IN THE FORM OF A GLEAMING WHITE ELE-PHANT, AND ENTERED HER WOMB THROUGH THE RIGHT SIDE. MĀYĀ EXPERIENCED THIS EVENT AS A DREAM, THUS CONCEPTION OCCURRED SIMULTAN-EOUSLY IN MIND AND BODY (cat. 3).

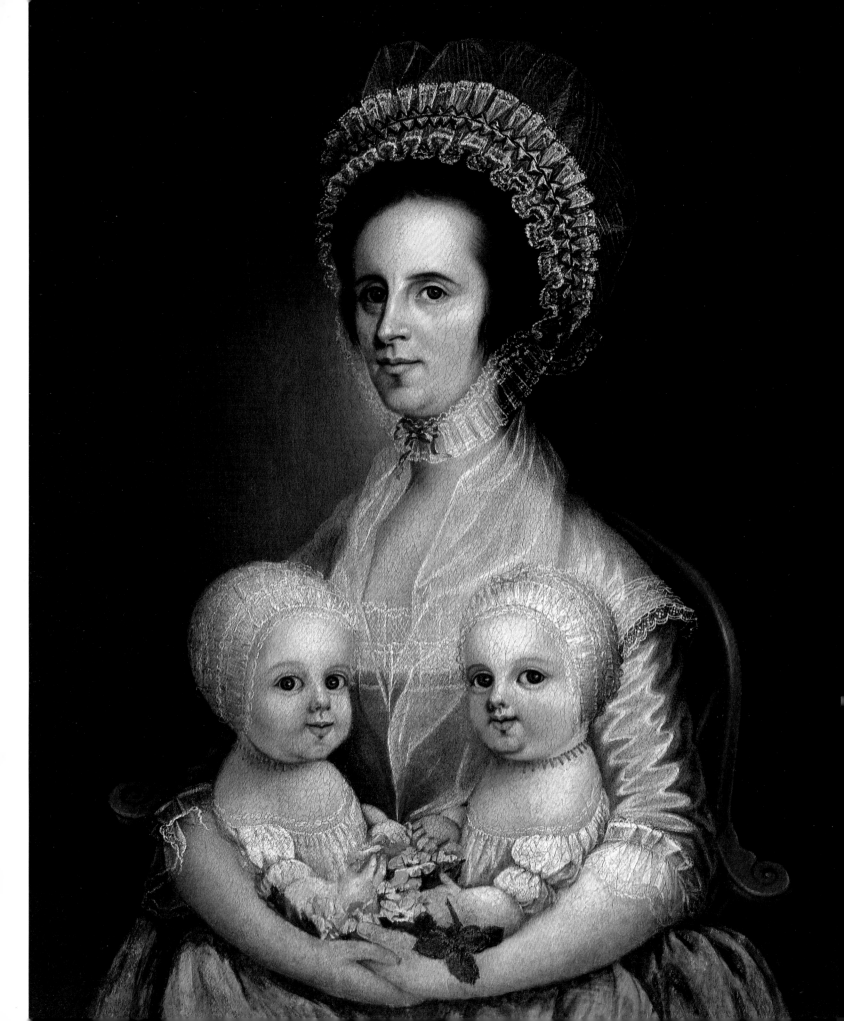

STEPHEN JAY GOULD   HUMAN BABIES AS EMBRYOS

Why are newborn humans far less developed and more helpless than the offspring of our primate ancestors?

No one will deny that primates are the archetypical precocial mammals. Relative to body sizes, brains are biggest and gestation times and life spans are longest among mammals. Litter sizes, in most cases, have been reduced to the absolute minimum of one. Babies are well developed and capable at birth. However, we encounter one obviously glaring and embarrassing exception—namely us. We share most of the precocial characters with our primate cousins—long life, large brains, and small litters. But our babies are as helpless and undeveloped at birth as those of most primitive altricial mammals.

Why did this most precocial of all species in some traits (notably the brain) evolve a baby far less developed and more helpless than that of its primate ancestors?

I will propose an answer to this question that is bound to strike most readers as patently absurd: Human babies are born as embryos, and embryos they remain for about the first nine months of life. If women gave birth when they "should"—after a gestation of about a year and a half—our babies would share the standard precocial features of other primates.

The initial impression that such an argument can only be arrant nonsense arises from the length of human gestation. Gorillas and chimps may not be far behind, but human gestation is still the longest among primates. How then can I claim that human neonates are embryos because they are born (in some sense) too soon? The answer is that planetary days may not provide an appropriate measure of time in all biological calculations. Some questions can only be treated properly when time is measured relatively in terms of an animal's own metabolism or developmental rate.

In astronomical days, human gestation is long, but relative to human development rates, it is truncated and abbreviated. A major feature of human evolution has been the marked slowing up of our development. Our brains grow more slowly and for a longer time than those of other primates, our bones ossify much later, and the period of our childhood is greatly extended. In fact, we never reach the levels of development attained by most primates. Human adults retain, in several important respects, the juvenile traits of ancestral primates—an evolutionary phenomenon called neoteny. Neoteny has been crucial in human evolution for two reasons.

One, it provides a morphology adapted to our mode of life. We have a large brain because rapid fetal growth rates continue in humans long after they have ceased in other primates. Our bulbous cranium and short face resemble those of juvenile primates, not the low-browed, long-faced adults. We can stand erect because our foramen magnum—the hole in our skull for attachment with the vertebral column—lies under our brain, not behind it as in four-footed mammals. The foramen magnum of fetal primates (and other mammals) lies under the brain, but migrates back during development.

Two, the slow rate of our development has been important in itself, quite apart from the juvenile morphology that it permits us to retain as adults. We are primarily learning animals; we need a long period of dependent and flexible childhood to provide time for the cultural transmission that makes us human. If we matured and began to fend for ourselves as early as most other mammals, we would never develop the mental capacity that our neotenic brain permits.

Compared with other primates, we grow and develop at a snail's pace; yet our gestation period is but a few days longer than that of gorillas and chimpanzees. Relative to our own developmental rate, our gestation has been markedly shortened. If length of gestation had slowed down as much as the rest of our growth and development, human babies would be born anywhere from seven to eight months to a year after the nine months actually spent *in utero*.

But why are human babies born before their time? Why has evolution extended our general development so greatly, but held our gestation time in check, thereby giving us an essentially embryonic baby? Why was gestation not equally prolonged with the rest of development?

From what I have seen (although I cannot know for sure), human birth is a joyful experience when properly rescued from arrogant male physicians who seem to want total control over a process they cannot experience. Nonetheless, I do not think it can be denied that human birth is difficult compared with that of most other mammals. To put it rather grossly, it's a tight squeeze.

There are not, I am confident, many human females who could give birth successfully to a year-old baby.

The culprit in this tale is our most important evolutionary specialization, our large brain. In most mammals, brain growth is entirely a fetal phenomenon. But since the brain never gets very large, this poses no problem for birth. In larger-brained monkeys, growth is delayed somewhat to permit postnatal enlargement of the brain, but relative times of gestation need not be altered. Human brains, however, are so large that another strategy must be added for successful birth—gestation must be shortened relative to general development, and birth must occur when the brain is only one-fourth its final size.

Our brain has probably reached the end of its increase in size. The paramount trait of our evolution has finally limited its own potential for future growth. Barring some radical redesign of the female pelvis, we will have to make do with the brains we have if we want to be born at all. But, no matter. We can happily spend the next several millennia learning what to do with the immense potential that we have scarcely begun to understand or exploit. ∎

Dr. Stephen Jay Gould teaches biology, geology, and the history of science at Harvard University.

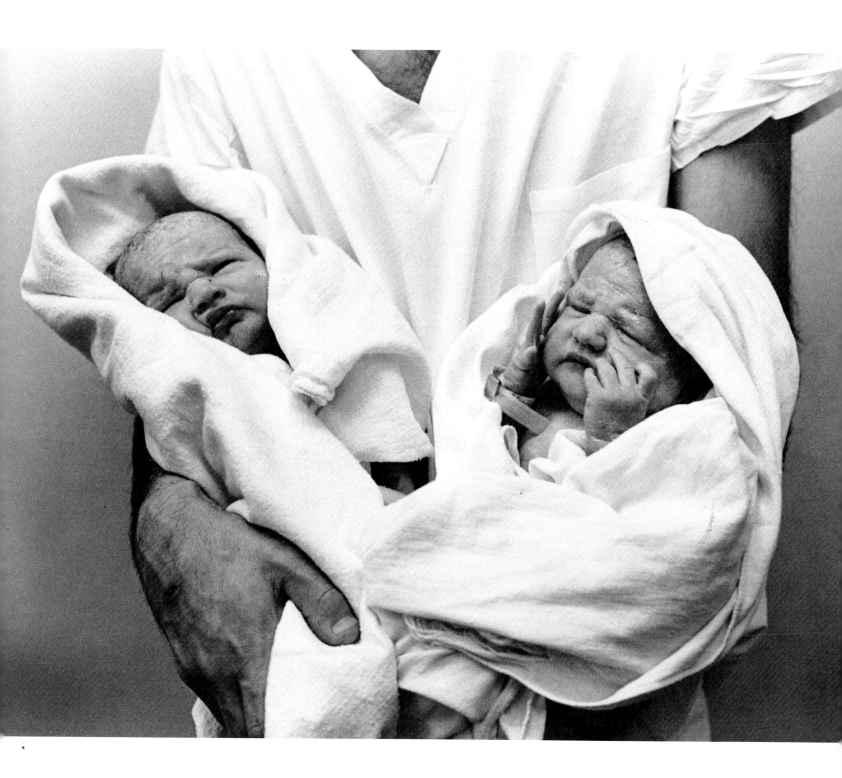

IN THE WESTERN WORLD, POPULAR CULTURE INSPIRED ALTERNATIVE EXPLANATIONS OF BIRTH EVEN AT TIMES WHEN SCIENTIFIC ADVANCEMENTS WERE BEGINNING TO CLARIFY THE BIOLOGICAL PROCESSES OF CONCEPTION. DURING THE VICTORIAN ERA AND INTO THE BEGINNING OF THE 20th CENTURY, FOR EXAMPLE, POPULAR BELIEFS ATTRIBUTED BABIES TO THE WORK OF THE STORK. THE POWERFULLY WINGED BIRD WAS ENCOURAGED TO BUILD ITS PLATFORM NESTS ON THE HOUSETOPS OF YOUNG COUPLES. LEGEND HAD IT THAT WHEN THE EGG HATCHED, THE BIRD WOULD DELIVER A BLANKET-WRAPPED NEWBORN IN ITS BEAK (cat. 12).

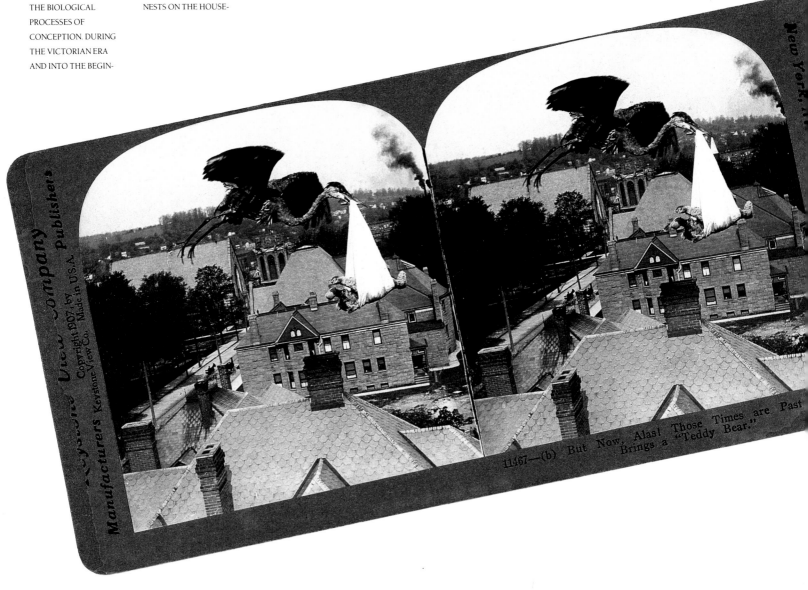

ERMA BOMBECK   WHERE BABIES COME FROM

Dear child, there is no story in this world more simple or beautiful in the telling than where babies come from.

Maybe that is because birth is as old as the universe and the process NEVER changes.

Imagine if you will a Sperm-mobile traveling the wrong way on a Fallopian expressway looking for a parking place. When the car is parked it is rewarded with a fertilized egg and life begins. Isn't that simple?

Well, actually, the Supreme Court is still out on exactly when life begins. It could be at that moment or it could be several weeks later, so for the time being, just stick to the parking lot theory. It's enough to know that the union of a male and a female is the ONLY way to produce an embryo.

Did I say "only way"? Actually, there have been some cases where the Sperm-mobile is frozen and doesn't have to make the trip until someone is ready to become a parent, but that gets confusing.

It will suffice to say that the female ALWAYS carries the baby until it is ready to be born. That's right. Always. Female snakes. Female gorillas. Female fish. Well, there is the seahorse where the male carries the offspring, but that is rare in the annals of reproduction. Or unless, of course, we're talking surrogate. That is when the Sperm-mobile has the advantage of valet parking. No, I would not like to explain that!

At any rate, let us just say for purposes of moving along that the embryo attaches itself to the inner lining of the uterus and starts to grow. Every gene is in place. A gene is a part of a cell that determines what you will inherit from your parents and what you will blame them for later. If you end up looking like Tom Selleck or Victoria Principal, you have Designer Genes. If you turn out short, with wiry hair and a werewolf smile, you must learn to play the piano well.

At five weeks, the embryo takes on a human look. Some mothers, like myself, find it necessary to go into maternity clothes at this stage.

At two months, all the internal organs have formed and the baby is now called a fetus. From here throughout the next seven months, the mother's body begins to change form to accommodate the life inside her. Her bustline falls to her waist, her shoulders and back arch, her knees never speak, and she looks like she has swallowed a thousand camels. There is absolutely NO WAY in the world to look otherwise…unless of course, you're on a soap opera. The gestation period of a baby born to a principal on a soap opera is three weeks…two if the ratings are in trouble and four if it's sweeps week and the kid's mother is demanding lines for him. But normally, it's nine months.

Where was I? Oh yes, once the baby is in the womb, there isn't a lot to do. Unless of course, you count the Lamaze classes where a wife goes with her husband to prepare for natural childbirth by learning how to relax with her contractions. (Some people, like myself, opted for a shot in the hip where I didn't regain consciousness until the kid was three years old, but that is considered cowardly.) And there are all kinds of tests, including ultrasound so you can see on a television screen what you've got going for you, and there is a current theory that babies who are read to and talked to while they're in the womb feel loved. If mommies have a history of instability, sometimes it's best to cool talking to your stomach.

But for the moment, let's just focus on a picture of mommie trapped in a chair for nine months because she is not sure her feet are still there.

Then one day, there is a signal that something is happening. The baby wants to be born. This is called labor. Here's the beautiful part. This is the time when a woman goes off all by herself in a private communion with the miracle inside her. She is frightened. She is exhilarated. She is alone with her mission.

Well, unless you count the husband who is hyperventilating and the grandparents who have been invited to the birthing room to witness the miracle and, of course, the doctor and nurses and the relative who is getting it all down on a video camera.

With each contraction, the baby makes its way out of the uterus, through the vagina, and out of the mother's body. The umbilical cord that connects the baby to the mother is severed. This is temporary. It will later be replaced by another lifeline called the telephone.

The child is born.

It will take the mother another 15 years for her body to return to the way it was before she conceived.

The baby is put into a small crib with a warm blanket to simulate the womb. Mommie gets to rest for 15 minutes. Then they get her to her feet, put her in a T-shirt with a red S on the front and a cape and she hits the ground running. Men have had longer good-byes at the bowling alley.

Despite all of this, it is the most wondrous thing that has ever happened to a woman or will happen in her entire life. Because of it she will never be the same again. A new dimension has been added to her. She has been privileged to produce another human being. That is something NO ONE ELSE but a woman can do.

Actually, there is in vitro fertilization where babies are developed in test tubes but… in that case the Sperm-mobile just cruises around and…

I know all this sounds like fun, but trust me when I tell you, you do NOT want a Sperm-mobile for Christmas. ∎

Erma Bombeck is a syndicated American humorist.

CONTENTED
INFANT, SWEDEN.
THOMAS BERGMAN

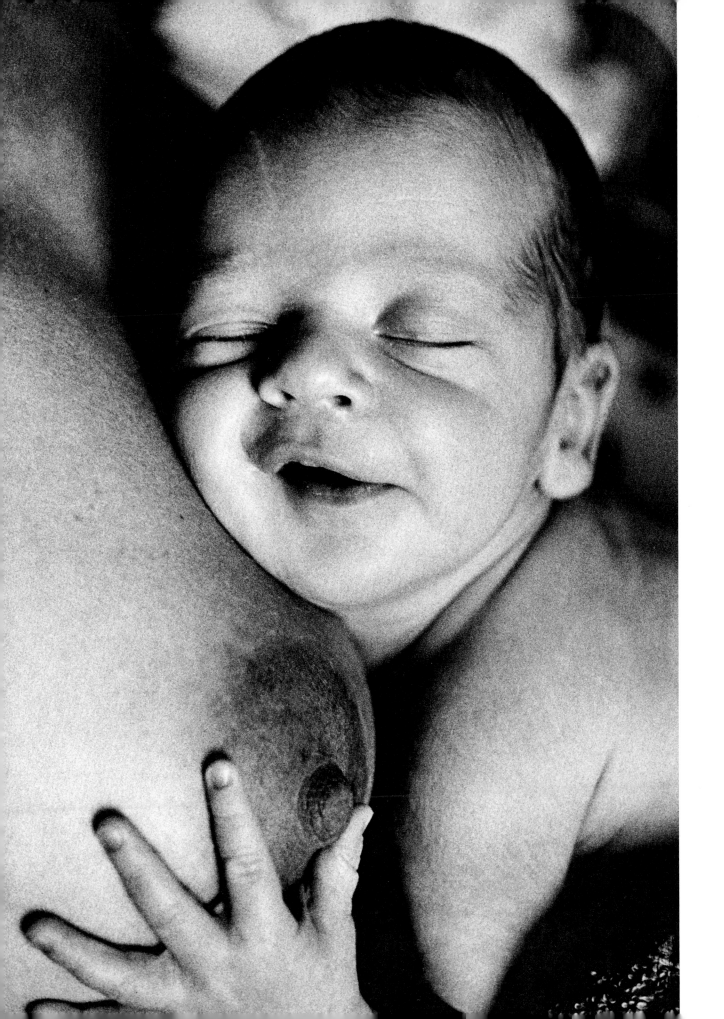

INTENT

What does an old wives' tale about hanging garlic

on the doorknob have to do with having children?

A good suggestion?

An odd prescription?

Something you might do yourself?

GERMANY.
GORDON GAHAN,
© 1974 NATIONAL
GEOGRAPHIC
SOCIETY

And why so much advice?

Why so much concern?

Because for many, new generations hold the promise of…

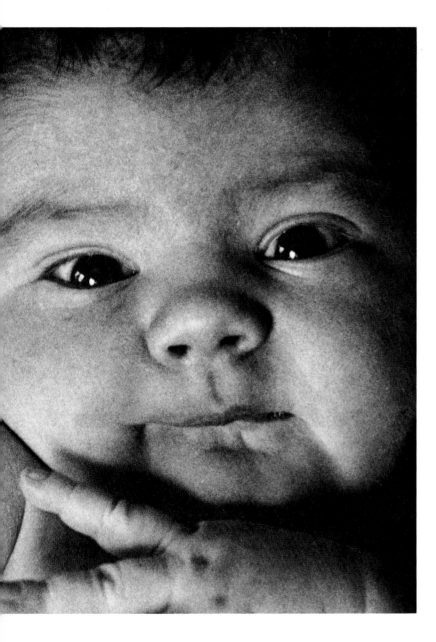

USA.
MIMI COTTER

PALESTINIAN
GRANDFATHER AND
GRANDSON IN
ZATARA, ISRAEL.
ALEXANDRA
DOR-NER

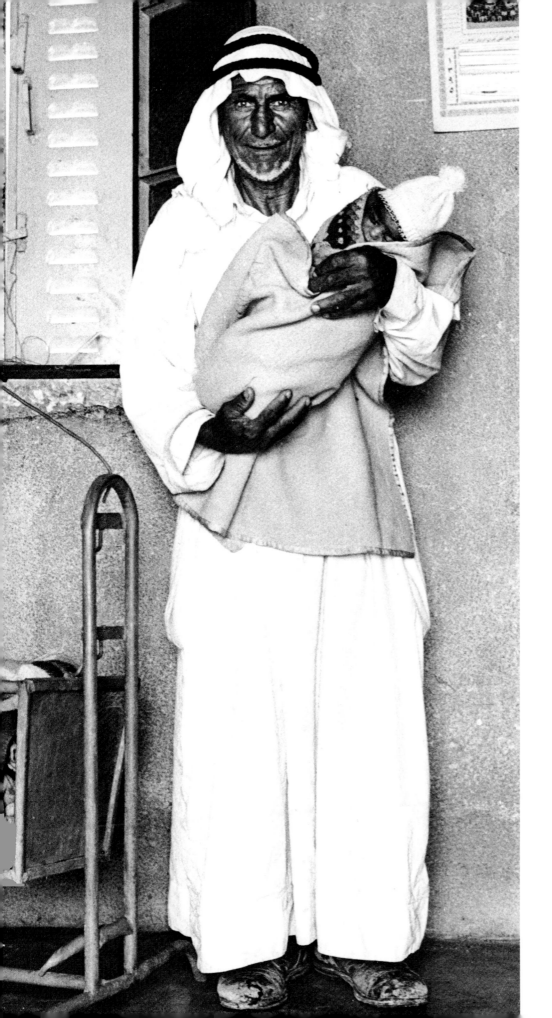

carrying on the family line,

herding the flocks,

inheriting the land,

fishing the seas,

hunting the forests,

running the business.

47

For others,

new generations would strain…

an overcrowded world,

the well-being of a family,

the rations of bread.

Children are riches: a child to bring status, proof of fertility and manhood, to inherit property, learn skills. A child as insurance for old age. A child to plough, to tend the goats, to replace another who has died, to be a companion to my mother and carry out the chores. A child for my sister who is barren, to give love in loneliness, to show that a girl is grown up now. A child to make a real family, a child before it is too late, a child for posterity, a child for fulfillment, a child by chance.

Childless, a woman may be pitied, blamed, feared. They point at her—the useless one, the alien punished by the gods, sin in her empty womb. The one who suffers from spells cast by a neighbor's malice. In some cultures her husband will divorce her to take another wife.

Even where families live crowded in cellars beneath ruined buildings, where shells smash daily, where the well is dry and the earth mud-cracked, where hands reach for the empty bowl and children add to hunger, birth still holds a seed of hope.

A child is proof of the future, evidence that it does not end with this. ■

Sheila Kitzinger

ONE SMALL
CHILD TAKES
RESPONSIBILITY
FOR ANOTHER IN
HONG KONG.
THOMAS HOPKER/
WOODFIN
CAMP, INC.

ABBY JOAN SYLVIACHILD   A PLANNED BABY

We have always been planners. We planned our educations, our travels abroad, our garden rows, and our childbearing. We planned to get pregnant when things were just right. We thought that having a child would be another accomplishment we could complete by choice, like the new house or job or degree. But the supposedly simple act of getting pregnant can sometimes turn out to be much harder than we think. Months and menstrual periods go by without any sign that our bodies are aware of our longings, dreams, and hopes. Our bodies betray us by being beyond our control. Like so many infertile couples, our feelings began with surprise and shock, then led to disappointment, denial of the reality, anger, isolation, depression, guilt, appeasement, then finally grief and mourning for the biological child never-to-be. Finally we came to some resolution as we planned, again, to reach our goal of parenthood another way.

The elevator ride up to the nursery floor of a small community hospital was the most intensely exciting moment of my life. I was about to meet my newborn daughter. After three and a half years of doctors, tests, temperature charts, drugs, surgeries, X-rays, a miscarriage, and the depression, sadness, and loneliness of being among dear friends with children, I was at last becoming a parent.

Although the events leading up to my daughter's being placed in my arms are certainly not the usual pregnancy-labor-and-delivery ones, I went through many feelings and emotional stages, some common to all expectant parents, as I waited for our first child. I wondered if the birth-parents would follow through with their plans to let us adopt this baby. I was scared that they would change their minds. I wondered when this baby would be born, since not knowing an exact due date meant not planning anything, not even telling anyone about the possibility.

Sometimes I wondered happy, lazy thoughts—as I weeded my vegetables more vigorously that summer than any summer since—about the baby's sex, size, and looks. I wondered in a worried way about the baby's health, since I had no control over the nutrition, vitamins, toxic substances, or other things affecting this pregnancy. Along with that, I also worried about the birth itself, hoping it would be spontaneous, non-traumatic, and unmedicated. I worried about Apgar scores and about fingers and toes like everyone else does. Things I didn't worry about, things I took for granted and assumed, were that I would love this baby, that she would be my own child, that we would be a family forever.

An 8:30 A.M. telephone call saying, "It's a girl, very big, very healthy," was our first information about our daughter. It came when she was about 15 hours old. A day later we told her four grandparents that, if all went well, we'd have our baby girl in two more days. We chose my grandmother's name for her but didn't dare to buy a single baby item until the papers were signed. It would have been too cruel to look at tiny new baby things in our home if the adoption hadn't taken place.

The morning of that exciting day, we were up and dressed early to go to the county courthouse. There we were interviewed about our ages, address, marriage, and state residency. The birth-parents had had a parallel experience before us. We had a quick hearing in front of a judge who asked us if we were aware that adoption meant our taking on the "care, custody, and control" of this baby for the rest of our lives. Of course we were aware! That was the whole object of becoming parents by adoption: to be our child's parents. At the time I couldn't believe the judge really asked us that, though I didn't make a peep in the courtroom.

From court we went to the hospital, an easy and familiar drive that seemed to take forever. We stopped only to call our parents. Mine were waiting back East for our call so that they could jump on the first airplane to be with us at this exciting time.

I will never forget riding up that hospital elevator, with our attorney who had to check the baby out of the hospital. Seeing our baby daughter for the first time, in a tiny examining room on the maternity floor, was dreamlike. Here was this *beautiful* baby who was going to be *mine/ours*. I watched the nurse dressing her. I was entranced, though holding back. I don't know why I didn't just pick her up and hug her, but I guess I still felt that maybe it was not going to happen, that something else would happen to keep me from being a "Mommy."

Finally all the paperwork of hospital checking-out was completed and a volunteer brought a wheelchair for me, just the way they do for every other new mom, even though I had walked in there by myself just 20 minutes before. A nurse held my daughter all the way down the elevator and out the front door to the car. Then, at last, she put the baby in my arms in the car and wished us good luck.

We had only one hospital pack of formula, so we stopped at our corner drugstore for our first baby shopping: formula, bottles, nipples, cotton and alcohol for her navel, a box of diapers until diaper service started, and a baby thermometer. We took several instant print photos and mailed them right away to her other grandparents, who would come to visit the very next weekend.

At home we just sat and looked at her sleeping. We couldn't take our eyes off her. We watched her breathing, her face movements, the flexing of her fingers and toes. We were fascinated, falling in love, amazed, and in awe of such a miracle. We also didn't know what to do until she woke up and needed to be fed or changed. We phoned a few more family members and a friend who started calling our other friends to spread the good news.

The baby was asleep on our bed when her grandparents saw her for the first time. They beamed; they exclaimed; they cooed about her beauty, her size, her loveliness, her skin, her hands. We all felt so filled with incredibly good feelings. After she woke up, we all worked on changing and feeding her, with much discussion of the right temperature for the bottle, whether the water to dilute the formula had to be boiled (yes, until she was four weeks old said the pediatrician later), and how often to burp her. She helpfully fell asleep after 2½ ounces, so we all could relax again and watch her sleep. This was a most fascinating activity and one which, before the day I became a mother, I had never even known about.

After about an hour, my parents borrowed our car to go shopping for "their baby." Our few borrowed clothes weren't enough. In two hours they returned with just about a full layette: a beautiful white wicker bassinett, blankets, little shirts, stretchies, washcloths and towels, diapers, sheets, pads, more toys, a diaper bag, and a clown mobile with a music box singing a song from my dad's childhood.

By supper, we were exhausted. We were all floating on clouds of happiness and incredibly high on this one little baby. We fed and changed her a few more times before we all went to sleep. The first time she woke us, at 1 A.M., I really didn't know where I was (in the living room on the sleeper sofa) or what was happening. Her cries seemed so loud in the otherwise silent house. She seemed so intensely hungry. We tried to get the bottle warmed up as quickly as we could, but she woke her grandparents anyway. My mom took over this feeding and I gratefully snuggled back under the covers for another three hours of sleep. By 4:30 A.M. my arms and legs felt leaden when I tried to move out of bed for her feeding. I wondered how anyone could continue to function after a night of being awake for 45 minutes every three hours.

In the morning, the most ordinary things seemed changed. Everything was revolving around the baby. My thoughts were: Is she up? Is she wet? Is the formula warm? Do we have more pins for the diapers? Can the bassinett go out on the patio? Do

ARTEMIS OF THE EPHESIANS IS A LATER GRAECO-ROMAN MANI-FESTATION OF THE ANATOLIAN FERTILITY DEITY, THE GREAT GODDESS. WORSHIP OF THAT GODDESS WAS CONNECTED WITH THE RISE OF AGRICULTURE AND THE NEED TO RITUALIZE THE PROCESSES OF REGEN-ERATION AND GROWTH IN THE NATURAL WORLD. ARTEMIS' LATER ASSOCIATION WITH FERTILITY WAS SYMBOL-IZED BY HER ROWS OF PENDULOUS BREASTS, AND BY THE HONEYBEES AND FLOWERS ON HER GARMENT (cat. 17).

we need mosquito netting? How busy we were—all four grown people not finishing our breakfasts without running to look at her, do some laundry of hers, wash and boil her bottles and nipples, call some more friends and family, get referrals for a pediatrician in town for her first visit. And in between, we all smiled at each other as we bent over the bassinett to look at her and listen to her breathe, watching her turn her head from side to side, yawn, or sneeze.

That day progressed like a carnival, with telephone calls ringing in with congratulations and friends stopping by to welcome our daughter. They brought with them treasured collections of their own children's out-grown baby equipment and clothes to share. A car seat, stroller, car bed, swingomatics, playpen, high chair, infant seats, baby bath, and changing table arrived until the patio looked like a babyland garage sale, with all the stuff being scrubbed clean and drying in the sun. My friends had saved their kids' stuff for my child-to-be, whenever she would arrive. Before, when I was suffering with my infertility and childlessness, they had agreed among themselves not to talk about their children when I was around. I did not know about their consideration until much later. I felt so much more connected to all of them now that we were sharing this mothering experience and now that they could talk "mother talk" freely with me.

Adoption is another way of building families; for after our child is with us, the same issues of sleeping through the night, parent exhaustion, learning to parent, coping with the first fever, bad diaper rash, ear infections, enjoying, worrying, teaching and learning with our child, and all the other wonderful and frustrating parts of being a family occur whether we have adopted or given birth to our child. ∎

Abby Joan Sylviachild (a pseudonym) has worked for feminist and women's health organizations for 20 years.

FULANI MOTHER
AND CHILD IN
SANGA, MALI.
ERIK HESMERG

54

At the family planning clinic, she was shown into a waiting room, where there were other women waiting. Two were undressed with their stockings rolled down around their ankles, just as you are when you are expecting, and the doctor wants to examine you. They reminded Adah of the prenatal clinics. She was now used to that sort of thing—stripping yourself naked to be examined. It did not bother her any more. She asked herself, why should it worry me? I've only got what you've got. Why should I be ashamed of my body? It did not matter any more.

Three screens were set up in the middle of the square room. Women were to undress behind the screen and then sit down and wait to be called one by one into the doctor's room to be equipped with birth-control gear.

Adah saw a young West Indian mother and purposely went and sat down beside her. She wanted to be on home ground because she was frightened and because the young girl was the only woman there holding a baby. Adah could look after her baby for her when she went in to be equipped, and she could look after Adah's. That would be fair. With such noble thoughts in her mind, she greeted the West Indian girl with a friendly smile. The girl smiled back, showing a golden tooth wedged in between her ordinary teeth.

They soon started to talk. She, the West Indian girl, was going to be trained as a nurse, so she needed some form of birth control during her training. Her husband did not mind. So, months before, she was given the Pill. But, she cried to Adah, see what the Pill had done to her. She pulled up her sleeves and showed Adah a very fine rash. The rash was all over her face and neck. Even her skinny wrists had not been spared. She was covered with the kind of rash that reminded Adah of the rash caused by prickly heat in Africa.

"Do they make you scratch? I mean, do you feel scratchy all the time?"

"Yeah, man. That's the trouble now. I don't mind the appearance. But they itch all the time."

Adah looked at her face again, and as she did the girl started to scratch the back of her skirt. She was trying to hide it from the other women, trying to hide the fact that her bottom was itching. God have mercy! thought Adah. Her bottom as well? Then she asked the girl, "Have you got the itch down there as well?"

The girl nodded. She had it all over her. Adah called to God to have mercy on her again. What was she to do now? She was not going on the Pill if she was going to end up

MAIDEN SPIRIT MASKS LIKE THIS ONE ARE USED BY THE IGBO OF AFRICA DURING ELABORATE MASQUERADE PERFORMANCES IN THE ANNUAL CYCLE OF AGRICULTURAL FESTIVALS, WHICH HONOR ANCESTORS AND CELEBRATE MOTHERHOOD, AS WELL AS HUMAN AND AGRICULTURAL FERTILITY (cat. 32).

looking like somebody with chicken pox, or scratching like this girl as if she was covered with yaws. No, she was not going to have the Pill, and she was not going home empty-handed with no birth control. She thought about the jelly and knew that it would only work when husband and wife are in agreement, for he would have to wait until it melted before coming on. So the jelly was out of the question for her. She could only go for the cap. That almighty cap which is specially made for one's inside.

It came to her turn to go and see the doctor and the midwife who fixed you up with your own special size of cap. It was a messy job. They kept trying this and that and kept scolding Adah to relax otherwise she would go home with the wrong cap that would not fit her properly and *that* would mean another child. The fear of what her husband, Francis, would say and what he would write to his mother and her relations loomed, full of doom, in her subconscious. Only she could feel it. The other two females, who were now tut-tutting at her and growing impatient and telling her to relax her legs, could not see the same picture that Adah was seeing. It was the picture of her mother-in-law when she heard that Adah went behind her husband's back to equip herself with something that would allow her to sleep around and not have any more children. She was sure they would interpret it that way, knowing the psychology of her people. The shame of it would kill her. Her children's name would be smeared as well. God, don't let Francis find out. In desperation, the two women, the doctor, and the midwife gave her a size of cap that they thought should fit. If it did not fit, it was not their fault, because Adah did not help them at all because she was feeling so guilty of what she was doing. First she had forged her husband's signature, now she had got a cap which she was sure was going to cause a row if he found out. But suppose he did not find out and suppose it worked? That would mean no children and she would keep her new job and finish her course in librarianship.

When she got home, she was faced with another problem. How was she to know what was going to happen on a particular night? Must she then wear the cap every night? That was the safest thing, but the cap was not very comfortable and Adah knew that it wobbled and she had to walk funnily to keep it in. And of course Francis would know. Oh, God, if only they had an extra room, then Francis would not have to see and watch and to make irritating remarks about her every move!

She ran down to their backyard toilet that had no electric light and fitted herself with her new cap. She fitted the cap in a hurry, almost going sick at the thought of it all. At that moment she felt really sorry for doctors and nurses. The amount of messing they have to do with people's insides! She dashed up, for Francis was already calling her and asking her what the hell it was she was doing down there in the toilet.

Adah smiled, a wobbly, uncertain sort of smile, for her heart was beating so fast and so loudly, the noise was like a Nigerian housewife pounding yams in her *Odo*. Her heart was going "gbim, gbim, gbim," just like that. She was surprised and shocked to realize that Francis could not hear the beating of that heart of hers. She thought everybody could hear it because it was so loud to her that it hurt her chest, making it difficult to breathe. But she managed a smile, that sort of lying smile.

Soon it was midnight, and the row which Adah had dreaded flared up. Francis got the whole truth out of her. So, she a married woman, married in the name of God and again married in the name of the Oboshi, the goddess of Ibuza, came to London and became clever enough within a year to go behind his back and equip herself with a cap which he, Francis, was sure had been invented for harlots and single women. Did Adah not know the gravity of what she had done? It meant she could take other men behind his back, because how was he to know that she was not going to do just that if she could go and get the gear behind his back? Francis called all the other tenants to come and see and hear about this great issue—how the innocent Adah who came to London only a year previously had become so clever. Once or twice during the proceedings she felt tempted to run out and call the police. But she thought better of it. Where would she go after that? She had no friends and she had no relations in London. ■

Buchi Emecheta was born of Ibuza parentage in Lagos, Nigeria. She currently lives and writes in London. Adah is a character from her novel, Second Class Citizen.

DJENNE MOTHER
AND CHILD DURING
A MARRIAGE
CELEBRATION IN
MALI.
ERIK HESMERG

MOTHER AND
CHILD ON THE
NEPAL-INDIA
BORDER.
DIANE LOWE/STOCK
BOSTON

SUDHIR KAKAR   THE CHILD IN INDIA

Within the wide diversity of India, its welter of distinct regional, linguistic, caste, and religious groupings, there is still a unified cultural awareness of the child that informs the behavior of parents and other adult caretakers. This cultural awareness, a specific Indian conception of the nature of children and the place of childhood in the life cycle, derives from many sources. There are passages dealing with children in the law books of the Hindus, while the section on the care and upbringing of children, the *Bālānga*, is an integral part of traditional Indian medicine, *Ayurveda*. There are references to children and childhood in such ancient epics as the Rāmāyana and Mahābhārata and descriptions of childhood in classical Sanskrit and medieval vernacular literature. In addition, the symbolic content of the various rites of childhood, and of the traditional folk songs that accompany them, provide some indications as to what Indians consider the chief characteristic of a given stage of childhood. While much of this material may seem to belong to the literate traditions of the Hindu upper castes, anthropological accounts have shown that such traditions are basically much the same in many lower groups, their continuous and continuing survival in large sections of society being one of the most distinctive features of the Indian culture.[1]

A major theme that stands out in the Indian cultural tradition is the intense parental longing for children, especially sons who can carry on the family line. This is important because of the emphasis placed on celibacy by the Buddhists and the Jains. A number of myths and didactic passages in the epics repeatedly emphasize that begetting a son is one of man's highest duties and the only way he can discharge the debt he owes to his ancestors. Consider the story of Jaratkuru:

The renowned ascetic Jaratkuru, full of merit and great spiritual power derived from his sustained asceticism, was wandering around the world when one day he came across a deep pit. In this pit, the spirits of his ancestors—the pitris—*were hanging head down, their feet tied to a tree trunk by a single skein of rope that was gradually being nibbled away by a large rat. It was evident that the pitris would soon fall down into the deep darkness of the pit. Moved by their pitiable condition, Jaratkuru inquired whether he could somehow save them from this fate, expressing his readiness to do so even if he had to give up all rewards to which his great asceticism entitled him. "Venerable ascetic," the spirits of his ancestors answered, "thou desirest to relieve us!...O child, whether it is asceticism or sacrifice or whatever else there be of very holy acts, everything is inferior. These cannot count equal to a son. O child, having seen all, speak unto Jaratkuru of ascetic wealth…tell him all that would induce him to take a wife and beget children![2]*

Another ascetic, Mandapala, is told in no uncertain terms that in spite of his most ascetic efforts, certain celestial regions will forever remain closed to him, for they can be reached only by those who have had children: "'Beget children therefore!' Mandapala is instructed, 'Thou shalt then enjoy multifarious regions of felicity!'"[3] Children in the Mahābhārata are not only seen as instrumental in the fulfillment of a sacred duty which, however agreeable and meritorious, still carries the connotation of religious necessity and social imposition. They are also portrayed as a source of emotional and sensual gratification. Listen to Shakuntalā, the forsaken wife of Dushyanta, asking the king to acknowledge his son:

What happiness is greater than what the father feels when the son is running towards him, even though his body is covered with dust, and clasps his limbs? Even ants support their own without destroying them, then why shouldst not thou, virtuous as thou art, support thy own child? The touch of soft sandal paste of woman, of [cool] water is not so agreeable as the touch of one's own infant son locked in one's embrace. As a Brāhman is the foremost of all bipeds, a cow, the foremost of all quadrupeds, a guru, the foremost of all superiors, so is the son the foremost of all objects agreeable to touch. Let, therefore, this handsome child touch thee in embrace. There is nothing in the world more agreeable to the touch than the embrace of one's son.

Sanskrit poets, too, have waxed lyrical over the parental longing for children and the parents' emotions at the birth of a child. In two well-known examples, Bhavabhūti describes Rāma's love for Lava and Kusha, while Bānabhatta rhapsodizes over Prabhakar-vardhana's love for his son, Harsha. The greatest of all Sanskrit poets, Kālidāsa, in his *Raghuvamsha*, describes Dilīpa's response to Raghu's birth thus:

He went in immediately (on hearing the news) and as the lotus becomes motionless when the breeze stops, he gazed at his son's face with the same still eyes. Just as tides come into the ocean when it sees the moon, similarly the King (Dilīpa) was so happy on seeing his son that he could not contain the happiness in his heart.[4]

FATHER AND
CHILD, INDIA.
CAMILLA JESSEL

The demands of objectivity compel us to report that the intense parental longing and pleasure at the birth of a child in the Indian tradition is generally limited to sons. Girls receive a more muted reception. Although a first-born daughter may be regarded by parents as a harbinger of good luck, the welcome accorded to further daughters declines markedly.

Contemporary anthropological studies from different parts of India and the available clinical evidence assure us that the traditional preference for sons is very much intact.[5] At the birth of the son drums are beaten in some parts of the country, conch shells are blown in others, and the midwife is paid lavishly, but no such spontaneous rejoicing accompanies the birth of a daughter. Women's folk songs reveal a painful awareness of their ascribed inferiority—of this discrepancy, at birth, between the celebration of sons and the mere tolerance of daughters. Thus, in a north Indian song, the women complain:

Listen, O Sukhmā, what a tradition has started!
Drums are played upon the birth of a boy,
But at my birth only a brass plate was beaten.[6]

And in Maharashtra, the girl, comparing herself to a white sweet-scented jasmin (*jai*) and the boy to the big, strong-smelling flower (*keorā*), plaintively asks:

Did anyone notice the sweet fragrance of a jai?
The hefty keorā however has filled the whole street
with its strong scent'.[7] ■

Dr. Sudhir Kakar is an internationally
noted psychoanalyst and a Senior Fellow
at the Centre for the Study of Developing
Societies in Delhi, India.

NANDI (GIVING DELIGHT) IS THE NAME OF THE GOD ŚIVA'S SACRED WHITE ZEBU BULL, WHOSE IMAGE APPEARS IN TEMPLES THROUGHOUT INDIA. AS AN IMAGE OF VIRILITY, NANDI CAN AID FERTILITY AND OFTEN IS WORSHIPPED BY BARREN WOMEN WHO DESIRE CHILDREN (cat. 16).

WERNER FORNOS FIVE BILLION AND COUNTING:
WE NEED MORE BIRTH CONTROL

The birth recently of the five-billionth human to share our planet brings attention to the rapid increase of global population. Moreover, it raises serious questions regarding the durability of the earth's natural systems and resources.

The world is growing by an unprecedented 1 million people every four to five days, 85 million a year. Population has doubled in the last 35 years and it is projected to double again in the next 40.

Dr. Norman Borlaug, Nobel laureate and father of the green revolution, doubts the world's ability to feed an additional five billion people within the next four decades. Lester Brown, president of the Worldwatch Institute, offers overwhelming evidence that our planet's carrying capacity is already bursting at the seams.

But even if it could be proved that there is no correlation whatsoever between rapid population growth and the earth's ecosystems and resources, there still would be compelling reasons for encouraging lower birth rates: the health and very lives of millions of women and children in the Third World where 90 percent of the world population growth occurs.

Ten million infants die each year in the developing world. A major expansion of family planning services could reduce those deaths by half or more, according to findings of the World Fertility Survey. An estimated 500,000 women in the developing world die each year as the result of pregnancy and childbirth complications. About one-quarter of these women could be saved if unwanted pregnancies could be avoided, according to a Columbia University report.

The World Fertility Survey concluded that children born less than two years apart are much more likely to die in infancy or in early childhood than those whose births are spaced at intervals of two or more years. The pattern was present in all 41 developing countries included in the survey. In Tunisia, Syria, Jordan, Yemen, and Portugal, infants born less than two years apart are about 2½ times more likely to die in their first year than children born 24 to 47 months apart. In these same countries, infants born less than two years apart are up to five times more likely to die in their first year than those spaced at intervals of four or more years. Children born less than two years apart are twice as likely to die before reaching their first birthday in Bangladesh, Morocco, and Turkey than those spaced 24 to 47 months apart.

Meanwhile, a substantial portion of developing world women already have all the children they want, according to the World Fertility Survey. The range varies from 12 percent in Ghana to 61 percent in Colombia and Sri Lanka. The average is about 50 percent. But a great majority of these women do not have access to family planning information or services.

A Columbia University report claims that avoiding unwanted pregnancies would have a considerable impact on reducing maternal mortality, especially since the proportion of women who want no more children rises sharply with age and with the number of living children. This is most significant because older women and those who already have many children stand a higher risk of dying as a result of childbirth than do women in their 20s and those with only two to four children.

Data on maternal and child mortality in the developing world should be an essential factor in the current political dialogue on U.S. funding for international population programs. If existing family planning services are cut back or withdrawn, there is every reason to believe that deaths among women during pregnancy and childbirth as well as among infants and children born at less than two-year intervals will escalate considerably.

The U.S. Agency for International Development has withdrawn its funding of the International Planned Parenthood Federation, the largest nongovernment provider of family planning services for Third World women. And the future of U.S. funding for the United Nations Fund for Population Activities, the largest multilateral organization providing such services, is in doubt. The blue-ribbon Committee on African Development Strategies has urgently recommended resumption of U.S. contributions to both IPPF and UNFPA as a key to slowing down population growth and preventing future famines in Africa, the region of the world with the highest fertility rates and the highest susceptibility to malnutrition, hunger, and starvation.

Today's unprecedented world population growth is due primarily to a combination of declining death rates and the young age structure of the developing world, where more than half of the population is either in or entering its childbearing years.

Lower mortality rates have resulted in large measure from improvements in nutrition and public hygiene and advances in medical technology—notably smallpox vaccinations, widespread use of antibiotics, and malaria control programs.

While the full consequences of continued rapid population growth may be unknown, the choice the United States and the industrialized world must make is clear. By drastically cutting back or withdrawing international population assistance, we would risk proliferating human suffering and chaos on a global scale and we would be signing the death warrants of countless women and children in the Third World.

Or we can substantially accelerate our longstanding commitment to the most effective and humane solution for reducing rapid population growth—voluntary family planning assistance—and reduce infant mortality by one-half and maternal mortality by one-quarter. If we are ready and willing to meet this monumental challenge, our legacy to future generations will be an opportunity for a better quality of life and the achievement of greater human dignity. ■

Werner Fornos is president of the Population Institute, a nonprofit public education organization.

INDONESIAN
MOTHER BREAST-
FEEDS TWO
CHILDREN AT
ONE TIME.
KEN HEYMAN

ESTHER BOOHENE   ZIMBABWE'S BATTLE WITH BIRTH CONTROL

Overpopulation is a serious concern in Zimbabwe, a small nation that must feed a populace of over eight million. Though the family planning program here has seen some success, its achievements have been not so much in limiting population as in improving the health of mothers and babies. Infant mortality dropped from 83 deaths per 1,000 births in 1982 (according to that year's census) to between 60 and 70 per 1,000 (as estimated by a later Ministry of Health study). Meanwhile, the population continues to grow unchecked, at a rate of 3 percent every year, threatening to cancel out even these gains.

In many cultures, birth control is still taboo. Fortunately, the idea has secured a foothold here: 38 percent of women in their childbearing years practice it; 27 percent use modern methods. But, despite this prevalence, fertility rates remain high.

In Zimbabwe, most mothers use contraceptives not to curtail the size of their families, but to allow them more time to recover between pregnancies. While the well-being of both mothers and newborn has improved as a result, family size has stayed about the same.

To most Zimbabweans, the concept of using contraceptives to limit the number of children they have remains a foreign one. Cultural norms and socioeconomic conditions encourage early and universal marriage, and exert powerful pressure on couples to produce many offspring. For a woman, bearing and rearing children is the primary source of prestige in the family and community; the more children she has, the more status she enjoys. What's more, a recent reproductive health survey reported that women still have more children than they want: The average most women desire is 6, while the current fertility rate (the average number of children women have) is slightly more than that—6.6. Obviously, family planning in Zimbabwe faces some serious obstacles.

Family planning was first introduced here in 1953—by the Pathfinder Association of Boston—when the country was still the European colony of Rhodesia. In 1965, the Rhodesian government set up the Family Planning Association, with the objective of improving the health of mothers and children. Although the association did some useful work, it also developed a reputation for trying to limit the African population while encouraging growth among European settlers. As a result, the association's effectiveness in promoting family planning was greatly diminished among the population of most need.

When Zimbabwe won independence, its leaders recognized the nation's need for coordinated family planning. So, in 1981, the government took control of the Family Planning Association, put it under the Ministry of Health, and renamed it the Zimbabwe National Family Planning Council.

The council's primary goals are to improve the health of mothers and children by encouraging longer waiting times between births, and to reduce population growth by promoting smaller families. To achieve these aims, the council uses administrative centers in all eight of the country's provinces. The program

TWO CHILDREN AT
A MARRIAGE
CEREMONY IN
SEGU, MALI.
ERIK HESMERG

69

uses the following family planning methods: voluntary sterilization, intra-uterine devices, hormonal injection, the pill, and barrier techniques. These methods are delivered by both larger institutions and centers based in the community. The institution-based system concentrates on the pill because there are few personnel trained in the semi-permanent and permanent methods, and most Zimbabwean women shy away from sterilization, because of cultural inhibitions. The community-based distribution system—the backbone of the national program—also focuses on the pill. Consequently, about 85 percent of the clientele use this method.

The main problem with relying on the pill, of course, is that its use—though prevalent—is not lowering fertility rates. A study by the evaluation and research unit of women in their childbearing years found that only 10 percent use contraceptives out of a desire to stop having children. Many of these are older women who have already borne as many children as they want, and sometimes more. It is only after eight children, on average, that women use the pill to limit family size rather than to allow more time between pregnancies.

Today, many women are using contraceptives to space their pregnancies further apart, but because of the widespread desire for large families, the time between births remains relatively short. Program feedback indicates that birth intervals are two years or less. But once the nine months for the pregnancy is subtracted from this interval, only fifteen months remain—on average—when a woman would be using the pill. And, for at least part of this time, the pill's effectiveness would be nullified by the contraceptive effect of breast feeding.

The effectiveness of the pill has also been questioned from other quarters. Though studies have yet to be done to confirm it, program feedback indicates that many women are not following instructions for using the pill properly.

The program's shortcomings are apparent—its overdependence on the pill and its inability to change attitudes toward the use of birth control, among others. Despite them, the program has made some great achievements. The strategy of using centers in the community to both spread birth-control information and to distribute contraceptives has made the idea of family planning acceptable to both urban and rural populations. And, as far as the national program is concerned, the goal of improving the health of mothers

THIS SMALL FIGURE IS CALLED *AKUA BA*, OR "AKUA'S CHILD," IN REFERENCE TO AN ASHANTI STORY ABOUT A BARREN WOMAN NAMED AKUA. AKUA CONSULTED A PRIEST, WHO TOLD HER TO HAVE A SMALL FIGURE OF A BEAUTIFUL CHILD CARVED THAT SHE COULD CARRY ON HER BACK AS SHE WOULD A REAL INFANT. FRIENDS LAUGHED AT HER, CALLING ON EVERYONE TO SEE "AKUA'S CHILD." BUT WHEN AKUA BORE A BEAUTIFUL DAUGHTER, OTHER ASHANTI WOMEN ADOPTED THE PRACTICE AS A CURE FOR BARRENNESS (cat. 24).

and children by giving mothers more time to recover between births is being achieved. This, together with other efforts by the Ministry of Health and similar agencies, has saved the lives of many women and children.

This broad-based interest in widening the intervals between births presents the opportunity for introducing more modern birth-control methods to help women achieve their preference— either increasing the time between their pregnancies or limiting the number of children.

The program has built a good foundation for the future. Although it has concentrated on the pill, it has at the same time convinced people that modern methods are more effective than traditional ones. And the council has developed a plan to deal with the program's deficiencies: Personnel in the community centers and health workers in villages will be trained to focus on educating and motivating couples in semi-permanent and permanent methods. Hopefully, this will eventually make the idea of limiting family size acceptable and more couples will adopt such methods earlier, improving the effectiveness of birth control in Zimbabwe. ∎

Dr. Esther Boohene is program coordinator for the Zimbabwe National Family Planning Council.

You will become pregnant if you let your husband hang his pants on the bedpost.

USA

"RICH MAN? POOR MAN?…" PEOPLE IN MANY PARTS OF THE WORLD TRY TO PREDICT THEIR CHILD'S SEX, FUTURE OCCUPATION, OR PROSPECTS FOR SUCCESS. THESE 18TH-CENTURY ITALIAN CARDS WERE ADAPTED TO AN INTRICATE FORTUNE-TELLING SYSTEM, *TAROCCHI,* THAT EMPLOYS TRUMPS IN DIFFERENT ORDERS AND NUMBERS TO YIELD SPECIFIC INFORMATION ABOUT THE FUTURE. SUCH SYSTEMS WERE OFTEN USED TO PREDICT ONE'S CHANCES FOR FERTILITY, CONDITION DURING PREGNANCY, AND THE OUTCOME FOR THE BIRTH OF A HEALTHY CHILD (cat. 49).

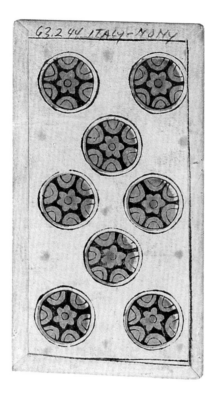

If you want a baby, get out of bed headfirst for four days. Present your backside instead if you do not wish to become pregnant.

USA

If you seem unable to bear children, then you should tie a red ribbon around the finger of a deceased relative or friend, who will be reminded to intercede for you when he appears before God.

CZECHOSLOVAKIA

If a woman leaves a diaper under a bed in the home where she is visiting there soon will be another birth at that house.

USA

MECHAI VIRAVAIDYA   HUMOR SELLS BIRTH CONTROL IN THAILAND

In Thailand, where the people are known for their kind smiles and sense of humor, the distribution of humorous promotional items was one important way to draw attention to the family planning services offered. The publicity campaign of the nongovernmental program included T-shirts emblazoned with slogans such as "Stop at two" or "A condom a day keeps the doctor away." These same slogans were also printed on cigarette lighters, matchbooks, pens, and a variety of other inexpensive but useful items. The family planning key ring that was attached to a plastic encased condom that beckons "In case of emergency, break glass" was an immensely popular item that has been sold all over Southeast Asia.

Although some readers may find all this silliness a little distasteful or even absurd, I would like to point out that if one can get people to laugh together about the topic of family planning, the battle is half over. The most important lesson to remember is that you are serving the people. If they can laugh and appreciate the humor, then you have effectively spread the word.

Additional campaigns to help people to better understand the "less attractive" yet more effective form of family planning, sterilization, are also necessary. The dilemma is how to make vasectomies and tubal ligations widely accepted.

Humor and fun, of course, was the method used in Thailand. By sponsoring "vasectomy festivals" on public holidays, where health and family planning displays, entertainment, balloons, and snacks helped create a carnival-like atmosphere, the public became more aware of the vasectomy as a safe and practical way to practice birth control for those couples that had completed their families. Of course, the media was attracted to these events, and this provided an important forum to spread the word of family planning.

Following up the humor with a concerted educational program completes the advertising strategy. The publication of pamphlets, colorful posters, and the use of radio campaigns, which in Thailand also included a cassette of "pop" family planning tunes, will inform a large segment of the population about the various methods that are available. Training programs for the grassroots distributors will allow them to be fully informed when curious villagers come to ask for family planning advice.

On a broader scale, the work of the family planning agency, whether successful or not, must be shared with the international community. For most family planning programs operating in the Third World, outside funding is necessary to implement a program that is large enough to fully meet the needs of the nation. Attention to the needs of the family planning agency must be sought through the preparation of proposals that feature sound project planning and realistic yet attractive targets. When it is able to meet these targets even on a small scale, the agency has proved itself to be capable and efficient.

In the case of Thailand, the coupling of family planning programs with other health services such as parasite control and environmental sanitation has proved to create greater incentives for the families to practice contraception. Family planning therefore becomes just one component in the overall development and improvement of the quality of life of the target population.

Family planning programs that espouse such wide goals are able to stand on their own merit. The publicity campaigns that first draw attention to the programs will need to continue, but the implementation of an effective and sound program will serve as the greatest public relations tool available for any family planning administrator.

My experience in Thailand has shown that the message of family planning can be shared with people of all ages, men and women, living in the rural and urban areas by backing up the seriousness of population growth with a little humor and fun. The attention that comes as a result of humorous publicity campaigns will serve as an important backup to the reliability and accountability that must be gained by the family planning agency with its local clientele and its domestic and international supporters.

Behind all the glitter and laughter, the people will fully understand the slogan that has been adopted in Thailand that "Many children will make you poor." ■

Mechai Viravaidya is founder and secretary-general of the Population and Community Development Association, the largest private, nonprofit family planning and development organization in Thailand, and serves as deputy minister of industry in the Royal Thai government.

SCOTT SULLIVAN   EUROPE'S POPULATION BOMB:
DECLINING BIRTHRATES CAUSE NEW
SOCIAL PROBLEMS

With much fanfare, the French government has announced a new program to encourage larger families: It will pay mothers who give birth to a third or subsequent child a "temporary maternal salary" of as much as $280 a month for three years. All over Europe, governments are beginning to feel the effects of a sharp decline in the birthrate. Britain is cutting university subsidies, and Belgium is laying off high-school teachers. West Germany plans to extend the period that draftees must serve in the armed forces from 15 months to 18. East Germany gives interest-free housing loans to young parents and forgives part of the debt each time they produce a baby.

On both sides of the East-West divide, Europe is in the throes of a demographic revolution. More young Europeans than ever are not getting married. Those who do are marrying later and having fewer children, and a significant number of two-career couples are deciding not to have children at all. As a result, the Continent's population will begin to decline in the 1990s. West Germany now has the lowest birthrate—1.3 children per woman—in its history. In Britain fertility has dropped by a third in the past 13 years. Even Catholic Italy will soon start to lose population if present trends continue. The birthrates of the Warsaw Pact countries, including the European portion of the Soviet Union, also have fallen sharply. The only Western European nations with enough births to maintain their size are Ireland and Greece. "In demographic terms, Europe is vanishing," says French Prime Minister Jacques Chirac.

The consequences of the demographic revolution will be far-reaching. Before long both NATO and the Warsaw Pact may be hard-pressed to find enough manpower to fulfill their military needs. Schools will be closed, and tens of thousands of teachers thrown out of work as the sparse classes of children born in the 1970s and '80s move through the educational system. By the end of the century, today's unemployment will be replaced by a shortage of workers, particularly of skilled labor. European governments will have to provide pensions and medical care for the 25 percent of their populations that will be older than 60, while the number of working taxpayers simultaneously shrinks.

Some of the direst predictions could be exaggerated. It usually takes three or four decades for major demographic changes to take effect. Today's working women who are postponing their childbearing still could turn out nearly as fertile as their mothers. But for over a decade, birthrates in every major European country have remained below the "replacement number" of 2.1 children per woman (the number required to replenish the existing population). Already West Germany, Britain, Belgium, Denmark, Luxembourg,

HENRY VIII's SECOND
WIFE, ANNE BOLEYN,
FAILED TO PRODUCE A
MALE HEIR. IN 1536, SHE
WAS BEHEADED (cat. 47).

East Germany, Hungary, and Czechoslovakia are certain to lose population in the first few decades of the next century. Italy, France, and the Netherlands may be in the same boat. (The U.S. birthrate is 1.8.)

With fewer babies being born, the "graying" of Europe is well under way. The average life expectancy for Western European men has shot up from 64 years in 1951 to 71 today. Thirty years ago European women could look forward to living to the age of 68; the figure now is 78, and it will rise above 81 by the year 2000. "France and Europe are entering a demographic winter," warns Gérard-François Dumont, a leading French demographer.

There is no clear agreement on why Europeans are having fewer offspring in prosperous times. Some demographers see the downturn as part of a long trend that began in the mid-19th century. Others argue that it is the product of a recent change in lifestyles and values. Most young Europeans still pay lip service to the family, but increasing numbers prefer cohabitation to marriage. Many young women want careers, to buy a better standard of living. "Children are no longer perceived as an investment in the future," says Christine Wattelar of the Catholic University of Louvain in Belgium. "They are seen as an extra expense, and the only return they offer is an emotional one." Michel Debré, a former French prime minister, complains: "We have destroyed marriage and the family as social values. We have erected greed and self-indulgence as our idols."

Government efforts to boost the birthrate generally haven't panned out. France has had vigorous pro-birth policies ever since the 1930s. All parents receive substantial payments and services to help with child-rearing. This year Chirac's government sweetened the pot with new benefits for parents who have three or more children. Despite all those efforts, France's birthrate fell from 2.7 children per woman in 1960 to 1.8 today.

East Germany also has had mixed results in its attempts to stimulate more births. In 1976, the government introduced a lavish set of pro-family incentives, including extra vacation time and six months of maternity leave. For three years, the birthrate shot up as young couples cashed in. But by 1980 the boom fizzled. Attempts to spur childbearing elsewhere in Eastern Europe also have provided no lasting results.

If a prosperous country cannot produce enough of its own children it can always import new citizens from abroad. In the booming 1960s all the major European countries imported labor, mainly from Turkey, Yugoslavia, and North Africa. European demographers note that the United States is more than compensating for its own demographic shortfall through massive immigration (both legal and illegal) from Mexico, the Caribbean, and Southeast Asia. Europeans resist immigration because of the current unemployment problem—and the 10 million foreign workers and their families who already need to be assimilated into their societies. But as European populations decline, more immigrants may be needed to keep industry going.

Europe has time to meet the demographic problem if it starts soon. A much wider use of flexible working time would enable national economies to cope with unequal flows into and out of the labor market. The introduction of more women into the armed forces and the use of private contractors to perform many routine military tasks would allow Europe to maintain its defenses. But such steps must be taken quickly. Otherwise Europe could be in for a very long demographic winter indeed, not so much due to a failure of activity "between the sheets," as the pro-natalists might put it, but to a multinational failure of imagination. ∎

Scott Sullivan writes for Newsweek.

ALTHOUGH POLITICAL ALLIANCES PLAYED A ROLE IN KING HENRY VIII's CHOICE OF MATES, THE STABILITY OF HIS MARRIAGES DEPENDED LARGELY ON THE SUCCESS OF A PARTICULAR WIFE TO BEAR A MALE HEIR TO THE THRONE OF ENGLAND. ONLY ONE OF HIS SIX WIVES—JANE SEYMOUR—BORE A SON (cat. 47).

For about a decade and a half now the peoples in the nations of the free, modern, industrial world—that's us in the United States, plus Canada, Western Europe, and Japan—*have not borne enough children to reproduce themselves over an extended period of time.*

We had a Baby Boom.

Now there is a Birth Dearth.

It is interesting, traveling to the nations afflicted by the birth dearth. In each country, someone—usually quite bright and educated—will inform you of one or two specific and unique reasons why the fertility rate has fallen so far, so fast *in that particular country.*

In Germany, you will be told that Germans don't really like children—there is even a word for it (*kinderfeindlichkeit*). In the Netherlands, people will tell you that there was a particularly big population explosion after World War II, that the country is geographically small, and so, very low fertility rates were bound to come. In Italy, one is told that while Italians love children, in the old days Italian women had so many children that their daughters saw how difficult it was, so they are having very few of their own.

In the United States, too, we hear some very specific tales of causation. It's said by some economists, for example, that real income didn't go up, or actually went down, starting in 1973, and the now-maturing baby boom generation really can't afford babies, and so aren't having babies. The trouble with that thesis is that the birthrate started falling 16 years prior to 1973, and by 1973 the total fertility rate (TFR) was down to 1.8, about where it is now. The fall in births came *before* the alleged fall in incomes.

More generally in the United States, it is said that the yuppies, American-style, are selfish materialists, interested only in themselves, their cars, their wines, their clothes, their jobs—but they don't have the social responsibility that yields either a caring society, or babies.

All these rather specific stories about specific countries make the question of causation an interesting one for a writer delving into the matter.

But, of course, there is a problem: for the birth dearth is not unique to Americans, Germans, Italians, and Dutch. It is going on everywhere in the developed world. It's happened on the small crowded island nation of Japan and on the big sparse island nation of Australia. It's happened during times of boom or recession. It's happened under liberal or conservative governments, in nations with allegedly permissive standards (Scandanavia) and nations that are allegedly somewhat more traditional (Japan). It's happened in countries with big prior population explosions (like the Netherlands) and in countries with small population explosions (like England.)

Not only is it happening everywhere in the developed world, but it's been happening for a long time. Theodore Roosevelt complained about America's falling birthrate during the 1890s, when lifetime births averaged over four children per woman. Mussolini complained about Italy's low birthrate. In the 1930s, sociologist Gunnar Myrdal viewed falling Swedish birthrates with alarm, in part to convince Swedish right-wing politicians to endorse welfare-state proposals, which he said would raise fertility. In fact, as noted, birthrates in the developed world have been declining since there has been a developed world. The Industrial Revolution apparently contained a fertility depressant. Demographers call it "the demographic transition"—the shift from high to low fertility.

What is new about the birth dearth is not its direction, which is down. What's new is its level—to a rate well below what is required to keep a population stable, and the fact that population decline is occurring when the nations involved are at peace and generally prosperous. Over the years, most demographers assumed that the decline would stop at the TFR of about 2.1 because the species would (in theory) eventually disappear if a 2.1 rate was not maintained. But just who is "the species"? They are just plain individuals, people who are in the bedroom making very personal, very individualistic decisions. The people in the bedroom are not thinking about "the species" at all. They are thinking about their own lives and beliefs, and how their lives and beliefs interact with the conditions they face.

Is their residence large enough for a baby? Is a bigger one available? Will Tom's salary be enough to support them if Sally stops working to have a baby? Does Sally want to stop working? Will they have enough money for college costs when the baby is no longer a baby? Won't their standard of living fall? Will Sally get maternity leave and get her job back? If she stays home for a few years, will she fall off the career track? Will Tom really share 50-50 in taking care of the baby? But doesn't he have to travel in his work? Can Sally cope with both a job and a child? Two children? Three?

So the history of fertility, and the fertility decline, is a history of very personal decisions that are often played out upon a backdrop of some conditions that are common to all the modern nations, many of which can be quite impersonal. Urbanization, job availabilities, contraception, and abortion come most immediately to mind.

But young people have not yet been educated that such private decisions may have a harmful public effect or a harmful personal effect. They do not know that the birth dearth may ultimately hurt them due to busted pension plans or economic dislocations or domestic turmoil. They do not know the ramifications of the birth dearth that can yield a world inhospitable to values they cherish. They do not know that in some nations (not the United States) the birth dearth could yield—let us say it—a withering-away. And my sense is that many are not fully aware of the potential personal sorrow that may befall them.

So, the first course of action is education. Accordingly, let us call a moratorium on calling yuppies and other young people "selfish" until they understand that their private choices will have public effects which they may not like. Once educated, they may act differently. ■

Ben Wattenberg is a Senior Fellow at the American Enterprise Institute and co-editor of Public Opinion *magazine.*

XIANGYING WANG   FAMILY PLANNNING IN THE
PEOPLE'S REPUBLIC OF CHINA

A profound revolution in human life is taking place in this vast land. For the first time in history, the men and women of China have succeeded in improving the quality of life—for themselves as well as for future generations. They have achieved this success through modernization and a nationwide population control program.

Since the founding of the Republic in 1949, fundamental changes have come about in the people's social, economic, and cultural lives. China's industry and agriculture have increased their gross output an average of 11 percent every year since 1973 (before then, the annual average was 2.2 percent). Per capita income also increased—by 9.2 percent per year—in the same period (again, the annual average before 1973 was 2.2 percent). China's population growth has slowed as well: from 2.1 percent yearly in 1973 to 1.15 percent by 1985. This slowdown demonstrates the success of China's intensive birth-control program, and is the rationale for its continuation.

Nowadays, the conventional wisdom remains that China is an immense territory rich in natural resources. Looking at our country on a per capita basis challenges this view. Per capita, China's arable land is only one-third the world average; grassland is one-fourth, and forestry one-ninth. The Republic has 7 percent of the world's total land area, but must feed 22 percent of the world's population. By the end of 1986, China's population stood at over one billion. Though the growth rate has declined somewhat in recent years, between 1981 and 1985 some 23,000 babies were born *every day*—a rate of 22 per minute.

The changing age structure portends even further growth. The children of the early 1960s baby boom are coming of age; between 1987 and 1997, about 11 million couples each year will enter their marriage and childbearing years. Nevertheless, it is more than reasonable for the Chinese people to have ardent hopes that their lives will continue to improve. To show its commitment to the people, the Chinese government has set national goals for development. From now to the end of this century, every effort will be made to quadruple the annual gross output of industry and agriculture, while holding the population to around 1.2 billion.

To meet these targets, China has been quickening its development process and, at the same time, fostering its intensive population program. The program encourages late marriage, delayed childbearing, and fewer, but healthier, births.

The specific policy since 1979 has been to advocate one child per couple. Those who wish to have a second child—with good reasons—can do so, but in a planned way. For national minorities, two children per couple is encouraged with an option for a third. Most urban couples of reproductive age give birth to one child, while some rural couples still have two children and some even more than two. Currently, of the couples of reproductive age, 15 percent nationally and 10 percent in rural areas have pledged to have one child only.

FAMILY IN XINJIANG
PROVINCE, CHINA.
HIROJI KUBOTA/
MAGNUM

Sustained efforts have been made to publicize population awareness through the mass media, workshops, and seminars. Since 1981, the program's message has also been put out through the junior and senior high school curricula.

A supply network has also made all kinds of contraceptives accessible, free of charge. Contraceptive and counseling services are provided by the family planning department in every hospital at and above the county level, by family planning clinics in cities, and by local doctors in towns and villages. In cities, every drugstore has a counter where free contraceptives are available.

In many localities, the one-child family is given preferred treatment in medical care, house allocation, and employment opportunities as well as in enrollment of the child in nurseries, kindergartens, and schools. A one-child family in urban areas is entitled to a cash subsidy for the child's health care until he or she reaches 14 years of age, and the mother is given extended maternity leave with full pay. For the rural population, a one-child family is allocated a larger share of land under contract or a reduced grain tax quota. Priority is given to them for loans, technical support, and other government assistance.

There is, however, no unified standard of disincentives. Usually, the parents of an unplanned child pay an amount equal to 5 to 10 percent of their total income, as a token of sharing the additional cost with the community.

CHINESE WORKERS MAKE THEIR DAILY COMMUTE. HIROJI KUBOTA/ MAGNUM

Socioeconomic development, improvement of health care and education, greater involvement of women in the labor force, a change of lifestyle—and the family planning program itself—have jointly paved the way for the acceptance of the small family. By 1985, the growth rate of the population had dropped from 26 percent in 1970 to 11 percent; the mortality rate decreased from 25 percent before 1949 to 7 percent, where it has stabilized. The total fertility rate (the average number of children per woman) dropped from 5.68 in the 1960s to 2. By the end of 1985, the prevalence of contraceptives had reached 74 percent, and the average age of first marriage for Chinese women had increased from 19 years old in the 1950s to 22. Life expectancy had increased from 35 years in 1949 to 68.9 years and the infant mortality rate had gone down from 200 per thousand in 1949 to 35 per thousand.

Surveys on sex preference and child value indicate that ideas on childbearing are changing swiftly. The traditional notions that "more sons equal more blessings" and "boys are superior to girls" are being replaced with "one child with a better education is a lot better than more children without education" and "boys and girls are equally valuable." To make life enjoyable for our own generation rather than raising more children is the common goal of most young people in China today. ∎

Xiangying Wang wrote this article while in Washington, D.C., as a visiting scholar with the National Academy of Sciences and the Population Crisis Committee. She lives in Beijing.

SANDY ROVNER   MAKING BABIES: HOW SCIENCE CAN
HELP INFERTILE COUPLES

Once it was simple. Boy meets girl, girl marries boy, couple makes baby.

But today, there are many ways to make babies.

Since 1978, an estimated 2,000 babies have been born worldwide whose conception is owed, one way or another, to something aside from—or in addition to—the conventional way such things are accomplished.

Although in some quarters there continues to be uneasiness, even serious qualms, about the religious and ethical issues involved, it looks as if these babies, wherever and however conceived—in whose womb with whose sperm and whose egg—are here to stay.

The technology is exploding. In this country alone, there are already almost 150 fertility centers specializing in IVF—in vitro fertilization.

In vitro means literally "in glass." In IVF programs, a human egg is fertilized by a human sperm in a laboratory petri dish. The resulting embryo is grown for a short period in the dish and then either implanted in a woman's uterus or frozen for later attempts at implantation.

Physicians are acquiring new skills. They have learned to pluck the ripe egg from the ovary at precisely the optimum second using a long aspiration needle guided by ultrasound, so surgery is often unnecessary. They are also becoming comfortable with older techniques, such as insertion of a thin tube—called a laparoscope—near the navel to diagnose and treat fertility-impairing conditions such as endometriosis, which causes blockage of the fallopian tubes.

Says veteran fertility specialist Dr. Howard Jones, whose pioneering Norfolk, Virginia, clinic is the universally accepted standard against which all others in this country are measured: "One of the most important developments is that in vitro fertilization and some of its alternatives have at last given us something more we can offer our patients who previously were at the end of the line."

The exquisitely timed and infinitely complicated physiological processes that create a healthy sperm and egg, plus the almost split-second timing required to synchronize their meeting during the few hours a month the egg is literally ripe and ready, make one wonder at the miracle of conception even in the natural scheme of things.

There are so many potential pitfalls along the way that it is not at all surprising that an estimated 4.5 million American couples—about one out of five—who want to have a baby are unable to after a year of trying, the time frame used to signify a "fertility problem."

When the natural process works, a woman's reproductive cycle is coordinated by a part of the brain called the hypothalamus. Among its many functions, the hypothalamus sends out hormonal signals directing the pituitary gland to produce two hormones—follicle-stimulating hormone (fsh) and luteinizing hormone (lh). They stimulate the ovaries to mature some of the 400,000 eggs each woman is born with, and they also stimulate the production of estrogen, which thins vaginal secretions, making it easier for sperm to reach the egg during intercourse. This thinning also prepares the lining of the uterus for the implantation of an egg once it has been fertilized.

In the male, a hypothalamic hormone called gonadotropin-releasing hormone (GnRH) affects both fertility and libido. The pituitary hormones, which act on a woman's ovaries, act in a male to stimulate the testes to produce sperm.

In the past, most research on fertility has involved the woman in the time-honored but erroneous assumption that "barrenness" was a female problem exclusively. But there is a matching set of disorders that can affect male fertility as well.

Although "the numbers game" is not always precise, Dr. Robert J. Stillman, director of George Washington University Medical Center's division of reproductive endocrinology and fertility, says that in general, 30 to 40 percent of fertility problems are related to the male and another third to the female. The rest are either a combination of both or cannot be pinpointed.

More and more formerly infertile couples can now bear children, Stillman says, as a result of advances in evaluation of both male and female factors, the possibility for both medical and surgical interventions and, finally, the options of in vitro fertilization with or without donor sperm, donor egg or, now, a donor uterus.

At the world IVF Congress in Melbourne, Australia, where IVF is virtually free or very cheap, the majority of patients who do not get pregnant quit the program before the third cycle.

In a single IVF try, the chances of achieving a pregnancy are generally deemed to be no more than 15 or 20 percent. The chances of a couple conceiving naturally in any given fertile period are only slightly higher.

To increase the odds, most IVF programs stimulate the patient's ovaries with drugs like Pergonal to produce multiple eggs, and three or four eggs are fertilized and implanted during each cycle. There are increasing numbers of cases in which more than one embryo implants, resulting in multiple births, usually twins.

IVF procedures usually cost between $3,000 and $5,000 for each try. Insurance carriers have been slow to include them in coverage, but gradually more and more plans are covering at least some of the costs.

Most experts agree that the newest breakthroughs in IVF technology involve techniques for freezing sperm, eggs, and embryos. For some years, sperm have been frozen in so-called sperm banks for artificial insemination. And most sperm for IVF are frozen now to provide a time lag that allows doctors to double-check the donor for acquired immune deficiency syndrome (AIDS) and avoid transmission to the embryo.

More recently, cryopreservation techniques have permitted the freezing of embryos and now, on an experimental basis, the successful freezing of unfertilized eggs. Egg freezing avoids the ethical issues or even scientific issues of what happens if you freeze the fertilized egg, which some people believe is more "human" than the unfertilized egg. The technology for freezing the egg has been difficult to perfect. It is, somehow, much more vulnerable to damage during the freezing and thawing processes than either the sperm or the embryo.

The Australians were the first to have to confront the "extra embryo" problem when an American couple, patients at an Australian fertility clinic, were killed in a plane crash leaving several embryos—the wife's eggs fertilized with donor sperm. After about a year of public controversy, Australian officials decided to permit the embryos to be implanted—anonymously—into the uterus of a surrogate mother and subsequently be put up for adoption. Had the egg alone been frozen, the question of disposition would have been free of the passions surrounding the "orphaned" embryos.

Says Stillman: "We may not know for years if you can have the egg frozen for long periods and have it fertilized later, and it is clearly still in the research phase."

"But," he added, "until about two years ago, all IVF was in a research phase, and the host uterus was just a dream." ∎

Sandy Rovner writes on health issues for the Washington Post.

CAPVT II.

De mixtura vtriusque sexus seminis, eiusque substantia & forma.

THIS ELABORATE DELIV-
ERY SCENE—RICH IN
INFORMATION ABOUT
16th-CENTURY CHILD-
BIRTH PRACTICES IN
GERMANY—SHOWS THE
EXPECTANT MOTHER
AND HER MIDWIFE, TWO
ASSISTANTS, SCISSORS
AND TWINE FOR THE
UMBILICAL CORD, A
TUB FOR WASHING
THE NEWBORN, AND
ASTROLOGERS WHO
PREPARE TO CAST THE
BABY'S HOROSCOPE
(cat. 48).

P Ostquam autem vterus, quod genitale fœminei sexus membrum
est, viri genituram conceperit, suum quoque semen illi admiscet,

Æ 3   ita:

Throwing old shoes at a newly wedded couple will bring many children.
ENGLAND

You will become pregnant right away if you put garlic in the keyhole of your honeymoon suite.
USA

You will become pregnant within six months if you lose a pair of earrings.
GUATEMALA

You will conceive if you mix an egg white and the white speck of an egg yolk with your husband's blood, stuff the mixture inside a dead man's bone and bury it.
HUNGARY

To prevent conception, have intercourse at dusk facing away from the setting sun.
CZECHOSLOVAKIA

Your husband will be sterile if there are three dust webs hanging from your bedroom ceiling.
USA

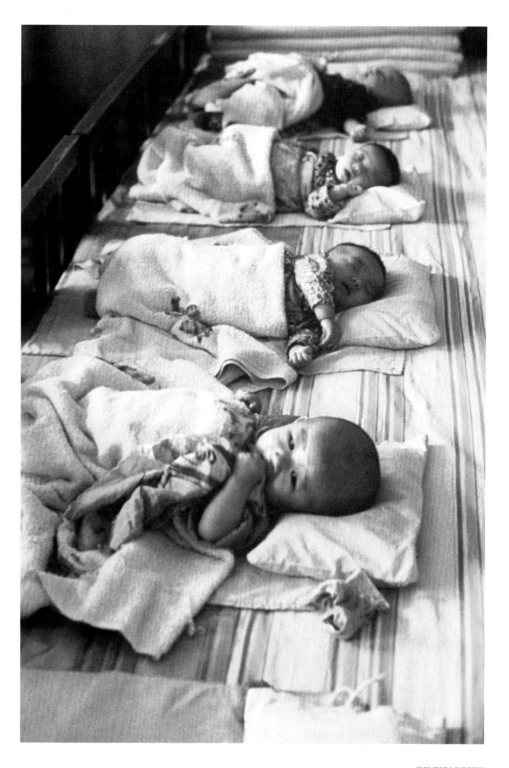

CHINESE NURSERY.
JACK LING/UNICEF

90

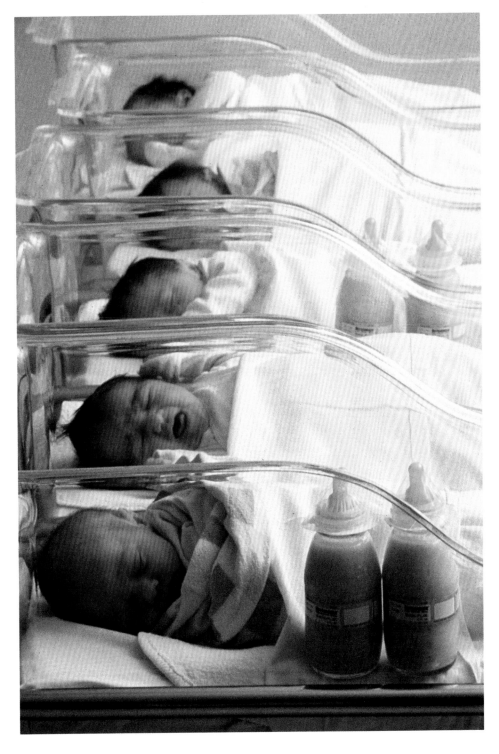

HOSPITAL NURSERY,
USA.
BURT GLINN/
MAGNUM

*You will conceive more easily if
you carry mistletoe.*
FRANCE

*Your child will be a boy if conception
occurs in the moonlight, but a girl if
conception occurs in the darkness.*
INDIA

*If you wish to conceive a girl, then lie
only on your right side during
intercourse. Lying on your left side
will bring a boy.*
WALES

*All your babies will be stillborn if you
meet a hearse on the way to the church
on your wedding day.*
GERMANY

*Tea brewed from the first wild
cornflowers will cause fertility in
a childless woman.*
USA

*Put your husband's pocketbook under
your pillow to insure fertility.*
USA

The woman on the table was straining to give birth. Her husband held her lovingly, as he had through her two other deliveries. Lynne and I stood and watched; we weren't taking part, and yet this event was happening for us. It was my baby that was being born, and it was Lynne, not the woman on the table, who was to be its mother.

Like most couples who choose surrogate parenting, Lynne and I believed that if we wanted a child we had no other recourse but to put our faith in people we barely knew—and in a procedure that had been barely explored. Lynne was born with a genetic neurological disorder, and she decided long ago that she would not risk passing the disease on. Her decision not to bear children had been painful. "I always wanted to have children," she says. "I always wanted to be a mother."

Soon after we were married, we began contacting adoption agencies. We had read about the dearth of available healthy white babies, but we weren't prepared for the other obstacles. Because I was 36 and Lynne 40, we were told by just about every agency that we were over their age limit. We also had been married for too short a time. Gradually we found ourselves leaning to surrogate parenting.

I contacted Michigan lawyer Noel Keane, who was known for his work with surrogates. Keane told me surrogate parenting had never been tested in court, and there were no laws protecting prospective parents. As a result, the contract between the surrogate and couple was not legally binding. The contract we would be required to sign with the surrogate and her husband called for her to be inseminated by my sperm, and if she became pregnant and delivered a child, to turn it over to me and my wife. The contract outlined our obligations to pay the surrogate's medical and other expenses and to put $10,000 in escrow. The money would be paid after she had fulfilled the contract. She would receive a partial payment if she miscarried, the amount determined by the length of the pregnancy. Her obligations included seeing an obstetrician regularly and avoiding illegal and nonprescribed drugs, alcohol, and cigarettes.

We could interview as many women as we wanted from the hundreds of applications Keane had on file. More than anything, we wanted someone who was warm, caring, intelligent, and healthy. If she had Lynne's coloring, that would be a plus. I wanted a woman who was 5 feet 6 or taller. Being 5 feet 5, I wanted to maximize the chances that my child would inherit tall genes.

We talked with several women the first day. Then we found Martha, who at 23 had two boys, ages two and three. "I would be helping someone else who could not have kids," she wrote on her application form. "Every home needs a child or it's empty." She made no bones about her other motive: "My husband is unemployed and I need the money to pay some bills." We wanted to meet Martha.

Martha came to Keane's office, accompanied by her two boys and husband, Peter. She was prettier than her picture, tall and thin, with reddish-brown hair. We asked if she would want any contact with us or the child after delivery. "Maybe a letter now and then and a picture at Christmas," she said. When we asked how they would feel if we were in the delivery room when Martha was to give birth, they both said that would be fine, and Peter added, "I'm going to be there, too." I felt that if Martha ever wavered about giving up the child, we could count on Peter to reinforce her commitment. By the end of the day, we had settled on Martha. Martha ovulated the following week, and I went to Detroit for the inseminations.

We were lucky. Within a month we learned that Martha was pregnant. From then on Lynne and I were typical expectant parents. We bought a crib, playpen, bassinet, changing table, and car seat. Every month I phoned Martha's doctor to see how the pregnancy was going and that she was keeping her appointments.

Many people asked us if we planned to tell the baby that she had been born to a surrogate. Yes, we answered, as soon as she was able to understand. We felt it was important to be totally honest.

In July Martha's physician told me that Martha was doing well. Her due date was set at around August 5. Lynne was determined to be there for the birth, and flew to Detroit on Sunday, July 28. I joined her on the weekend before the due date. The next two days dragged by. The baby had dropped lower, but Martha was not going into labor. The doctor scheduled an induction for the morning of August 8. We went to Martha's room after she was given labor-inducing drugs and waited for them to take effect. After several hours she was in great pain despite an injection of Demerol. I felt helpless. Had she been my wife I could at least have comforted her. Instead, Lynne took that role, holding Martha's hand and rubbing her back. I moved to the other side of the room and tried to watch "All My Children," which Martha had turned on, but I cringed as Martha's groans worsened.

Martha cried out for more pain medication, but the doctor said it might be bad for the baby and left. I followed her into the hall, needing reassurance that Martha was okay. But there was something else I wanted to discuss. The hospital staff had never had a surrogate birth before. I wanted them to be aware that Martha was not going to keep this baby. I suggested that the doctor tell the delivery-room nurses not to put the baby in Martha's hands immediately after it appeared because I didn't want the mother to bond with the child. The doctor said she understood and would speak to the staff.

An hour later the doctor returned, examined Martha and announced that it was time. Nurses wheeled Martha into the delivery room and Lynne and I put on scrub suits. At Martha's request, I stood behind her out of respect for her modesty. Lynne stood at the foot of the table, behind the doctor, and Peter leaned over the table and held Martha, who was screaming with pain. "I'm dying!" she yelled. "Take it out, cut me." Finally, the baby's head emerged. Lynne looked over at me, her eyes glowing. The nurses were also looking at me and smiling. "One more push, Martha," the doctor said, "here it comes…and it's…a baby girl."

Peter looked over at me. I could tell he was smiling broadly through his mask. One of the nurses motioned for me to go over to where they were cleaning the baby. I couldn't tell if she was pretty or not, or even if she was clearly mine. Her mouth, however, was definitely familiar—exactly like one of my niece's.

Lynne had moved to Martha's side and was holding her hand. Martha turned toward her and said, "Lynne, go see your baby." ■

Daniel Shapiro is Houston correspondent for Newsweek.

It's possible to be horrified by what happened to Mary Beth Whitehead in the Baby M case and still think that contract motherhood can be a positive thing if carefully regulated. If there had been better screening at the clinic, if the contract had included a grace period, if actual infertility had been required of Elizabeth Stern, the contracting mother, we would never have heard of Baby M. If, if, if.

Regulation might make contract motherhood less haphazard, but there is no way it can be made anything other than what it is: an inherently unequal relationship involving the sale of a woman's body and a child. The baby-broker's client is the father; his need is the one being satisfied; he pays the broker's fee. No matter how it is regulated, the business will have to reflect that priority. That's why the bill being considered in New York state specifically denies the mother a chance to change her mind, although the stringency of the Stern-Whitehead contract in this regard was the one thing pundits assured the public would not happen again. Better screening procedures would simply mean more accurately weeding out the trouble-makers and selecting for docility, naïveté, low self-esteem, and lack of money for legal fees. Free psychological counseling for the mothers, touted by some brokers as evidence of their care and concern, would merely be manipulation by another name. True therapy seeks to increase a person's sense of self, not reconcile one to being treated as an instrument.

Even if the business could be managed so that all the adults involved were invariably pleased with the outcome, it would still be wrong, because they are not the only people involved. There are, for instance, the mother's other children. Prospective contract mothers, Mrs. Whitehead included, do not seem to consider for two seconds the message they are sending to their kids. But how can it not damage a child to watch Mom cheerfully produce and sell its half-sibling while Dad stands idly by? I'd love to be a fly on the wall as a mother reassures her kids that of course she loves them no matter what they do; it's just their baby sister who had a price tag.

And, of course, there is the contract baby. To be sure, there are worse ways of coming into the world, but not many, and none that are elaborately prearranged by sane people. Much is made of the so-called trauma of adoption, but adoption is a piece of cake compared with contracting. Adoptive parents can tell their child, Your mother loved you so much she gave you up, even though it made her sad, because that was best for you. What can the father and adoptive mother of a contract baby say? Your mother needed $10,000? Your mother wanted to do something nice for us, so she made you? The Sterns can't even say that. They'll have to make do with something like, Your mother loved you so much she wanted to keep you, but we took you anyway, because a deal's a deal, and anyway, she was a terrible person. Great.

Oh, lighten up, you say. Surrogacy fills a need. There's a shortage of babies for adoption, and people have the right to a child.

What is the need that contract motherhood fills? It is not the need for a child, exactly. That need is met by adoption—although not very well, it's true, especially if the parents have their hearts set on a "perfect baby," a healthy white newborn. The so-called baby shortage is really a shortage of those infants. What William Stern wanted, however, was not just a perfect baby; the Sterns did not, in fact, seriously investigate adoption. He wanted a perfect baby with his genes and a medically vetted mother who would get out of his life forever immediately after giving birth. That's a tall order, and one no other class of father —natural, step-, adoptive—even claims to be entitled to. Why should the law bend itself into a pretzel to gratify it?

The Vatican's recent document condemning all forms of conception but marital intercourse was right about one thing. You don't have a right to a child, any more than you have a right to a spouse. You only have the right to try to have one. Goods can be distributed according to ability to pay, or need. People can't.

It's really that simple. ∎

Katha Pollitt, a poet and writer living in New York City, is a contributing editor of The Nation. *The Baby M case (a name used in court) was a custody battle between surrogate mother Mary Beth Whitehead and the couple who had contracted her to bear a child for them, Elizabeth and William Stern. Whitehead was artificially inseminated with William Stern's sperm, making them both the biological parents of Baby M. This article was written in response to New Jersey Judge Harvey Sorkow's 1987 ruling granting custody to the Sterns.*

FATHER AND BABY
GIRL, USA.
JEFFREY MacMILLAN

In a few years you can bet on it. Baby Girl Who is going to turn to her parents and ask, "Where did I come from?" This question won't bring on the normal, scaled-down, blushing nursery lecture about sex. Oh, what a different tale these parents have to tell.

Baby Girl Who (as in "Who" does this baby belong to?) was conceived last August. The egg and sperm of a couple from New York got together in a petri dish in Cleveland. What came from this union was an embryo. The embryo was implanted into the womb of a woman from Detroit.

The genes of the first woman and her husband were nourished and carried in the uterus of the second woman, who was paid $10,000 for fetus care. Then, on April 13 in Ann Arbor, Michigan, Baby Who was delivered into the arms of the couple from New York.

This is a story complex enough to make the average parent long for the stork system. In the origin of this member of the species, the birds and the bees had less to do with reproduction than doctors and lawyers had. For the very first time, the word "mother" was defined not in the delivery room but in the courtroom.

Baby Who was the product of one woman's genes and another woman's womb. She had in effect a genetic mother and a gestational mother. These two women were not in conflict; they were in cahoots. The genetic mother was fertile but had no uterus. The gestational mother had a womb for rent.

Nevertheless, they all went to court to clear up the question of parenthood before delivery. There a Detroit judge ruled that the genetic mother and father would be the *real* parents of the baby in the other mother's womb.

Is this beginning to sound like something out of Gilbert and Sullivan? *Brave New World?* Does it remind you of Margaret Atwood's *The Handmaid's Tale*?

Slowly, one step at a time, we have been separating reproduction from sexual intercourse. Artificial insemination, in vitro fertilization, surrogate motherhood. Now, in logical sequence, we have the surrogate motherhood of an in vitro fertilization. It requires a very tiny leap, more of a hop, to imagine a future embryo created from a sperm donor and an egg donor, implanted into a second woman, all for adoption by a third.

Who is the mother in that case? The one who provided the genes, the one who supplied the womb, or the one who set up the whole project in order to raise the child? We have never before had so many motherhood options. More to the point, we have never before said that a woman who gave birth to a baby is not its mother.

I am uncomfortable enough with a technology that reduces the pregnant woman to the status of a commercial vessel carrying genes to term for her employer. I am more uncomfortable when the courts take the motherhood title away. If the egg donor is the "real" mother, she might even win the right to protect her embryo if the "vessel" was smoking or eating improperly, or resisting medical treatment.

The situation is even more unnerving from the point of view of the baby, who has come from the egg and out of the womb. For two or three days Baby Girl Who was in legal limbo while the physicians did tests to confirm that the baby was the offspring of the genetic parents.

"It's intolerable to have a newborn baby and not know who its parents are," says medical ethics lawyer George Annas of Boston University, "If the question is what's best for the child, I would argue for the gestational mother. You know who that is. There is never any question in anyone's mind."

The presumption that the woman who carried the baby is the mother is common law in most states. It should be everywhere. The genetic parents can always adopt the baby. It may sound odd to adopt your own genetic offspring—what if the woman decided to keep Baby Who?—but it is the lesser risk.

All of these quandries, like the babies themselves, are born as we attempt an end run around nature. We don't accept limits, even the limits of fertility. Men and women who cannot conceive or carry children expect science to figure out a way for them to have babies, even their "own" babies. Science is most obliging.

By now we are so far removed from nature that we need a law to determine mother-hood. How odd that we find ourselves arguing about the definition of the very first word in any baby's vocabulary: "Mama." ∎

Ellen Goodman is a syndicated columnist living in Boston.

STEPHANIE MANSFIELD   A WOMB OF HIS OWN

Men and women are finally about to become wombmates if a British magazine's prediction is correct. Recently the general-circulation weekly *New Society* reported that the technology now exists for men to give birth.

That's right. Have babies.

Think of it. Magazine editors probably already are. (*Esquire:* BREAST FEEDING AND THE THREE-PIECE BUSINESS SUIT. *Sports Illustrated:* JOE MONTANA'S SUPERBABY.)

How could men have babies, you ask? Simple. A donated egg would be fertilized with sperm outside the body. The embryo would then be implanted in the bowel area, where it could attach itself to a major organ.

"It can be done," Dr. John Parsons, senior registrar and lecturer in obstetrics at King's College Hospital in London, was quoted as saying. "And undoubtedly, someone will do it."

The magazine said candidates for male pregnancy might be homosexuals, transsexuals, or men whose wives are infertile. To achieve pregnancy, males would have to receive hormone treatment to stimulate changes that occur naturally in females during pregnancy, according to the magazine. The treatment would enable the embryo to attach itself to a kidney or the wall of a large intestine, where it would create its own life-sustaining placenta.

"It could be done by getting an embryo to implant in the bowel," Dr. Alan Trounson, an expert in embryo freezing, was quoted as saying. Trounson, director of the Institute of Early Human Development at Monash University in Melbourne, Australia, also warned that male pregnancies would pose significant technical and ethical problems. "I think those risks are too big to try to establish pregnancy in man," he was quoted as saying. "But with careful evaluation of pregnancy those risks could be reduced."

Unfortunately, pregnant men would miss out on the joys of natural childbirth; according to the magazine, the babies would be delivered by Caesarean section.

For women, the news may come as a shock. For one thing, Burt Reynolds can now have his own babies. Worse, we'll have to rub our mates' backs, soothe their swollen ankles, and schlep out in the middle of the night to fetch them olives and Oreo Cookie ice cream.

Pin-striped suits will now come with optional Velcro closings. Paternity jockey shorts will have a special stretch panel. Having a baby will become a status symbol; Lee Iacocca will have twins. A pregnant David Hartman will finally beat Jane Pauley in the ratings as Dan Rather ponders career versus fatherhood.

And the next time the boss gets testy, we can sit back and shake our heads. "It's just his hormones." ∎
Stephanie Mansfield is a staff writer for the Washington Post.

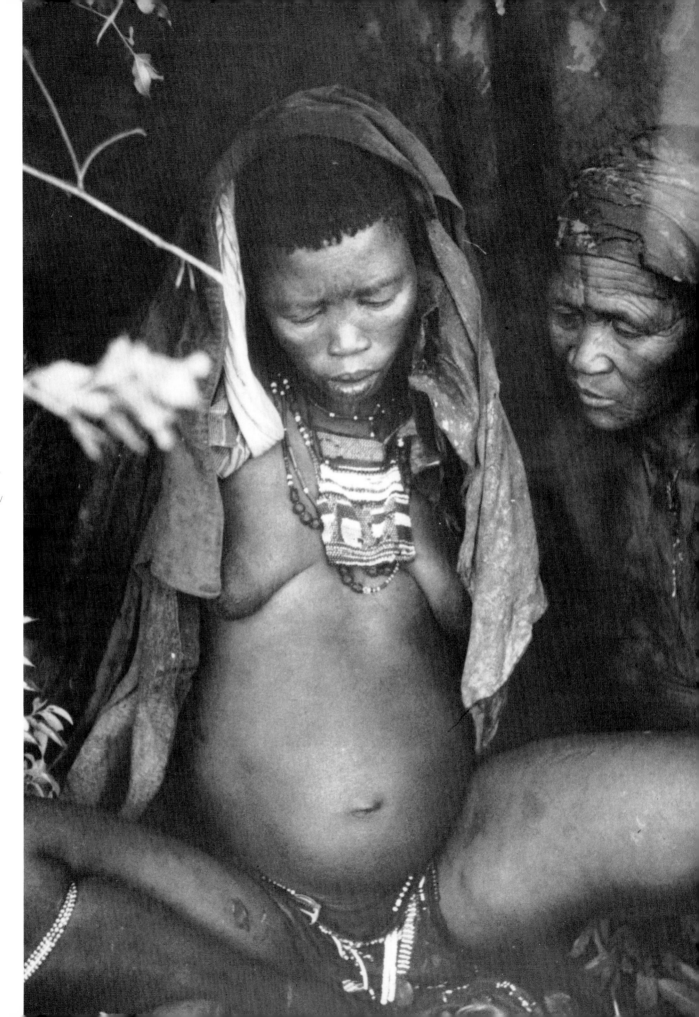

!KUNG SAN
EXPECTANT
MOTHER IN LABOR,
BOTSWANA.
MARJORIE SHOSTAK/
ANTHRO-PHOTO

100

TRAVAIL

Uncertainty circles the expectant mother and child.

Hope and fear accompany the nine-month wait…

Will we lull the child to sleep with song,

or mourn beside an empty cradle?

Will the child be born an heir,

a keeper of the family name?

Will the mother's body be strong enough for both of them?

Will she be able to endure the pain?

Will the child be graced with eyes that see,

with strong and sturdy limbs?

Will this waiting ever be over?

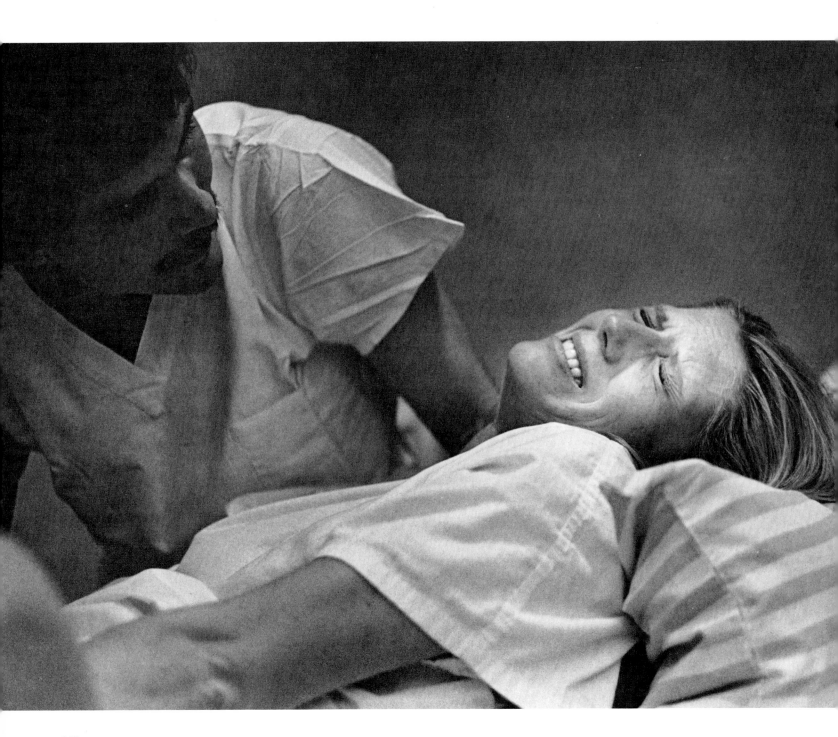

Birthing women kneel, squat, crouching, stand rooted in thatched hut or beneath palm-leaf awning, where water sluices the stones in a village bathhouse, in the forest clearing, by the river, or awash at the edge of the sea. The birthing woman is cradled in the strong arms of her sisters, women who have made this same journey and know it well. She draws strength from the eyes of the midwife, calling to Allah, Mary, mother, or biting her lips in silence as the womb energy sweeps through her.

When the birth is hard and weary, there is help to give. Unstop bottles, open doors, fling wide windows, pour rice grains through the shirtsleeves of the man who fathered this child, stream water through the chimney of the borning room. Take the eagle's feather and signal the four points of the compass, or cup your hand to capture corn, life-staple, and blow the spirit down through the passageway of life.

The man who waits murmurs a prayer, holds fruit with which to greet his child, to place on the newborn's tongue so that life may be sweet, or sits, staring blankly: "What can be going on in there? It's been so long. Was that her scream?" Perhaps he waits to take the placenta and bury it under a tree, which shall from then on be a symbol of his child's life. Or he lies in his hammock simulating pain, wracked by pantomime groans, squirming in agony. Thus he demonstrates publicly his fatherhood, thus deflects bad spirits from the birth.

Older siblings play unaware that another is coming to take their place, one who will be offered as a gift, a friend, someone they are bound to love.

The helping women knead back and belly, urge her onward. "Be brave…not long." Her breathing quickens, stops, and the hard bud of the child's head is urged toward light. ■

A WOMAN IN
LABOR IS
COMFORTED BY
HER HUSBAND, USA.
MARY MOTLEY
KALERGIS

Sheila Kitzinger

When a baby is still inside you, before you give birth, you have many thoughts. You think, "The day I give birth, will I be courageous? Will I be afraid? Will I live? The day I feel the pains will my heart be strong enough to withstand it?"

Sometimes your heart is filled with rage. You think, "What am I going to do about this?" But another part of your heart says, "My pregnancy is going very well and maybe I'll give birth very well. One day I will feel it moving, because I am a woman and not a man; one day I will feel the labor."

Other times your heart is miserable. You think, "A baby isn't itself a painful thing. Why should a painless thing hurt so much when it comes from your insides, hurt like a sickness, hurt with such a big pain?"

You live and live and listen to yourself. You watch as your body changes. One day you feel the baby moving, rising high inside you. Another day you feel it elsewhere. You live, feeling the baby as it does things.

You soon start to feel the movements more often—near your back and everywhere. Then it moves to where it is going to be born. That's when it first hurts; that's when the two of you meet up against each other. You struggle with each other, and the baby grabs at your heart. Your heart throbs; the strength of the pain grabs your heart away from you.

Then the pains start to come, again and again. There's hurt and pain and it comes like it's fire! Again and again it comes, then it rests. It's quiet, lying still. Then it rises again, jabbing and hurting, bigger and bigger, coming over and over again. There's another rest; even if it's already pushing out, it just rests. But it rises again and there's more pain and pushing and it starts to come out from the mouth of your stomach. It's on its way out. Another quiet and another rise. Then a pain like fire is at the lips of your vagina and the head and the hair on the head start pushing through. Those are the things that hurt; not the body, that doesn't hurt at all. Then more quiet and more pushing. With the next rise, it pushes against and rushes out.

That's the birth of a baby. ■

Nisa is a !Kung San woman living in a remote corner of Botswana on the northern fringe of the Kalahari Desert. Her words were transcribed and translated by Marjorie Shostak.

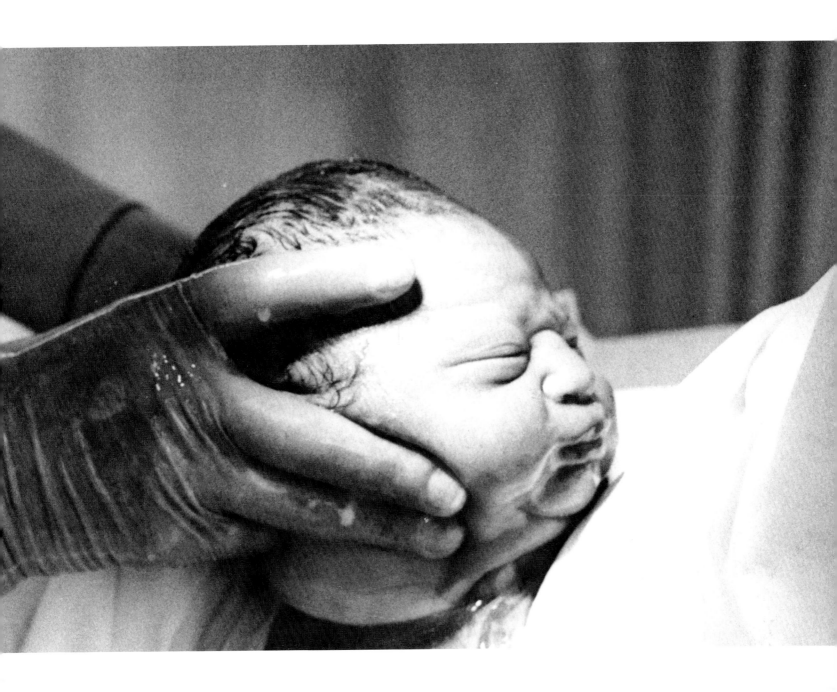

BABY'S HEAD
EMERGING FROM
BIRTH CANAL,
GERMANY.
CORNELIUS
MEFFERT/STERN

ELIZABETH MARSHALL THOMAS   BIRTH AMONG THE !KUNG BUSHMEN

Day or night, whether or not the bush is dangerous with lions or with spirits of the dead, Bushman women give birth alone, crouching out in the veld somewhere. A woman will not tell anybody where she is going or ask anybody's help because it is the law of Bushmen never to do so, unless a girl is bearing her first child, in which case her mother may help her, or unless the birth is extremely difficult, in which case a woman may ask the help of her mother or another woman. The young woman was only 50 feet from the werf [the space surrounding a homestead] when she bore her daughter, but no one heard her because it is their law that a woman in labor may clench her teeth, may let her tears come, or bite her hands until blood flows, but she may never cry out to show her agony. Bushmen say a woman must never show that she is afraid of pain or childbirth, and that is why a woman goes alone, or why a young girl goes only with her mother, for then if she shows her pain and fear, only her mother will know.

When labor starts, the woman does not say what is happening, but lies down quietly in the werf, her face arranged to show nothing, and waits until the pains are very strong and very close together, though not so strong that she will be unable to walk, and then she goes by herself to the veld, to a place she may have chosen ahead of time and perhaps prepared with a bed of grass. If she has not prepared a place, she gathers what grass she can find and, making a little mound of it, crouches above it so that the baby is born onto something soft. Unless the birth is very arduous and someone else is with the woman, the baby is not helped out or pulled, and when it comes the woman saws its cord off with a stick and wipes it clean with grass. Then the mother collects the stained grass, the placenta, and the bloody sand and covers them all with stones or branches, marking the spot with a tuft of grass stuck up in a bush so that no man will step on or over the place, for the ground where a child has been born is tainted with a power so strong that any man infected with it would lose an aspect of his masculinity, would lose his power to hunt. The woman does not bury the placenta, for if she did she would lose her ability to bear more chidren.

The moment of birth is a very important one for the child and for the mother; it is at this moment that the child acquires a power, or an essence, over which he has no control, although he can make use of it. It will last him all his life; it is a supernatural essence that forever after connects the person born with certain forces in the world around him: with weather, with childbearing, with the great game antelope, and with death, and this essence is called the *now*.

Now is intangible, mystic, and diffuse, and Bushmen themselves do not fully understand its workings. They do not know how or why *now* changes weather but only that it does. They watch the changes carefully, though, and by observing have discovered the limits of their own *nows*. When the fluid from a mother's

AMONG MANY CULTURES, FERTILITY IS A SIGN OF ABUNDANCE AND IS LINKED TO OTHER SOURCES OF ACCOMPLISHMENT. SPOONS LIKE THIS ONE ARE USED BY DAN WOMEN WHO HAVE DISTINGUISHED THEMSELVES THROUGH MERITORIOUS ACHIEVEMENTS (cat. 19).

womb falls upon the ground the child's *now* is determined, and it is partly for this reason that birth is such a mighty thing.

Birth is usually joyous. Bushmen of all ages adore their children and grandchildren, placing a child's health and wishes uppermost in their minds. Orphans are eagerly adopted by their aunts or grandparents, and a newborn baby is welcomed as though it were the first baby the werf had ever seen.

When one young woman came back to the werf with her baby she sat down and calmly washed the blood from her legs with water from an ostrich eggshell. Then she lay on her side to rest with her baby beside her, and covered the baby from the sun with a corner of her kaross. She put her nipple in the baby's mouth and let her try to nurse. The young woman still said nothing to anyone, but she did open her kaross to show the baby, and one by one we all came by to look at her, and she was not brown, not gold, but pink as a pink rose, and her head was shaped perfectly. At the bottom of her spine was a Mongolian spot, dark and triangular, and her hair, which she shed later, was finely curled and soft as eider down.

The father had been away, but he came home a little later and sat stolidly down on the man's side of the fire, his hands on his knees. He pronounced the baby's name softly to himself. Later, when he had no audience, he slipped his finger into the baby's hand. Of course the baby grasped it strongly, and the father smiled. ■

Elizabeth Marshall Thomas made these observations between 1951 and 1955 during three expeditions to the Kalahari Desert in Botswana, where she studied the way of life of the !Kung San people (previously called Bushmen).

Eskimo women used to talk about giving birth as being "inconvenient." This is not to say that it was any fun, but they had a remarkably short period of confinement. The women used to sit on their knees while giving birth. If the woman was in a tent or a house when her time came, she would most often dig a hole in the ground and place a box on either side of it to support her arms, and then let the baby drop down into the hole. If she was in an igloo, the baby had to be content with the cold snow for its first resting place. If the birth seemed to take long, the husband would very often place himself behind his wife, thrust his arms around her, and help press the baby out.

Navarana was true to form regarding these things. One day, while I was sleeping, she came to tell me that Itukusuk had caught a narwhale. Did I want to go down there and eat *mattak?* I said that I was sleepy, I had just returned from the hunt, but I would come later. It was during the summer, daylight lasted through 24 hours, and every man had his own sleeping period in that part of the world. Later I woke up again when she came back home. I asked if the mattak feast was over already, but she said that she had an upset stomach, and so she had come home to sleep. She went into our other room, and I resumed my sleep. After a while, Arnanguaq came to report that Navarana was in labor.

I became very excited and called Knud. He said that, as far as he knew, coffee had always played a role in the proceedings. It was during the First World War, we had not received supplies (especially coffee) for a long time, so I said that this was quite impossible. Knud then revealed that he had preserved some coffee beans tied up in a piece of cloth for the occasion. Consequently, we resolved to go to the brook for water.

Before we could leave the house, though, we heard a loud yell: *"Anguterssuaq!* A big boy!" It was Arnanguaq, acting as midwife. Somewhat dazed, I went with Knud for the water, and when we returned, we went inside to see Navarana. She said that it was more tiresome than she had imagined to bear boys and so she wanted to be left alone. It was only three in the morning, she still had time to get a nice sleep.

I was too happy to sleep. I went outside and sat down on a rock and started laying all kinds of plans for my boy. I resolved to stay in Thule the rest of my days, to teach him hunting, economy, and industry, and to be to him everything that a father could be. He was to avoid all the stumbling blocks I had run into myself. In short, I sat there daydreaming about my newborn boy that I hadn't even seen. And I stayed there until Navarana came out herself and told me to come in and see him. She got out of bed at the usual hour and tidied up the house.

In the evening, Knud threw his coffee party. The entire Thule population was there, of course, and he opened the dance with Navarana. She didn't stop dancing till very late. Our first-born had arrived in style. ∎

Peter Freuchen, for many years an Arctic explorer and adventurer, married an Eskimo woman, Navarana, while operating a Hudson Bay trading post in the early 1900s. Here he describes the birth of their son, Mequsaq.

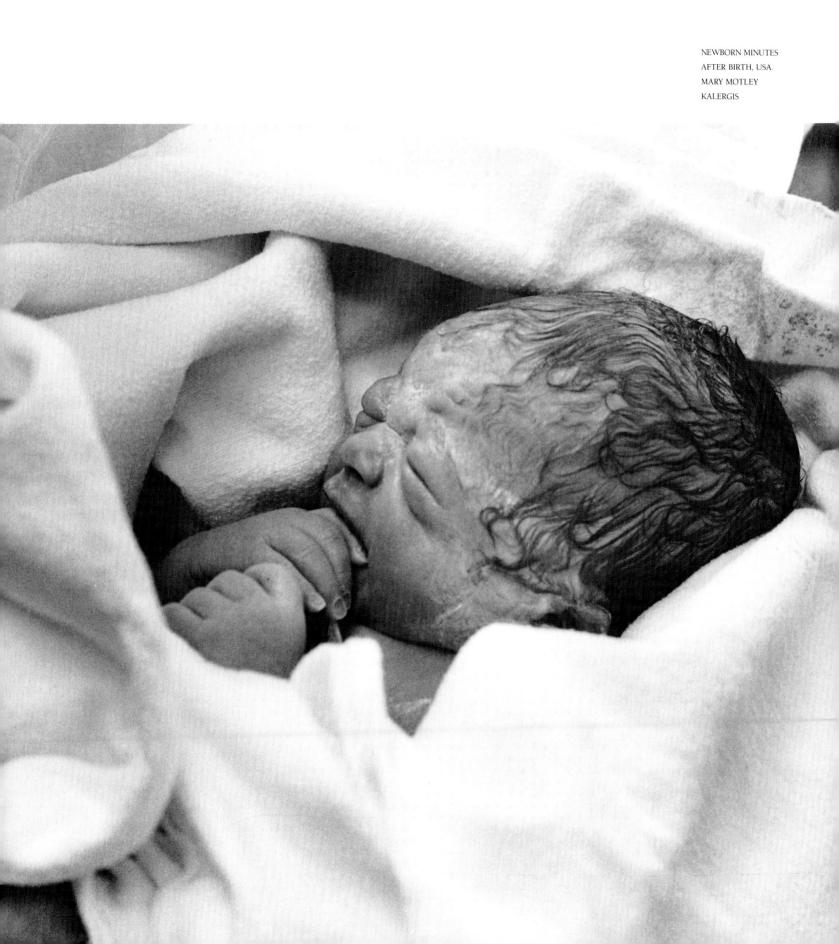

"You have given birth to a rock," Mai Hajjan, a midwife from a Punjabi village in Pakistan, tells new mothers upon the delivery of a daughter. This, says the midwife, "gives the woman strength to recover from the trials of labor and delivery." If the mother believes she has delivered a baby and thus fulfilled her duty, she might just die, happily, rather than summon the resolve needed for recovery. If a boy is born, Mai Hajjan tells the mother she has given birth to a girl. Hence the woman will want to live in the hope of bearing a son the next time.

The practice of this verbal rite speaks to the dangers of childbirth, and to the importance of a mother's survival for her child. Among Pakistanis and indeed throughout much of the Muslim world, the breast feeding of the infant is an extension of the life-nurturing begun in the womb. Breast milk is conceived of as a form of blood. Mothers willingly sacrifice this blood, and hence their vitality, in order that their offspring may be strengthened and grow. Should the mother not survive childbirth, another woman would have to make this sacrifice—and would become a "mother" to the child.

Various postpartum practices ensure the health and safety of the newborn. Mother and child are relatively isolated from communal life for 40 days. The infant is bathed, massaged, and fumigated with herbal preparations of henna and benzoin. Lampblack is applied to soothe and beautify the eyes. Amulets are strung to keep away *jinn*—mischievous fire-beings—and the body marked to avoid the evil eye and black tongue of envious neighbors.

Parents, relatives, and others in Mai Hajjan's village safeguard the newborn and attempt to impart worthy characteristics. When Bhai Khan's son was born, Mai Hajjan circled a water-holder over the baby's head, then poured water on her feet, saying, "May this child's misfortune beset me." Bhai Khan then asked his father, a respected elder and successful cultivator, to feed the infant *gutkī*, by putting a finger tip of molasses into the baby's mouth. This would instill in the child the virtues of his grandfather. When Sajvarah's daughter was born her first clothes were made from the shawl of an elderly relative in the hope that the infant too would be long-lived.

An infant is formed not only with the blood and characteristics of its parents and relatives but also with the *rūh,* or spirit of Allah. Progeny are regarded as *tabarak,* living blessedness, endowed with the light of God, which enters the fetus in the fifth month of pregnancy. Parents, relatives, and indeed the entire community are charged with the responsibility for guiding this light in the proper direction. To accept this spiritual trust is both an act of duty and kindness. Soon after the birth of his son, Bhai Khan recited into his infant's ears the call to prayer (*azān*) and the credo (*takbīr*) "Allahu akbar" ("God is great"). He arranged for the *'aqiqa,* a sacrifice of goats—two for a boy, as in this case, or one for a girl. Standing in the dusty courtyard of a mud-built domestic compound, surrounded by well-wishing neighbors, Bhai Khan replicated the sacrificial Abrahamic rite of hundreds of millions of Muslims the world over: "Almighty Allah, I offer in the stead of my own offspring, life for life, blood for blood, head for head, bone for bone, hair for hair, skin for skin. In the name of God do I sacrifice this goat."

Pakistanis recognize both the tenuousness of earthly life and its continual dependence upon Allah's blessing. Their belief that, according to the Qor'an, "Allah is closer to you than your own jugular vein" indicates the preeminence of spirit in making bodily existence possible. Life, while a blessing, is in its earthly form *majāzī*, or ephemeral. Death occurs when the spirit leaves the body. But spirit life, extant before birth, is *haqīqī*, or eternal, and continues after death. Pakistanis speak of this as a *wāpasī*, or return, eloquently stated in the Ya Sin Sharif, the Qor'anic verses intoned in the presence of the dying:

> *If we grant long life to any,*
> *We cause him to be reversed in nature…*
> *So glory to Him in whose hands is*
> *The domination of all things,*
> *And to Him will ye be all brought back.*

Islamic eschatology posits a moral universe with a heaven, hell, and day of judgment. Spiritual training provides a guide for living an earthly life, but also provides for a birth to an afterlife. An often-quoted Qor'anic saying affirms that "heaven lies at the feet of one's mother." In order to pass tranquilly to the next world, some Urdu-speaking Pakistanis, like Ali Ahmed, practice the custom of *dūdh bakshvānā*. Before his mother died, Ali Ahmed thanked her for sacrificing her own vitality on his behalf. He asked for and received her forgiveness for as an infant having drunk and been sustained by her milk-blood.

Many Pakistanis prepare for the afterlife by establishing relationships with a *pīr*, or spiritual preceptor. The *pīr* initiates the follower and guides his or her spiritual development. On judgment day, the arising spirit may depend upon the *pīr* to intercede with God. Sings a Punjabi villager about his *pīr*,

> *He is the head of the pīrs,*
> *He has freed those with chains,*
> *He can bring up the sunken boats,*
> *He is the owner of paradise,*
> *He can make the dead alive.*

Parturient, physical birth separates offspring from parents and spirit from Allah. Through spiritual birth, in the afterlife, that which has been separated is rejoined. Rehamani Shah, a *pīr* from the Sind province, is highly regarded by thousands of followers who refer to him as their *rūhānī bap,* or spiritual father. As he succinctly defines his birthing role, "He [one's biological father] helps the spirit come down into the body. My job is to help it go back up." ∎

Dr. Richard Kurin is an anthropologist who has conducted intensive field research in rural and urban India and Pakistan. He is deputy director of the Office of Folklife Programs of the Smithsonian Institution, and professorial lecturer at Johns Hopkins University School of Advanced International Studies. Dr. Kurin served on the curatorial committee for the Smithsonian's Generations exhibition.

FUNERAL FOR A
BABY WHOSE
MOTHER USED
HEROIN DURING
HER PREGNANCY,
TULSA, OKLAHOMA,
USA.

GEORGE WILL   REQUIEM FOR INFANT DOE

The baby was born in Bloomington, Indiana, the sort of academic community in which medical facilities are apt to be excellent. Like one of every 700 babies, this one had Down's syndrome, a genetic defect involving varying degrees of retardation and, sometimes, serious physical defects. The baby needed major but feasible surgery to enable food to reach its stomach. The parents refused the surgery. Instead, they chose to starve their baby to death.

An Orwellian euphemism—"treatment to do nothing"—was concocted for this refusal of potentially lifesaving treatment. Indiana courts refused to order surgery. The baby's death was thus the result of premeditated action, in the hospital and in court.

Such killings can no longer be considered aberrations, or culturally incongruous. They are part of a social program to serve the convenience of adults by authorizing them to destroy inconvenient young life. The parents' legal arguments, conducted in private, reportedly emphasized freedom of choice. There is no reason to doubt that if the baby had not had Down's syndrome the operation would have been ordered without hesitation by the parents or, if not by them, by the courts. Therefore the baby was killed because he was retarded.

Indeed, the parents' lawyer implied as much when, justifying the starvation, he emphasized that, even if successful, the surgery would not have corrected the retardation; that is, the Down's syndrome was sufficient reason for starving the infant. But the broader message of this case is that being an unwanted baby is a capital offense.

In 1973 the U.S. Supreme Court legalized abortion.* Some critics were alarmed because, in their view, the Court offered no intelligible reason why birth should be the point at which discretionary killing stops. They feared what the Indiana affair demonstrates: The killing will not stop. The trick is to argue that the lives of certain kinds of newborns are not sufficiently "meaningful"—a word used in the 1973 Supreme Court ruling—to merit any protection that inconveniences an adult's freedom of choice.

Hours after the Indiana Supreme Court had upheld the right to choose "treatment to do nothing," the lawyer for the baby's parents publicly praised his clients' "courage" in making a difficult decision. He said it was a "no-win situation" because "there would have been horrific trauma—trauma to the child, who would never have enjoyed a quality of life of any sort, trauma to the family, trauma to society."

*The Court's decision in *Roe v. Wade* upholds a woman's constitutional right to privacy in deciding whether to terminate a pregnancy during the first trimester; within limits thereafter, the states may impose restrictions.

The *Washington Post* headlined its report: "The Demise of 'Infant Doe'" (the name used in court). The story began: "An Indiana couple, backed by the state's highest court and the family's doctor, allowed their severely retarded newborn baby to die late Thursday...."

But "severely retarded" is a misjudgment that is both a cause and an effect of cases like the one in Indiana. There is no way of knowing, and no reason to believe, that the baby would have been "severely retarded." A small fraction of Down's-syndrome children are severely retarded. The degree of retardation cannot be known at birth. Furthermore, such children are dramatically responsive to infant stimulation and other forms of early intervention.

When a commentator has a direct personal interest in an issue, it behooves him to say so. My son Jonathan, age 10, fourth-grader, Orioles fan, and the best Wiffle-Ball hitter in southern Maryland, has Down's syndrome. He does not "suffer from" Down's syndrome. He suffers from nothing, except anxiety about how the Orioles will finish the season.

He is doing nicely, thank you. But he is bound to have quite enough problems dealing with society—receiving rights, let alone empathy. He can do without lawyers laying down the law about whose life does and whose does not have "meaning," without people and courts asserting the principle that children like him are less than fully human. On the evidence, Down's-syndrome children have little to learn about being human from the people responsible for the death of Infant Doe. ∎

George Will is a syndicated columnist and social commentator in Washington, D.C. "Infant Doe" (a name used in court) was born and died in 1982.

MOTHER MOURNS OVER HER DEAD CHILD, BANGLADESH. STEVE RAYMER, © 1975 NATIONAL GEOGRAPHIC SOCIETY.

JERRY ADLER   EVERY PARENT'S NIGHTMARE

The father remembers the birth of his first son, who sprang into life with a ferociousness that unnerved even the most hardened delivery-room nurses; and then his second son, born in silence, his chest quivering with the effort to draw air that would not come, his face the color of dusk. His muteness was astonishing, as if his body had somehow become separated from his soul and preceded it into the world. The obstetrician bent over him with a bulb syringe to clear the mucus from his mouth. Suddenly he stood up straight. He scooped the baby up in his arms and ran with him out of the labor room, yelling as he went.

The doctor was calling for a pediatric resident. Ordinarily such help would be at least five minutes away—the pediatric floor was in another wing of the hospital—but as it happened a third-year resident was nearby, having been called a few minutes earlier to help with another newborn. Also, she was a former pediatric nurse, experience that at the moment was more useful than the sum of knowledge of the entire faculty of the Yale School of Medicine. Quickly, skillfully, she threaded a narrow tube through one nostril and down into Max's trachea and began pumping air into his lungs. When the father looked in a few minutes later he saw the baby, who had gone to pink and was waving his arms and legs, and he felt much better. Only then did he notice the doctor standing alongside, counting to herself as she squeezed the bellows of a hand-held respirator.

There is a problem, the obstetrician told the father. The baby's lower jaw was abnormally small, and the hinges did not function; the effect was that his tongue was forced back toward his throat, blocking his airway. "We can't stabilize him," the doctor said. "He has to have a tracheotomy. They will make a hole in his throat and put in a tube so he can breathe. There is a risk. A baby's trachea is very small. They will be operating close to the thyroid gland. But you really have no choice." The father remembers a nightmarish trip in and out of elevators and along empty corridors, two nurses wheeling the baby while the doctor walked behind, squeezing the bag that pumped air into his baby's lungs. The father held open a door, helped lift the cart over a threshold. *I'm doing something for you, son,* he thought, absurdly. *Your father is with you.* Over the rumble of the casters he could hear the baby crying feebly. Since that day it has been nine months. The father has never again heard his son make a sound.

How could it happen? How could a human embryo, the product of 10,000 generations of evolution, depart so radically, so catastrophically from the well-marked path of ontogeny? Even a relatively common and—as birth defects go—minor affliction such as cleft palate is a mystery buried in the newborn's past, a memento of a dim moment when two soft folds of tissue, groping toward each other in the darkness of the womb, somehow failed to fuse.

The major constraints on Max were these. He was unable to suck and therefore had to be fed—breast milk, which his mother expressed with a mechanical pump—through a tube in his stomach. At first this tube was passed through his nose at each feeding, but it didn't take long for him to learn to hate that. (His father secretly, subversively, cheered this sign of independence, even as it pained him to see Max in such discomfort.) When he was about a month old, doctors performed a gastrostomy: an incision into his stomach into which a small plastic button with a removable cap was fitted. When he needed to eat, a tube was inserted into the button, and milk was forced through the tube from a syringe. He could not use his voice, owing to the tracheotomy, which diverted his breath below the vocal chords. A silent baby goes against nature because he cannot cry out for help. Max could cry tears, but his only sound was the hiss of his angry breathing through the tube in his throat.

He also had the alarm on his cardiac monitor. This device, connected to his torso by three electrodes, projected a record of his breathing and heart rate on a small oscilloscope. The father spent an inordinate amount of his time in the hospital watching the phosphorescent outline of his son's vital functions. The real value of the monitor was that it would sound an alarm if the baby showed signs of cardiac distress, defined as a heart rate of below 80 or above 180 beats per minute. The only time this happened was when he got mad. After a few moments of crying, his pulse would shoot up to 220 or so, a raucous bleat would sound above the routine wails and beeps and rumbles of the busy ward and a nurse would come along to see what was bothering Max.

Another problem posed by a tracheotomy is the accumulation of mucous secretions in the trachea. Since the baby cannot easily cough these up, they must be suctioned out frequently during the day and night with a sterile catheter inserted through the trachael opening. The catheter must be handled with sterile gloves, purged with sterile water, used once and then thrown away. The secretions must not be allowed to dry out and thicken, so an artificial supply of warm mist must substitute for the moisture that normally would be provided by air passing through the nose and mouth. Lying asleep under the strong hospital lights, with the mist swirling around his head, the baby took on a faintly demonic air, his mother thought. His five-year-old brother looked at him once and went running for a nurse, yelling that the baby was on fire.

Yet when he awakened, his mother could see that his eyes were large and deep blue and expressive, like his brother's. His hands were very beautifully formed, with long tapered fingers. When he cried, he could be plucked from his tangle of wires and tubes and take comfort from being held against the breast from which he could not nurse. And he could smile; as between eating and smiling, there is no question which is more important for a baby to do.

Two days after Max was born, the father went to a little ceremony marking his first son's completion of nursery school. The other parents must have thought it odd that he found this occasion so moving that he cried through most of it. "It is so hard to be strong," he says. "You face a new weakness each day."

And of course it changes one's outlook on life, insofar as virtually everything else becomes subordi-

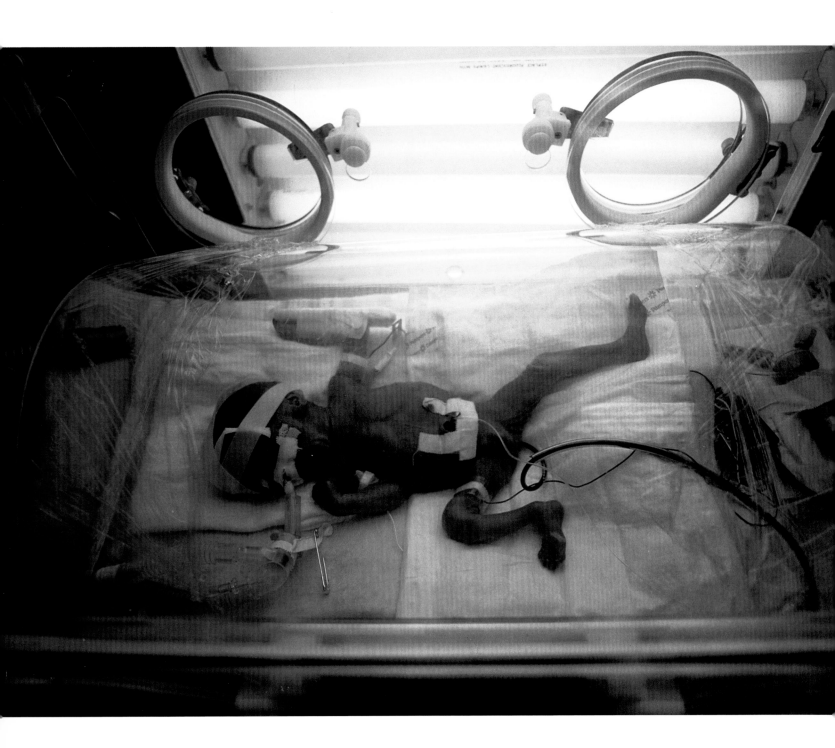

nated to the need to keep one's medical insurance in force. Max's hospital bills, from birth until the day he went home, came to just under $50,000, and that of course is just the beginning. His father paid almost none of this. He works for a large corporation that provides excellent insurance benefits. But he wonders why one's life has to be subject to these contingencies and happenstances of fate. What if he were a farmer, or a laid-off millworker? As it happens, he is a journalist, and therefore by definition a chronic malcontent, always threatening to go off to a farm in Vermont and write a novel…but that ambition has been shelved indefinitely. "Harold Robbins couldn't pay my medical bills out of royalties," he says.

During the long days the mother spent with him in the hospital, she had developed a fantasy that if only she could bring her baby home with her, to his own room and crib, he would be normal. Shortly after his birth, it was suggested to his parents that Max might have to spend a year in the hospital, or more, until his tracheal tube could come out.

The decision to let Max go home after two and a half months was based on his general medical progress, on the hospital being satisfied that he could be cared for at home and of course his rate of gaining weight. Almost everything that happens with a sick baby is dependent on his weight. The price of bringing Max home was to fill his parents' house with enough medical equipment to open a small clinic. He went home with a compressor the size of a medium dog, which rumbles and vibrates as it provides the air pressure that carries mist to his tracheal tube. He has a cardiac monitor, a suction machine, cases of sterile water for making mist, quantities of catheters, feeding syringes, sterile surgical gloves, gauze in three different sizes, hundreds of yards of tubes, and hoses of various kinds. The electric bills in this home have gone up 50 percent since he came home. Nurses sit by his crib on 12-hour shifts. When he awakens in the middle of the night, his breathing hard and raspy, it is a nurse that he sees.

His father was worried about going out of doors with Max. His first son had been an exceptionally friendly, beautiful baby, and even so the father found it maddening to be among strangers who were invariably lured by the baby's smile into prodding and poking him. He declared that he was preparing for Max's first encounter with strangers by lifting weights.

There came a day when he looked at his son and saw a serene intelligence in his clear blue eyes, and he dared to think that the happiness that his first son had as his birthright, his second son might yet gain by courage. And he was moved to say to his wife:

"You know, it could have been a lot worse."

And she answered, immediately, instinctively, out of a love that looks through pain and grief: "Yes, it could have been much worse. We could have not had him at all." ∎

Jerry Adler writes for Newsweek.

A PREMATURE BABY IS KEPT ALIVE IN AN ISOLETTE IN THE NEONATAL INTENSIVE CARE UNIT OF A BOSTON HOSPITAL. ALEXANDRA DOR-NER

In Middlesbrough General Hospital in England, an unborn baby kicks inside its mother's womb. Twenty-four-year-old Deborah Bell, who suffered a brain hemorrhage when she was five months pregnant, is as unaware of these movements as she is of everything else. She is now being kept alive by machine so that her baby has a fighting chance.

In nearby Harefield Hospital, Jane and Ian Paterson spend as much time as possible with their three-month-old baby Jem, the world's youngest heart-transplant patient, now recovering from the operation that was necessary to save his life.

In Texas, a one-year-old boy, known only as Baby Mitchell, is learning to talk, unaware of the controversy that surrounds him. He was "born" twice—the first time when a surgeon took him half way out of his mother's womb to operate so that a urinary blockage did not kill him before he grew to term.

Three different babies, three different stories about survival against the odds. But together they raise a question: How far should we go to keep a baby alive? It is a question that today more and more people—both parents and professionals—are being forced to ask themselves.

In Victorian times having a baby was a gamble with fate. Even if the mother survived childbirth, many babies failed to reach childhood. Only 55 years ago, in 1931, the first year that perinatal mortality rates were calculated, there was 1 death for every 16 births; now the rate is about 1 in 80 (13 per 1,000). Rationally we know that babies can still die or be born handicapped, but, because the tragedy is no longer commonplace, we are not prepared emotionally for it to happen to us. Not only do we expect to be able to produce our 2.4 children without difficulty; if anything does go wrong we assume that the wonders of medical science will put things right.

But there is a growing concern that we are moving too fast. Is it worth risking a woman's life, not to mention her ability to carry subsequent children to term successfully, for the sake of an operation that other doctors feel, as in the case of Baby Mitchell, could have waited? And what effect would it have had on the baby? Being born once, after all, is supposed to be traumatic enough.

Kypros Nicolaides is senior lecturer at King's College Hospital in London, involved in perinatal diagnosis and fetal therapy. Like many of his colleagues, he is very much aware of the social and ethical problems raised by the development of new techniques and technology that can be used on very young—even unborn—babies.

Dr. Nicolaides said: "There has been considerable discussion in the field about these

PREMATURE INFANT,
USA.
DAVID HURN/
MAGNUM

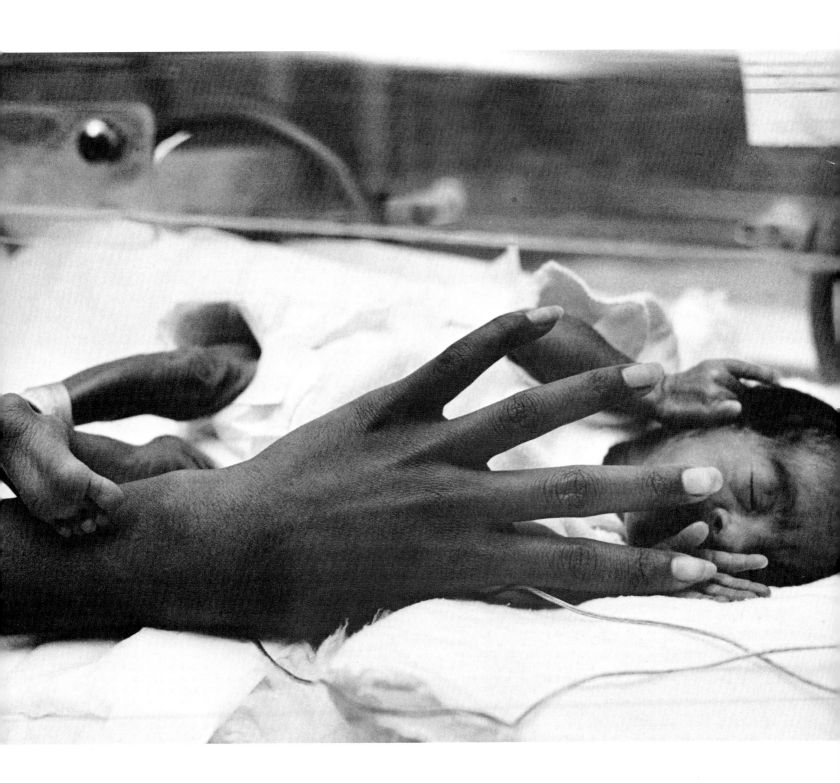

matters. They are quite controversial. I've adopted the attitude that we try everything we can, provided it is the wish of the parents, and we are very honest with them as to the outcome for the baby. Perhaps adopting the technician's approach is an easy way out. We have the techniques, we offer them to you, you decide."

Cliff Roberton, a consultant pediatrician at Addenbrookes Hospital in Cambridge, England, sounds a note of caution about much of baby surgery, in particular about the prospects of heart-lung transplants, and raises questions about the long-term prospects. He said: "We don't know how ultimately successful a transplant would be. While it would be useful to give someone of, say, 45 an extra 10 years, to do that for someone of nought poses different philosophical problems." So should they be done at all? "If there were enough donors, I would be happy for a small number of operations to be carried out on carefully selected patients in hi-tech centers. But you need 5 to 10 years to answer the question as to whether the technique is viable."

Put another way, the argument is not simply about how far you should go to keep a baby alive, but how you decide whether the quality of the life or the length of the life you have offered it is acceptable. Should we battle on to preserve some kind of life at any cost?

A DOLL FROM KENYA,
A FERTILITY SYMBOL
AND A CHERISHED
PERSONAL POSSESSION
THAT MOTHERS CRAFT
FOR THEIR DAUGHTERS
(cat. 31).

Dr. Roberton also points out that the pressures on parents and professionals are different, depending on whether a child faces a mental or a physical handicap. He says that he has never had a parent question whether or not a baby should be operated on for a kidney or a heart disorder, whereas it is very common to question the idea of an operation when a neurological handicap is involved: "By and large I'm inclined to go along with the parents' wishes."

Better techniques of prenatal diagnosis—including methods like chorionic biopsy and the improved application of ultrasound—mean that more and more parents will be asking themselves, even before their babies are born, how far they want the medical profession to go to try to save their child's life.

Would it be better to leave it all to nature? Kypros Nicolaides says: "Nature is very clever at times, but also very cruel. Humanity developed weapons to deal with snakes and lions, a primitive technology to deal with nature. We have developed medicine. As new scientific advances are made we go through an interim period where we assess new methods of treatment. We shall make mistakes, we shall have unreal hopes, but things will balance out." ■
Lee Rodwell is a freelance writer in England.

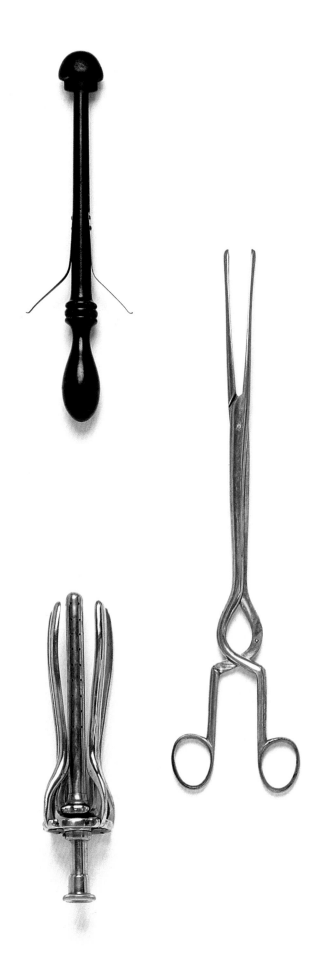

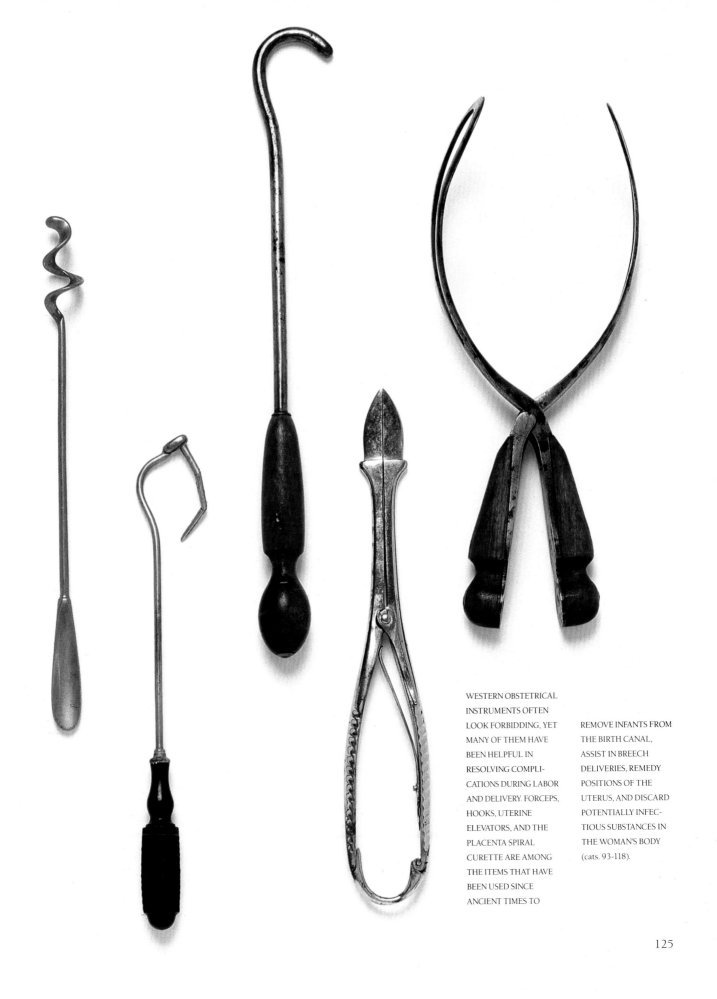

WESTERN OBSTETRICAL INSTRUMENTS OFTEN LOOK FORBIDDING, YET MANY OF THEM HAVE BEEN HELPFUL IN RESOLVING COMPLICATIONS DURING LABOR AND DELIVERY. FORCEPS, HOOKS, UTERINE ELEVATORS, AND THE PLACENTA SPIRAL CURETTE ARE AMONG THE ITEMS THAT HAVE BEEN USED SINCE ANCIENT TIMES TO REMOVE INFANTS FROM THE BIRTH CANAL, ASSIST IN BREECH DELIVERIES, REMEDY POSITIONS OF THE UTERUS, AND DISCARD POTENTIALLY INFECTIOUS SUBSTANCES IN THE WOMAN'S BODY (cats. 93-118).

BARBARA MELOSH   THE POLITICS OF BIRTH IN AMERICA

THE RISKS AND
UNCERTAINTIES
ASSOCIATED WITH
LABOR AND CHILDBIRTH
ARE ILLUSTRATED IN
THIS BALINESE WOOD
SCULPTURE. THE
MOTHER-TO-BE IS IN AN
ADVANCED STAGE OF
LABOR. SHE IS ASSISTED
BY HER HUSBAND,
YET HER EFFORTS
TO DELIVER ARE
DISTRACTED BY THE
PRESENCE OF A *LEYAK*,
A LONG-HAIRED DEMON
THOUGHT TO
FREQUENT BIRTHING
ROOMS, WAITING FOR
THE OPPORTUNITY TO
DEVOUR A BABY AS
SOON AS THE CHILD IS
FULLY BORN (cats. 68, 69).

In a large university hospital, a woman lies in a brightly lit white room, strapped onto a narrow bed. Plastic tubing runs into a vein in her hand, and wires trail from her vagina to the fetal monitor next to her. Waves on the screen and blips from the monitor record the fetal heartbeat and the woman's muscular contractions. Down the hall, another woman pants in the prescribed rhythms of Lamaze, coached by her husband who lies next to her in a double bed. A nurse-midwife encourages the two and prepares gauze, scissors, clamps, and suction bulb, ready to assist the laboring woman and the newborn infant. Furnished with a television, rocking chair, rugs, and curtains, the birthing room offers a homey enclave surrounded by the bustling activity and sleek equipment of an American hospital. Outside the window, an ambulance careens to the emergency room door, its cargo a frightened teenager. She denies vehemently that she is pregnant even as her baby is born. Meanwhile, a mile from the hospital in a comfortable old Victorian house, another woman labors in her own bed, attended by a lay midwife and comforted by close friends and expectant father. Advocates of Leboyer's "gentle birth," they will dim the lights as the newborn baby emerges, play soothing music, and immerse the infant in a warm bath.

American women give birth in all these settings, their circumstances shaped by their choices and by the constraints of nature, class, and culture. The collage of births described above stands as a microcosm of contemporary health care in the United States, which in turn suggests much about the diversity, conflict, and inequality of America itself.

In barely a century, birth has moved from home to hospital, and the pregnant woman, once attended by female relatives and friends, is now surrounded by a dizzying array of hospital workers. In the late 19th century, doctors replaced the traditional midwives at the bedside of the parturient woman; in the 1920s and 1930s, middle-class women began to give birth in hospitals, but the transition was not complete until after World War II. Although it is relatively recent, medical management of birth has assumed a striking dominance. In most states today, a woman risks arrest and prosecution for giving birth without medical supervision.

Though the medical profession has assumed a sweeping authority over birth, that control is not monolithic or uncontested. The vignettes above suggest both the powerful influence of the medical model and its uneven hold. The birthing room and the home birth illustrate the consumer revolt of the last 15 years. The critique of medical authority is itself diverse and various. In part it derives from the counter-culture of the '60s, a movement that expressed revulsion from technology and rejected a way of life mediated by machines

A SPECULUM, AND
15th-CENTURY OVUM
FORCEPS USED TO
REMOVE THE BABY
FROM THE BIRTH CANAL
(cats. 43, 47).

and experts, alienated from nature. Only a few people followed the prophets of the New Age back to the land, and yet the counter-culture cast ripples through much of American society, in part because its critique resonated with a traditional American self-reliance and suspicion of expertise. In the wave of reform of the 1960s and 1970s, critics undermined the professional claim to objectivity by exposing a health care system that reflected class, sexual, and racial inequality. The women's movement has mounted a far-reaching challenge to medical authority. Controlling our bodies was both a metaphor and an agenda for change: Women demanded safe and effective birth control, legal abortion, and better health care services as part of a larger vision of female autonomy. Though the woman's movement held no single position on technology, feminists were united in outrage against the paternalism and sexism of much health care, and the image of an unconscious woman restrained and "delivered" by a male obstetrician powerfully summarized women's subordination.

Beset by consumer rebellions, physicians also confronted unrest within the ranks of health care workers. Nurses chafed under medical authority, expressing aspirations nurtured by three-quarters of a century of professionalization and encouraged by the support of a resurgent feminism. Baccalaureate programs imbued students with a sense of nursing's distinctive practice and legitimate sphere of autonomy. Discontented with the hier-archy and bureaucratic discipline of hospitals, nurses struggled to develop training and niches for independent practice. In state after state, nurses chipped away at the legal restrictions that constrained their practice. One prominent example is contem-porary nurse-midwifery, a post-graduate nursing specialty that prepares a nurse to attend normal labor and delivery without direct supervision of medical colleagues. Such practitioners represent an intermediate response to the critique of medical

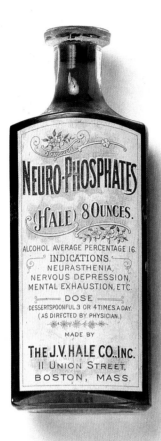

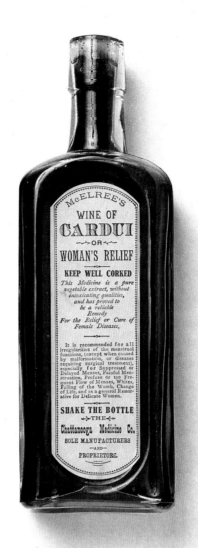

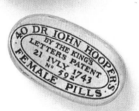

DURING THE 19th
CENTURY, GYNE-
COLOGICAL AND
OBSTETRICAL
CONCERNS PROVIDED
AN ENORMOUS MARKET
FOR PATENT MEDICINE
MAKERS. ITEMS MADE
FOR "LADIES'
DISORDERS" WERE
THOUGHT TO SOOTHE
THE AILMENTS OF
PREGNANCY (cats. 50-61).

authority. Lay midwives, representing a more thoroughgoing rejection of medical expertise, have yet to gain legal sanction, while nurse-midwives are gradually winning legitimacy.

Other social forces abetted the challenge to medical authority. The rapidly falling birthrate, combined with the expansion of hospitals and the medical profession, created a buyers' market. Obstetricians and hospital administrators, once secure in their supreme control, became newly responsive to consumer demands as they began to compete for clients. At the same time, the fiscal crisis of the health care system created new pressures for cost control. Though doctors might be committed to maximum use of new technology, hospital administrators, pressured by third-party insurers (including the federal government), began to pay closer attention to the bottom line. Even as feminists applauded birthing centers and nurse-practitioners for their sensitivity to female clients and a less interventionist approach to birth, administrators and planners recognized that such strategies were cost-effective as well.

The other two vignettes—of the high-tech delivery and the birth to a teenage mother—represent the contradictory character of a health care system that is at once overzealous and neglectful. The fetal monitor is often taken as a symbol of the American medical profession's bent for technology. It can perhaps be seen as representing both the resources and the limitations of such technology. Few would contest its usefulness in high-risk labors. And yet critics have noted its role in encouraging aggressive intervention in labor, perhaps increasing the rate of Caesarean section that is already the highest in the world. Technology has also contributed mightily to consumers' unrealistic expectations of perfection. The high rate of Caesarean births can be partly explained by American obstetricians' practice of "defensive medicine"—overtreating patients to avert possible legal claims in a climate of drastically increasing malpractice suits.

The boundless faith in technology has another kind of cost. Though the resources of medicine can shield us from many of the dangers of birth, not every pregnancy will end with the joy of a robust infant. Ironically, because the real progress of medicine has raised our expectations, we are perhaps less well prepared than our foremothers to face the sorrow and loss that sometimes attend birth.

Meanwhile, even as one woman labors under the electronic vigilance of the monitor, the young woman in the ambulance travails without benefit of any intervention or support. The comparison is more than rhetorical, for the fetal monitor and the teenager's plight both demonstrate the workings of the political economy of medicine. Our investments in health care have been consistently skewed to expensive technology designed for aggressive intervention; the simple and less glamorous work of preventive care has rarely captured the imaginations of taxpayers, policymakers, or medical practitioners. The human and economic costs of such neglect are high. This teenager's baby is more likely than others to start life in the intensive care unit. For this painful and uncertain beginning, someone will have to pay a tab that could run to a quarter of a million dollars. Yet in the Alice-in-Wonderland economies of the 1980s, the Reagan administration has cut funding for the prenatal care that has been proven to reduce such outcomes.

The language of choice pervades American culture, a language rooted in the historical experience of economic bounty and political freedom. But these four scenarios of American birth in the 1980s point to the limits as well as the exercise of choice. The United States stands alone among highly industrialized nations in its failure to develop comprehensive national health insurance. Poverty and racism blight the futures of many mothers and children. And though 20th-century American women may face birth with new confidence in their own survival and the health of their infants, still we remain vulnerable to the uncertainties of nature. ■

Barbara Melosh is curator of medical sciences at the National Museum of American History, Smithsonian Institution, and associate professor of English and American studies at George Mason University. She was a member of the curatorial committee for the Smithsonian's Generations *exhibition.*

BETWEEN THE YEARS 200 AND 700, THE MOCHE PEOPLE OF PERU CRAFTED THIS VESSEL THAT INCLUDES A BIRTH SCENE WITH THE LABORING MOTHER, HER ASSISTANT, AND A MIDWIFE (cat. 71).

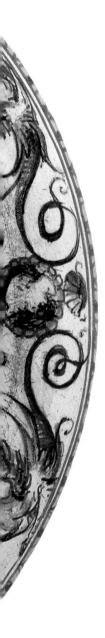

DECORATIVE VESSELS
LIKE THIS ITALIAN
PLATTER WERE USED TO
SERVE BROTH TO THE
WOMAN IN LABOR, AND
LATER WERE GIVEN TO
HER AS A GIFT (cat. 70).

A woman in her early 30s, pregnant for the first time, is well into her ninth month and rather tired of waiting. She wants to spend a day or two relaxing with her husband in the mountains, three hours from the hospital, and they ask their midwife for permission. Although the woman is, in the terminology of obstetrics, an "elderly" primigravida, she is healthy, and the pregnancy has gone well. There is little chance that a first labor would have progressed very far within three hours of the first clear signs, so permission is cheerfully granted.

The couple considers childbirth a natural process and has gone to a midwife in reaction against its "medicalization." The midwife will deliver their baby in a hospital, with a trained obstetric surgeon sleeping down the hall, but the surgeon will not be called unless needed. Otherwise labor and delivery will go as the pregnancy has gone: with respect for the risks, with, as doctors say, "a careful, watchful waiting pose," but with strict avoidance of unnecessary medical meddling.

At eight in the morning, the cramps begin in earnest. Even the first one doesn't seem like a false alarm, and by the third (they are equally spaced, 20 minutes apart) the man and woman get into their car and are on their way. There is a bad moment in a gas station when the gas cap is stuck (it would be funny, if this were a movie), and the contractions are increasingly painful all the way home. Still, the breathless arrival at the hospital doesn't impress anyone. Examination reveals a typically slow first labor, with only a centimeter and a half or so—one finger—of dilation. The midwife shows them into the birthing room and notes that there is medicine for pain on hand. She seems to be preparing them for a long haul.

The midwife, as always, offers the medication apologetically. All her patients are people like these, dedicated to natural childbirth. They have attended classes that blur the colossal distinction between the roles of the man and of the woman; thus, "they" have exercised, been taught to breathe rhythmically (one way during the contractions, another way between them), learned that conquering pain is a matter of mind over body, and all in all come to mistrust the intervention of obstetricians as intrusive and self-serving. In medical terms, they conceive of pregnancy and childbirth as physiological, not pathological.

The couple waits for nature to take its course. Dilation progresses by millimeters. Contractions get longer, stronger, and closer together. After nightfall, fatigue sets in, and there is little sign of progress. There is back labor—pain referred from the uterus to the lower back—and the man presses on the sore spot, as instructed, with all his might, but to no avail. The breathing exercises increasingly seem to him a paltry device. One A.M., two, three. Dilation has progressed only five or six centimeters. The pain is tremendous. Medication is offered and refused again and again.

The pain becomes worse. The man has long since decided that medication is in order, but his wife continues to refuse. Since the cervix appears to be stretching lopsidedly, the woman changes position, which seems to accelerate labor. When the head crowns, it looks so purple and misshapen that the husband is sure it is malformed. But at 6:30, after more than 22 hours of labor, as the sun comes up over the river near the hospital, a perfect baby girl is born, introduced to her mother (who is now grinning instead of cursing), and put to the breast.

Although it was eight or ten hours longer than the average for a first labor, the ordeal was not beyond the acceptable range, and no decision made by the midwife or the obstetrician was objectionable. Yet, in many hospitals, medication would have been virtually forced on the laboring woman. In most large hospitals, fetal monitoring would have been performed, to make sure that the fetus was not suffering from oxygen deprivation or some other complication. And some physicians would have done a Caesarean section, lest prolonged labor injure mother or child. This was a marginal case; it turned out well, but it needn't have.

The various risks that this couple averted are summed up in a venerable epigram of obstetrics: Childbirth may be physiological for the species, but it's damned near pathological for the individual. In other words, childbirth, seen from an evolutionary perspective, is a normal, clearly essential process, but for the mother it can be painful, sometimes traumatic, even fatal. In this paradox lies the tension between the old-fashioned approach, with the attendant needles and drugs, and the newer, low-technology approach with its abiding faith in nature. And in it lies the question of whether the return to "natural" childbirth has been carried too far.

Watching dogs and cats give birth seems to underscore its naturalness. Rarely does the mother need assistance, and the same is true for nearly all other mammals. Among many primates, though, things are more difficult, partly because evolution has endowed them with such large brains. (Primates typically have a brain-to-body weight ratio of 12 percent at birth, as against 6 percent for other mammals.) The problem is not just that large brains imply large skulls, which pass through the birth canal only with difficulty, but that larger and more complex brains—and, indeed, larger and more complex infants— call for a longer gestation period, and the longer the gestation period, the more difficult the birth can be. The sophistication of mammalian placentation—the biological intimacy of the connection between mother and fetus—increases as gestation progresses. In monkeys, the placental tissue (genetically a part of the fetus) so thoroughly invades the maternal domain that part of the uterus wall itself must be sacrificed in the afterbirth. A substantial number of mother and infant monkeys die as a result of cephalopelvic disproportion—heads that are too big for birth canals.

The great apes—chimpanzees, gorillas, and orangutans—suffer much lower rates of cephalopelvic disproportion, and birth for them is usually easy. Why do the great apes have it so easy? They expel the fetus at a relatively early stage in its development and thus avoid the crunch faced by monkeys, albeit at the expense of having a more fragile infant to care for. But the apes in this sense are an evolutionary island. The hominids, our post-ape ancestors, seem to have followed the monkey model; their rise was associated with an incredibly rapid advance in brain size, much of it achieved *in utero*. To further complicate matters, those ancestors began to walk upright, and the pelvis was thus being selected for weight-bearing: It became shorter and stubbier, and the birth canal narrower and less pliant, while the fetal head became larger. For a time, it appears, this tension between the anatomy of mother and of child was eased in the manner of the great apes: Fetuses were expelled proportionately earlier. But that trend could go only so far, and it never compensated fully for the growth in head size. We have ended up with an uneasy balance—a newborn infant of questionable viability and an unprecedentedly difficult birth, longer and riskier even than that of monkeys.

The natural childbirth revolution has achieved many of its goals, and, in some sectors of society at least, its tenets are the new gospel. Laboring women are no longer surrounded by medical technology.

They are fully conscious during childbirth, and many of them love it—at least in retrospect. Nature, not convenience, determines the onset of labor. Medications are minimized and designed to avoid infant sedation. Fathers or other companions are encouraged to stay in the delivery room, and evidence suggests that their presence shortens labor.

But there remain reasons for questioning the revolution. The first is that, like any revolution, it has its excesses and its ideologues. There are those who insist on home birth, for example, and this simply is dangerous. In one study, 20 percent of normal pregnancies resulted in unpredictable high-risk births.

More objectionable, perhaps, than any single practice favored by the natural childbirth school is the dogma that sometimes emanates from it. In some circles, women are ashamed to ask for painkillers of any kind, even in the most dire circumstances. Aside from the needless suffering that such asceticism entails, there is the risk that extreme pain could throw the woman into panic, making more difficult the birth and the treatment of any complications, such as profuse bleeding. Even if most births are more physiological than pathological, pathology is never far away, and it often appears on short notice. Though the rate of Caesarean section may have dropped at some medical centers, nationwide it has continued to rise, and now it exceeds 20 percent. Even as some women reject all sorts of medical intervention, others blindly obey instructions, unaware that they have some say in the matter.

Whatever its shortcomings and excesses, though, the return of natural childbirth has been basically good and probably inevitable—our evolutionary heritage reasserting itself after a hundred years of growing technological intervention. I was the father in that 22-hour birth, and it scared the living daylights out of me. Still I would not have missed it for the world—and neither (or so she insists) would my wife. Later, as a medical student, I delivered 36 babies. Nearly all of them were born to conscious mothers, in the presence of fathers or other helpers. And, as I gazed across the site of what had been such intense pain—at the father, holding the baby I handed him; at the mother, face to face with that baby for the first time—the smiles on their faces said as much as any obstetrics text. To be sure, the rite of passage we have evolved in the 1980s has its idiosyncracies—as what ritual shouldn't? It belongs to our optimistic, overly romantic culture. But it also has something in common with the rites of passage in any number of ancestral human societies. And it echoes, too, certain rhythms of reproduction that must have surrounded the first live-born young as they wriggled out of the wombs of early mammals more than a hundred million years ago. ■

Melvin Konner teaches anthropology at Emory University, in Atlanta, and is a non-practicing physician.

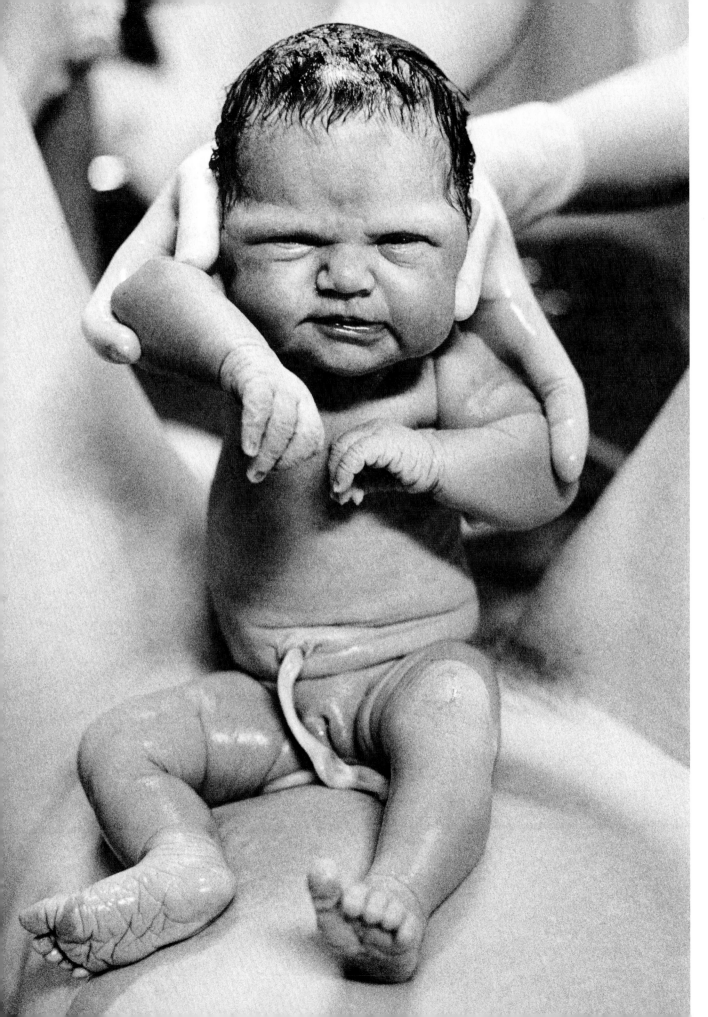

137

ANNIE MAE HUNT   GRANDMA WAS A MIDWIFE

My grandmother was a midwife. Every white man or black man born in that country that's my age, my grandma *caught* him. They called it *catch em*. Yes, a many a one down there right today.[1]

Grandma would go and stay three and four weeks with a family, according to how rich they was. The Hodes, the Yahnishes, the Wobblers, they all were rich people, Bohemian, German, Polish people. Yeah, that's what that country's made out of.

She was woke up many a night, and stayed right there with that woman until she got up. There wasn't nothing they could do for pain. Grandma kept quinine. Now they had a doctor in there, was a doctor named Kanale, and one that name Wooskie. They'd give them quinine. They knew just how much to give them. Now what that quinine was for, I don't know.

And Grandma had another little medicine in a bottle, real dark red. I don't know what it was. Grandma kept also a black bag, just like a doctor did, she kept it. And we wasn't allowed to touch it. We couldn't even look at it too hard, cause everything she needed was there. She had her scissors and her thread that she cut the baby's cord, and she had it right there. Where the doctors tie the baby's cord now with certain plastic and catguts and stuff, Grandma had big number-eight white spools of thread, and she kept it in this bag.

Everybody paid her—except sometimes the colored people didn't. It wasn't no more than three dollars to *catch* a baby. She stayed with the rich white people, doing their washing and ironing, and taking care of the woman's baby and her chores. Those Polish and German people had a hell of a chore. Those women worked like dogs. They'd do anything a man would do, go out and plow. Now the rich women didn't do this, but the rich white woman's daughter got out and plowed like her brother did. And when the mamas didn't have no small babies, they worked in the fields too. Grandma didn't do that; she'd wash and iron.

And when Grandma came home, they would give her 25, 30 dollars, and that was a whole lot of money. She'd have everything she needed, all kinds of clothes and meat, and she'd bring light bread home, and we was there to gobble it up 'cause we loved it.[2]

She *caught* everybody in that country, white or black. You better know she did. She had a name for herself. She was good and she was recognized. ■

Annie Mae Hunt told this and other stories about her own and her family's experiences to Ruthe Winegarten, who recorded them in a book, I Am Annie Mae, The Story of a Black Texas Woman.

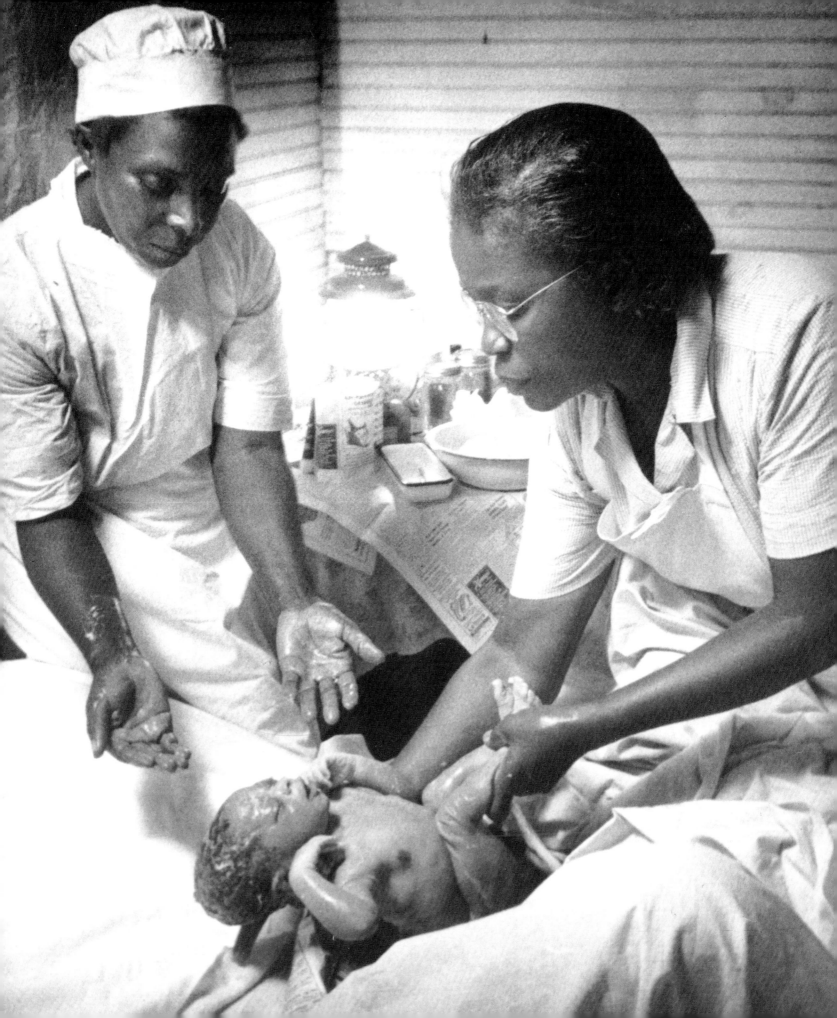

GRANDFATHER,
OVER 100 YEARS
OLD, ROCKS HIS
GRANDCHILD, USSR.
JOHN LAUNOIS/
BLACK STAR

WELCOMINGS

How did they greet your arrival?

Did they tell you

that you would till the fields?

Hunt for food? Mind the store?

Did they offer you special gifts if you slept?

If you ate well?

If you smiled?

Did they assure you

    that you had inherited your father's eyes?

Your grandmother's hands?

    The musical talents of a distant relative?

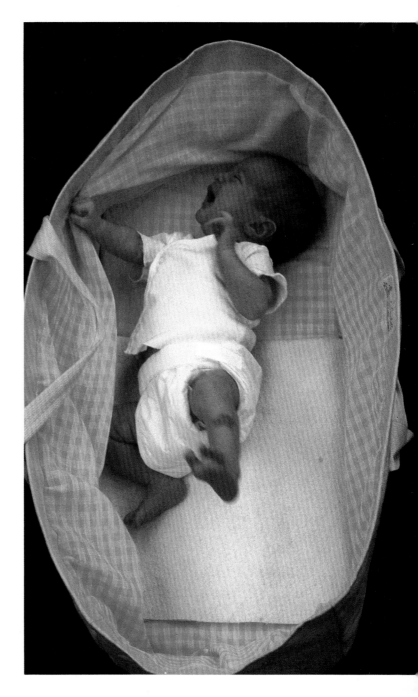

    Did they say that goblins would take you

      if you cried through the night?

FRANCE.
J.H. LARTIGUE,
COURTESY OF
L'ASSOCIATION DES
AMIS DE J.H. LARTIGUE

BABY FUSSES IN
HER CANVAS
CARRIER, USA.
ALEXANDRA
DOR-NER

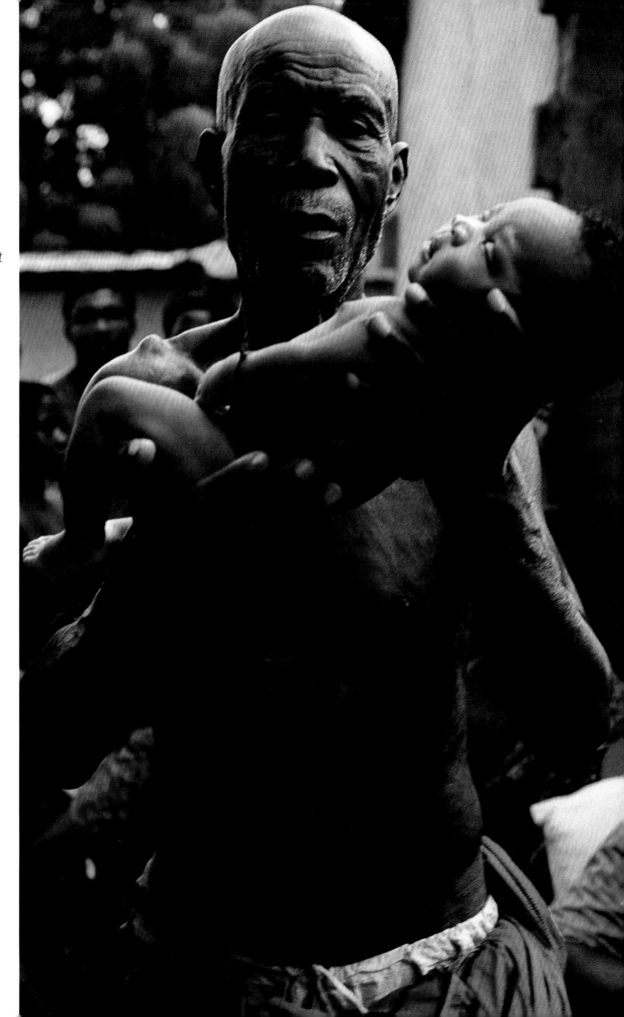

Did they promise you

success if you sought

the wisdom of

your ancestors?

The patience of

the saints?

The bravery of

your village leader?

What did you learn

as they rocked you

to sleep?

Expectation leaps. Those at hand move closer, lean forward. Eyes shine. Women busy themselves with preparations, pour water in the bowl, warm the receiving blanket, wind swaddling bands, make the mother's strengthening broth. An astrologer eyes the stars. The diviner readies himself to interpret omens in the placenta.

Then comes that first strange animal cry in the night, a child's astonished salute to life. Hands reach out to lift and cradle the little one, to rest it on the ground where all may marvel, to offer the sweet closeness of the mother's body, or to suspend it upside down, measure length, check reflexes.

Fresh from the waters of the womb, the child opens eyes onto a new world. Faces, seen as if through frosted glass, loom close, recede again, the intricate variety of the human, its curves and lines, the movement of lips, cheeks, lids, brows.

Wherever a baby is born—in gleaming hospital, in thatched hut, under the open sky, in the mother's bed—it is in the mosaic of faces, voices, hands that are the first lessons of culture. Thus starts the patterning of thoughts and behavior on this new being, who will traverse the bridge from nature into culture. ■

Sheila Kitzinger

GRANDFATHER AND
BABY GIRL, GHANA.
DENNIS STOCK/
MAGNUM

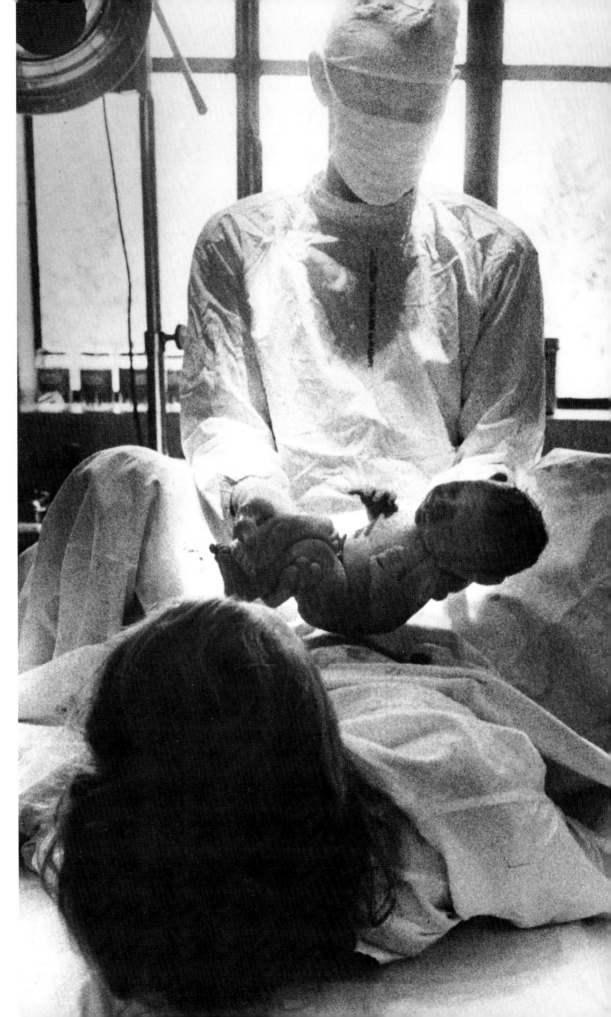

My heart is joyful,
My heart flies away, singing,
Under the trees of the forest,
Forest our home and our mother,
In my net I have caught
A little bird.
My heart is caught in the net,
In the net with the bird.

SONG SUNG BY A WOMAN GIVING BIRTH
PYGMY—CENTRAL AFRICA

Sleep my child,
and do not cry.
The angels will come
and the night is near.
The moon is shining
with silvery light,
shining right in
my darling's cradle.

LULLABY—EL SALVADOR

A heart to hate you
Is as far away as the moon.
A heart to love you
Is as close by as the door.

LULLABY—BURUNDI

146

MAYA ANGELOU   THE BIRTH OF MY FIRST CHILD

After a short labor, and without too much pain (I decided that the pain of delivery was overrated), my son was born. Just as gratefulness was confused in my mind with love, so possession became mixed up with motherhood. I had a baby. He was beautiful and mine. Totally mine. No one had bought him for me. No one had helped me endure the sickly gray months. I had had help in the child's conception, but no one could deny that I had had an immaculate pregnancy.

Totally my possession, and I was afraid to touch him. Home from the hospital, I sat for hours by his bassinet and absorbed his mysterious perfection. His extremities were so dainty they appeared unfinished. Mother handled him easily with the casual confidence of a baby nurse, but I dreaded being forced to change his diapers. Wasn't I famous for awkwardness? Suppose I let him slip, or put my fingers on that throbbing pulse on the top of his head?

Mother came to my bed one night bringing my three-week-old baby. She pulled the cover back and told me to get up and hold him while she put rubber sheets on my bed. She explained that he was going to sleep with me.

I begged in vain. I was sure to roll over and crush out his life or break those fragile bones. She wouldn't hear of it, and within minutes the pretty golden baby was lying on his back in the center of my bed, laughing at me.

I lay on the edge of the bed, stiff with fear, and vowed not to sleep all night long. But the eat-sleep routine I had begun in the hospital, and kept up under Mother's dictatorial command, got the better of me. I dropped off.

My shoulder was shaken gently. Mother whispered, "Maya, wake up. But don't move."

I knew immediately that the awakening had to do with the baby. I tensed. "I'm awake."

She turned the light on and said, "Look at the baby." My fears were so powerful I couldn't move to look at the center of the bed. She said again, "Look at the baby." I didn't hear sadness in her voice, and that helped me to break the bonds of terror. The baby was no longer in the center of the bed. At first I thought he had moved. But after closer investigation I found that I was lying on my stomach with my arm bent at a right angle. Under the tent of blanket, which was poled by my elbow and forearm, the baby slept touching my side.

Mother whispered, "See, you don't have to think about doing the right thing. If you're for the right thing, then you do it without thinking."

She turned out the light and I patted my son's body lightly and went back to sleep. ∎

Maya Angelou is an author, poet, actress, and civil rights activist, whose work speaks particularly to the black experience in America. She holds a lifetime appointment as Reynolds Professor of American Studies at Wake Forest University.

DOCTOR HOLDS
NEWBORN UP FOR
MOTHER'S FIRST
LOOK, USA.
EVE ARNOLD/
MAGNUM

Moved by the birth of his son, a Bedouin put together a series of ideas that could be termed his secular creed. The poet counsels his son on the importance of independence, prudence, clan ties, the right choice of wife, disciplining children, proper relations with one's neighbors, the proper reception of guests, the dismissal of gossip, the care of weapons, and the acceptance of one's fate. The poem was recited to the present writer by Bedouins from three different confederations in southern Sinai (the Ahaywat, Tarabin, and Muzayna), but its origin and framework apparently stem from the Arabian peninsula and an earlier date.

O king, hear my advice, you who're born today
*   You're small enough to order yet, and vigilance convey*

Be mindful of your lifestock, they will shield you from disgrace
*   The wealth of anybody else will not afford you face*

Though governed by your brother's son, don't settle in a town
*   If you should need but five dinars, he too would turn you down*

When starting on a journey, make provisions as behooves
*   Prepare sufficient water, and a fire-steel and shoes*

One never knows where night will find him, traveling all the day
*   Or if, by chance, some circumstance will lead him off his way*

Be mindful of your brother's son and father's brother's boy
*   It's they who'll share your worries and take pleasure in your joy*

Don't take a wife who'll make you be remiss in social virtue
*   And will, if you consult her, harm your brother, though it hurt you*

Don't take a wife who'll keep you from the folk that you hold dear
*   Though her face be like the sun and moon, so gloriously clear*

Don't take a little mountain-goat capricious, quick, and thin
*   And surely if she's not been raised by your paternal kin*

Take instead a cousin, you'll be comforted and eased
*   She'll not complain when you're away, yet when you're back be pleased*

An outside girl will have no mind to soothe you when you grieve
*   And if your wealth should disappear, she'll make accounts and leave*

Be not loathe to strike your son, to have him grow up right
*   And keep the upper hand, although his mother burst with spite*

And keep your children from your neighbor, lest you rouse his scorn
*   He may anger well disguise, but in his thoughts it's borne*

Your neighbor's wife, of her beware, though in the waste she call
*   A tryst with her may cost a herd of bent-hocked camels tall*

Indeed, your neighbor's dog forbear, although your leg he bite
*   Even if he tears your shoes, and you're unshod at night*

Don't show a guest approaching where your neck's two muscles meet
*   Look friendly and be cheerful, like he's one you gladly meet*

And even if the guest offend you, treat him like a dear and friend
*   Even if, at times, his talking brings your patience to an end*

Guests don't come and tire with a long, eternal stay
*   Most will spend the black of night and leave at break of day*

Don't let men's untrue reports arouse you to concern
*   Just as gossips bring you news, they carry yours, in turn*

Thus I'll have slandered you, and me you'd denigrate
*   I'll have made you angry, and you'll be full of hate*

And don't neglect your sword's sharp edge, it's there to save your life
*   Your right hand will yet seek its aid, the hour of great strife*

The sword is not a brother always there to be your shield
*   The sword is but a weapon for your own strong arms to wield*

Finally, when God wills war, and puts us to the test
*   And the fighters call on you for aid, don't flee from their request*

Once the battle has begun, with God's your preservation
*   He'll save you from the pit of death, if that's his inclination*

Your written fate is bound to reach you, even if you hide
*   Another's fate will miss you, though you're standing by his side.* ∎

Dr. Clinton Bailey has studied Bedouin poetry and culture in Sinai and the Negev Desert for 20 years. He is professor of Arab history and culture at Tel Aviv University in Israel.

MICHAEL DORRIS   A SECOND ADOPTION

I was already a seasoned unwed father. In 1971, when I was twenty-five years old, I had managed to adopt a three-year-old son. At first, I had been met with some skepticism: Why would a single man wish to be a parent? How well could a male nurture a young child? Who would care for him while I worked? Was this decision an impulse, a passing whim?

At the time, I answered those questions, to myself and to a series of social workers, with an uncharacteristic certainty. Why *wouldn't* a person want a child? Wasn't that the very basis of society? Besides, I argued, I come from a long line of single parents—most of them women, it was true, but nevertheless I had no delusions about the demands of the responsibilities I sought. Daycare centers were expensive and of varying quality, but I was prepared to find a good one, and as a college teacher I had a measure of schedule flexibility that would allow me to juggle my hours when necessary. Finally, I requested if possible that my child be of Native American ethnic background. As a mixed-blood Modoc who taught American Indian studies, I believed I could provide an environment in which boy or girl could grow up both proud and comfortable with his or her heritage.

One by one, the Catholic social services of Alaska and New Hampshire, a national adoption place-ment agency, and a western state's department of child welfare were persuaded, and just over nine months after my initial inquiry, I was awarded temporary custody of my son, Abel.

Predictably, our adjustment to each other was full of surprises, full of events that could not have been anticipated: I changed my employment from a small, experimental college to a larger institution; after only five months in my care, Abel was discovered to have a chronic, inherited medical problem. Yet the important things—my desire to care for a child, my satisfaction in being a parent—remained constant. As with any experience that alters one's future permanently (in this case for the better), it was impossible to realize in advance how large the vacuum in my existence had been before Abel came. Nor could I imagine, once he was with me, what my life would have been like without him.

There is one feature of single parenthood that any man or woman solely responsible for a young child knows, no matter how that arrangement evolved: Dating is next to impossible. By the time a babysitter is found, picked up, given instructions, checked upon by telephone, driven home, and paid, your partner for the evening had better have been True Love. If not, you have to wonder: Was it worth it? Furthermore, you become a kind of package deal—like me, like my child, or forget it.

In 1974, with a demanding job, a six-year-old son with special needs, and no fiancé on the horizon, I realized the time had come to recontact my adoption agency. If I was going to spend the next 12 or 13 years of my life as a single parent—a distinct possibility—I wanted to do so with a larger family.

Denis Daigle, Abel's case worker, was not encouraging. There were so many couples waiting for

USA.
N. JAY JAFFEE

151

placements, he said, that it was unlikely that any agency would approve a second child for a single male, especially since this time I required a toddler. He would submit the paperwork at my request, but I should not count on anything, not get my hopes up.

Okay, I promised, and pasted yellow wallpaper with a small green-and-red teddy-bear design in the spare bedroom of our house. I watched yard sales for cribs and basinets, and found a used rocking horse in mint condition. I put my name on the waiting list for a child care center and arranged for a lighter teaching load. When Denis called, his voice incredulous, I was ready.

"You won't believe it," he said. "There's a little Sioux boy, just over a year old, who's available. They've approved your application."

"When does it happen?" I asked. I felt the stirrings of the male analogue of labor.

"He's in South Dakota."

I did some geographical calculations. "I'm presenting a paper at a one-day conference in Omaha next Tuesday," I said.

"Could you be in Pierre on Wednesday?"

Could I. I had already chosen his name, Sava, after a Native Alaskan friend who had taken me on as a salmon fishing partner for two summers.

On Tuesday afternoon the weather turned nasty. All planes were grounded, so I rented a car, called the case worker in South Dakota to tell her the name of the motel where I had a reservation, and drove all night from Nebraska. I checked into my room exhausted, unbathed, and bleary-eyed at 9 A.M., and before I had a chance to unpack my suitcase there was a knock on the door. I opened it to a smiling young blond woman in a green parka.

"Hi, I'm Jeanine from S.D.D.S.S.," she announced. "Are you ready to meet your son?"

"Can you wait a few minutes? I want to take a shower, change my clothes, maybe pick up a present for him someplace on the way."

An uneasy expression crossed her face.

"Is something wrong?"

"Well…*actually* he's in the car right now." Jeanine glanced to her left, and, following her look, I saw a baby carseat and the top of a purple knitted cap. I didn't want to give the impression of the slightest hesitation, so I said, "Great! Bring him right in."

The instant she turned her back I dashed to the bathroom, splashed water on my face, and dabbed some aftershave on my neck. First impressions are important and at least I could smell good.

When I emerged Jeanine was standing in the room holding a bundled, solid-looking baby with incredibly dark, intelligent eyes that regarded me with wary suspicion.

"He's very friendly," Jeanine said. "He's been so anxious to meet you."

I held out my arms, savoring the tender moment of first encounter. He was no lightweight. I cradled him in my arms and lowered my face close to his to get a good look. "Hello Sava," I whispered.

His eyes widened, then closed tightly, and simultaneously his jaws opened and opened and opened, revealing a space more like the Grand Canyon than a mouth. I felt him draw a long breath into his lungs, and when he released it in a howl, my mind pictured a cartoon image of pure sound, strong as a hurricane, blowing everything—furniture, hair, trees—in its wake.

Jeanine made a step toward us as if to retrieve him, but I shook my head and spoke more confidently than I felt. "Just leave us alone for an hour or so. We'll get used to each other." I nodded encouragingly to underscore my words and she reluctantly departed.

Sava's yells did not abate, but he didn't struggle as I sat down on the bed, and sat him on my lap. He was not in the slightest afraid but was simply registering a protest, a review, of what he had just seen. I unsnapped his coat and removed it, spoke softly in what I hoped was a comforting tone, and after a few long minutes he opened one eye and took a second look.

He was a beauty: feathery straight black hair, a sensuous mouth, a strong, broad nose, a clean, sweeping jaw. His torso was wide and his hands were square-shaped with thick, tapering fingers. He opened the other eye and, as abruptly as he had begun to cry, he stopped. We stared at each other, amazed in the sudden silence.

"Hello Sava," I tried again, and this time he only blinked.

Late the next day we boarded a plane back to New Hampshire. By then, I knew Sava's favorite food—mashed green beans mixed with cream of mushroom soup and canned fried onions sprinkled on top—and that he hated to have his hair washed. I knew he was a sound sleeper, had a long attention span, and was ticklish just below his rib cage on his right side. I knew that he and my oldest son were profoundly different in their personalities—Abel would leap headfirst into any strange lake, but Sava would always test the water first—but that they would be compatible brothers. And I knew all over again, as if for the first time in human history, the experience of becoming a parent: I had already forgotten what it felt like *not* to be Sava's father. ∎

Michael Dorris is now the parent of five children (Sava is 15) and husband of writer Louise Erdrich. He is a novelist and teaches Native American studies and anthropology at Dartmouth College.

It's my fat baby
I feel in my hood,
Oh, how heavy he is!
Ya ya! Ya ya!

When I turn my head
He smiles at me, my baby,
Hidden deep in my hood,
Oh, how heavy he is!
Ya ya! Ya ya!

How pretty he is when he smiles
With his two teeth, like a little walrus!
Oh, I'd rather my baby were heavy,
So long as my hood is full!

ESKIMO LULLABY—GREENLAND

The little girl will pick wild roses,
That is why she was born.

The little girl will dig wild rice with her fingers.
That is why she was born.

She will gather sap of pitch pine trees in the spring.
She will pick strawberries and blueberries.
That is why she was born.

She will pick soapberries and elderberries.
She will pick wild roses.
That is why she was born.

TSIMSHIAN LULLABY—CANADA

NURSERY IN
MOSCOW, USSR.
MARC RIBOUD/
MAGNUM

155

THE BIRTH OF TWINS
AMONG THE YORUBA OF
SOUTHEAST NIGERIA
USUALLY IS A JOYOUS
OCCASION. YET SOME-
TIMES IT ALSO IS CAUSE
FOR CONCERN, FOR
TWINS ARE REGARDED
AS SPIRITUAL BEINGS
WHO CAN BRING THEIR
PARENTS BAD LUCK AS
WELL AS GOOD FOR-
TUNE. TWINS AT BIRTH
OFTEN ARE MORE FRAIL
THAN SINGLE INFANTS.
THEY ALSO HAVE A
HIGHER MORTALITY
RATE. WHEN TWINS DIE
AMONG THE YORUBA,
TWO FIGURES ARE
CARVED AND CARED
FOR JUST AS REAL
INFANTS WOULD HAVE
BEEN WITH THE HOPE
THAT THEY WILL BRING
GOOD LUCK TO THEIR
PARENTS (cat. 92).

MARY JO ARNOLDI   THE LEGACY OF A NAME AMONG
THE BAMANA OF MALI

Our names contribute in large measure to who we are, and we often hear people speak of children growing into their names. This is certainly true among the Bamana of Mali. The Bamana are farmers who live in the south-central region of Mali (although some Bamana also work as traders and craftsmen). They share a language and many customs—naming practices among them—with closely related neighboring groups such as the Malinke, Mandingo, and Jula.

A child's naming ceremony, *Den togo da,* is an occasion for celebration and joy within the family and the community. It is the formal recognition of the child's birth as well as his or her welcome into the community. The ceremony generally takes place seven days after the baby's birth. Prior to the ceremony, people speak of the newborn child only as *cekura* (the new boy) or *musokura* (the new girl). Although there have been many social changes in Mali in the last century, the Bamana and their neighbors still follow many of their time-honored customs in selecting a child's name.

Among the Bamana, the elders of the father's family—rather than the infant's biological parents—enjoy the perogative of naming the child. In Malinke families, however, the elders of the father's family choose the name for the first two children born while the elders of the mother's family name every third child.

The custom on the naming day in many Bamana communities used to be that the elders of the father's extended family would each bring a *kala*—a small gift for the newborn's household—which could be a stick, a pot, or a tool. The child's mother would then select one from among these objects and the elder who had brought it would be given the honor of naming the child. Today, in many regions, this custom has been abandoned, but the selection of a child's name still rests in the hands of the elders. One important exception occurs if a stranger is visiting the family during the birth of a child. Since his visit is regarded as an important and noteworthy event, the visitor will often be given the honor of selecting the child's name.

Certain children come into the world "with their names." In deciding the newborn's name, the elders first consider whether the child's birth coincided with an auspicious occasion, such as the annual festival of a particular spirit, as a sign that the child has brought his name with him. Thus, in this instance, the newborn would likely be named for that spirit, and placed under its protection.

If a woman is having trouble conceiving or is experiencing a difficult pregnancy, the family may promise to dedicate the as yet unborn child to a particular spirit. At the naming ceremony, the child would be given the spirit's name in recognition of this promise.

Sometimes complications arise. I was told of an important blacksmith whose family had dedicated him to two spirit protectors before his birth, and who was subsequently born during the annual festival for a third spirit. At his naming ceremony, he was named for all three spirits, signifying his personal relationship with all of these powerful forces.

Among Islamized Bamana, a similar practice occurs. If a male child is born on the feast day honoring

Mohammed's birth, the infant boy will generally be named for the prophet. Throughout the boy's lifetime, his name—Mohammed—will evoke the event surrounding his birth.

Another common practice is to name a child after the day of the week on which the baby is born. Thus the name Kari literally translates as "Sunday," while Sibari means "Saturday." These children are also considered to have come into the world with their names.

Throughout this region, twins are honored and special people. Both twins and the sibling born after them come into the world with their names. Twin names for boys are Shoba, Sine, and Ceba and for girls are Wasa and Kasa. In Islamized families, male twins are generally named Alassane or Ousseini; females are named Bintufine, Sitafine, or Kafune. In both non-Islamized and Islamized families, the child who is born after the twins is usually named Koni or Sayo, which means "the little one who comes after."

Another important practice involves naming a child after a respected person, generally an elder. Children who are given the name of an elder take on the elder's status within the family. For instance, in many Bamana families the first son and the first daughter are given the name of the paternal grandfather and the paternal grandmother. Out of respect for their own parents, the child's father and his generation of brothers and sisters will always address this child by the term "father" or "mother" rather than using the child's real name. When a young boy is called Baba, the term of endearment for father, it generally signifies that his grandfather is his namesake.

Bamana consider that having a namesake is both a great honor and a responsibility for an elder. As children grow up, a special relationship often develops between elders and their namesakes, and it is the responsibility of these elders to pass on all of their knowledge and skills to this new generation.

For the Bamana, the legacy of a name is very important; a person's name is a significant part of his or her identity. It can invoke the memory of an important event associated with the child's birth. It can allude to the circumstances surrounding the birth, or can mark a special relationship across generations. Along with character and destiny, a child's name will contribute to his or her potential and accomplishments in Bamana society. ■

Dr. Mary Jo Arnoldi is associate curator of African ethnology at the National Museum of Natural History, Smithsonian Institution, and was a member of the curatorial committee for the Smithsonian's Generations *exhibition.*

WODAABE MOTHER
BATHES HER BABY
AS AN OLDER
CHILD LOOKS ON,
NIGER. CAROL
BECKWITH, FROM
NOMADS OF NIGER,
PUBLISHED BY
HARRY N. ABRAMS,
INC., 1983

So how shall we name you, little one?
Are you your father's father, or his brother,
  or yet another?
Whose spirit is it that is in you,
  little warrior?
Whose spear-hand tightens round
  my breast?
Who lives in you and quickens to life, like
  last year's melon seed?
Are you silent, then?
But your eyes are thinking, thinking, and
  glowing like the eyes of a leopard
  in a thicket.
Well, let be.
At the day of naming you will tell us.

DIDINGA OR LANGO POEM—UGANDA

VLADIMIR NABOKOV THE EARLY YEARS WITH OUR SON IN BERLIN

You remember the discoveries we made (supposedly made by all parents): the perfect shape of the miniature fingernails of the hand you silently showed me as it lay, stranded starfishwise, on your palm; the epidermic texture of limb and cheek, to which attention was drawn in dimmed, faraway tones, as if the softness of touch could be rendered only by the softness of distance; that swimming, sloping, elusive something about the dark-bluish tint of the iris which seemed still to retain the shadows it had absorbed of ancient, fabulous forests where there were more birds than tigers and more fruit than thorns, and where, in some dappled depth, man's mind had been born; and above all, an infant's first journey into the next dimension, the newly established nexus between eye and reachable object.

Whenever you held him up, replete with his warm formula and grave as an idol, and waited for the postlactic all-clear signal before making a horizontal baby of the vertical one, I used to take part both in your wait and in the tightness of his surfeit, which I exaggerated, therefore rather resenting your cheerful faith in the speedy dissipation of what I felt to be a painful oppression; and when, at last, the blunt little bubble did rise and burst in his solemn mouth, I used to experience a lovely relief while you, with a congratulatory murmur, bent low to deposit him in the white-rimmed twilight of his crib. ■

Vladimir Nabokov fled his native Russia after the Bolshevik Revolution. He studied at Cambridge, and later lived in Berlin until 1937, writing fiction, criticism, and poetry in Russian. In 1940, after coming to the United States, he began to write in English. By the time of his death in 1977, Nabokov was a writer of universal acclaim.

KRIS HARDIN ROCK-A-BYE BABY…

What's in a lullaby? Nothing much, you might say, just kid stuff. And yet, if you take a closer look at the songs used to lull infants to sleep, you will be surprised by the range of lyrics and rhythms used by people around the world to accomplish the same task.

Compare the words of these four lullabyes:

Siembamba, momma's little child,
Wring his neck, throw him in the ditch.
Trample on his head,
Then he is dead.

That I shall not do.
I like to keep my little child,
So why should I cut his head off?[1]

USA.
JIM RICHARDSON

This song was recorded in South Africa. Siembamba, the infant, was being cared for by an older sister, who sang this song. As she sang she was reassuring Siembamba that no harm would come during sleep.

The following is typical of Vietnamese lullabyes, which often include cooking tips and moral tales or parables:

To make a soup of fish and pumpkin
Add some pepper and chives to bring out the taste.
Sleep soundly, my baby,
So I can work to feed you.
The bridge is made of nailed planks,
And crossing a rickety bamboo bridge is the most
  difficult of all.[2]

This song, recorded in the United States, may make reference to American Indian traditions, but at the same time it predicts that if the child sleeps he will grow to acquire the things that a man should have:

Go to sleep, little baby, do not cry,
You should be a big boy by and by.
You should have a boat and a hatchet, too.
You should ride on the water in your own canoe.[3]

In this Kuna lullaby an infant is told about social roles and the occupations appropriate for a man:

You are a little man
You go fishing for small fish
When you are bigger you will go walking in the
  mountains

When you are a man
When you grow up you will work [harvest]
  coconuts
Your mother wants you to go but when you
  are bigger

You are a little man
In the canoe you go fishing
Mother is cooking

You are a little man, you are not a woman
When you go to the mountains you will be
  farming in the sun all day
Every day you are a little man.[4]

These songs represent variations of four kinds of lullabyes used around the world—those that use rhythm and soft sounds to mesmerize a child to sleep, those that swath the child in endearments, those that predict or promise good things in return for sleep, and those that threaten a child into sleeping. Of course, any kind of song can be used to put a child to sleep. The most improbable American sleep-inducers I have heard of are "Casey Jones" and "Slewfoot Sue,"[5] but most Americans do not recognize these as lullabyes.

Differences in imagery and content within lullabyes can serve as windows onto the cultural worlds in which they are used. For example, the lyrics of the songs above show some of the fears and aspirations mothers or caretakers from different parts of the world have for their children: They describe social relationships, roles, and occupations, and they give some insight into what mothers might feel is important for a child to know. The phrases of other lullabyes encapsulate some of the moral tenets and metaphysical knowledge of particular places.

Who sings a lullaby can also provide valuable insights into the social relationships of another culture. While Americans generally rely on mothers to do this job, in other places it may be a sibling, a grandparent, a father, or another relative who takes on this responsibility. Among the Kono of Sierra Leone, a mother will scold an overly tired child, while a grandmother is likely to take the time to rock the young one to sleep. Apparently, Kono grandmothers take the role of the ones who nurture and spoil the child; thus they usually develop very close bonds with their daughters' children.

While infants cannot really be said to "learn" such things as morals or social roles and behavior at an early age, lullabyes are one of the first settings where these kinds of social principles are expressed. These principles are repeated in a variety of contexts as children grow, affecting their personalities, world view, and other kinds of "taken-for-granted" notions that form people's ideas of how the world ought to be and how they, as individuals, fit into it. Lullabyes are one of the first introductions an infant has to the social world, and as such they have a major role in constructing culture, as well as in transmitting that culture to future generations. ■

Dr. Kris Hardin is assistant professor of anthropology at the University of Pennsylvania. She was curator of ethnology and a member of the curatorial committee for the Smithsonian's Generations *exhibition.*

USA.
McCOY/BLACK STAR

IVAN KARP   TRAGEDY IN BIRTH: AN AFRICAN VIEW

During the last 18 years I have been visiting the Iteso and conducting field research among them. The Iteso are a Nilotic-speaking people who live on the border between Kenya and Uganda. In spite of the extra-ordinary changes that have visited their society during the time I have known them, they have chosen to keep certain aspects of their lives constant. Today, as in times past, the religious rituals and medical practices of the Iteso display an almost obsessive concern with the health and well-being of their children.

The birth, growth, and maturation of children are essential to the continuity of any culture. It should be no surprise, then, that the customs and practices connected with producing and raising children—and training them in their society's ways—are of paramount importance to all peoples. What does surprise perhaps is that even though cultures attribute great meaning to the customs and practices necessary to their survival—parenting, birth, and the initiation of children—the specific meaning of these activities can vary greatly from culture to culture.

The rationales for these customs and practices are the beliefs that peoples hold in common. These beliefs are not just abstractions—theories isolated from experience. They express what people value most about their lives and, at the same time, contain rules and recipes for managing the dangers of the world in which they live.

The Iteso live in a hostile environment. As in most parts of Africa, the rate of infant mortality during the pre-colonial period was 50 percent. Kenya is a rich country by African standards, yet during the drought of the early 1980s perhaps half of the people of Kenya's northern deserts died of starvation.

So, becoming a parent—having children—is no automatic or easy procedure among the Iteso. Yet their very definition of an adult is tied to parenthood. No one can be called a man (*ekiliokit*) or a woman (*aberu*) until he or she is married. Even this status is only a way station to parenthood. Only then can people assume the full rights and duties of adults.

Anthropologists have often shown how reproducing the culture is the latent agenda of any society's beliefs and institutions. Less often they point out how much this is an overt goal, defined and expressed by a people in their rituals. Iteso women, in all their important rituals, dramatically reenact their forms of domestic labor—tasks associated with producing food and feeding children. Infants born to a family after an earlier child has died must undergo a special ritual in which they are named for one of the intrusive animals of the "bush"—such as a hyena or a jackal—that invade the home and destroy what the people have produced.

If rituals associated with birth following death express the dangers that daily threaten the Iteso, the birth of twins is the occasion for rituals celebrating the felicity of procreative powers. Called *Mamai* and *Eja*—maternal uncle and paternal aunt—twins stand for all the blessings of the successful and orderly production of the world. Twins are a gift, the Iteso say, and twins are required to be the first to taste the

DOGON CHILDREN,
MALI.
ERNA BEUMERS

166

fruits of the harvest and to drink this ritual's newly brewed alcohol. The ceremonies surrounding the birth of twins are the most elaborate in the Iteso repertoire, and it may take years for a family to store enough wealth to sponsor such a celebration. Twins are named to commemorate the Iteso sense that surviving is a cooperative effort, with high value placed on kin and community.

Still, the scent of death taints even the celebration of twins, the high point of Iteso culture. "If twins are not separated," a wise old woman said, "sickness swells in your home, at the very least until one of you leaves." What she is telling us here is that if a twin doesn't die, someone else will. There is a sense expressed in this that bodies cannot occupy the same conceptual and social space.

The Iteso view of birth is essentially tragic. Their customs and beliefs assert that even the most successful births allow only temporary relief from the material world against which they struggle. For the Iteso, birth is also one of the moments at which death is most likely to intervene. In any case, averting death at birth is at one and the same time temporary and the highest good they can imagine. They acknowledge the inevitable at the same time as they struggle against it.

My American students used to ask me what purpose there was in studying exotic societies such as the Iteso. American ideas dispose us to believe that we can escape our fate through technological means. We may have something to learn from the tragic view of Iteso culture, which acknowledges that life and death are inexorably intertwined. ∎

Dr. Ivan Karp is curator of African ethnology at the National Museum of Natural History, Smithsonian Institution, and was a member of the curatorial committee for the Smithsonian's Generations exhibition.

Sleep my son,
my good son,
my lovely diamond.
Sleep, and that the girl,
which shall be your wife,
enjoys you some day.
Sleep sweet in my arms,
which are surrounding
you like a soft silk.

LULLABY—GREECE

USA.
HELLA HAMMID

168

Sleep, sleep.
Be a good child and sleep.
Your nana went over the mountains
to reach her village.
When she comes back
she will bring you drums
and flutes as a gift to you,
and with these toys
she will bring you to sleep.

LULLABY–JAPAN

You son of a clear-eyed mother,
You far-sighted one,
How you will see game one day,
You, who have strong arms and legs,
You strong-limbed one,
How surely you will shoot, plunder the Herreros,

And bring your mother their fat cattle to eat,
You child of a strong-thighed father,
How you will subdue strong oxen between your thighs one day,
You who have a mighty penis,
How many and what mighty children you will beget!

LULLABY—SOUTH AFRICA

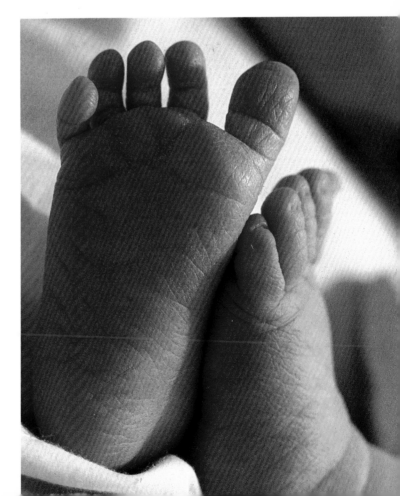

I have made a baby board for you daughter
May you grow to a great old age.
Of the sun's rays have I made the back
Of black clouds have I made the blanket
Of rainbow have I made the bow
Of sunbeams have I made the side loops
Of lightning have I made the lacings
Of sun dogs have I made the footboard
Of dawn have I made the covering
Of black fog have I made the bed.

NAVAJO CHANT—USA

CHARLES KRAUTHAMMER   TEN POUNDS OF POETRY

Three weeks ago Daniel Pierre Krauthammer, our first, entered the world. It was a noisy and boisterous entry, as befits a 10-pound Krauthammer. It has been just as noisy and boisterous since. I had been warned by friend and foe that life would never be the same. They were right.

Of course, like all exhausted newborn fathers, I am just looking for sympathy. It is my wife, Robyn, whose life has been fully merged with his, in a symbiosis profound and delicate. His sucking, did you know, causes the uterus to contract and helps shrink it back to normal size. Twenty days old, and he is healing her.

What she does for him, of course, would not fit in a month's worth of my columns. What do I do? It seems my job is to father, a verb which must count as one of the age's more inventive creations. How exactly to father? I don't really know. The women's movement, to which the idea owes its currency, is right to insist that the father do more.

But more of what? I have been asking myself that lately as I rock him and hold him and speak to him in the gravest of tones. But we both know, we all three know, the truth: Nature has seen to it that anything I can do, she can do better. Mine is literally a holding action.

Of course, the imperative to father is only the last of the social conventions one must bend to on the road to parenting. (I am learning the language.) First, there is Lamaze, the classes that teach you to be natural. Robyn does not fancy oxymorons. And I, as a former psychiatrist, know a placebo when I see one. We said no to Lamaze.

We said yes to the Volvo. In fact, on the Volvo we went all the way. We got the station wagon with roof rack: the ultimate yuppie conveyance. "For safety reasons only," I explain to friends, a protest that meets with knowing smiles.

Finally, there is the supreme modern convention: the now absolute requirement that father, in surgical gear, attend the birth. Of course, you don't have to if you don't want to. You can, if you wish, wait outside, like Dagwood Bumstead, pacing and smoking and fretting until it's over. You have the perfect right to betray your wife, spurn your child, and disgrace your sex. It's a free country.

The transformation of expectant father from nuisance—packed off to boil water, find towels, and generally get out of the way—to conscripted co-producer of the birth epic is one of the anthropological wonders of the age. And on the whole, apart from the coercion, a good thing. Father's presence serves two purposes. One is to reduce the anguish of the mother. The other is to increase the anguish of the father. Both seem to me laudable goals. It makes up a bit for the extraordinarily unfair balance of suffering that attends childbirth.

Thank God, the new convention does not (yet) command fathers to attend a Caesarean delivery. I speak from experience. Robyn needed a Caesarean and, hoping I could comfort her, I was with her in the operat-

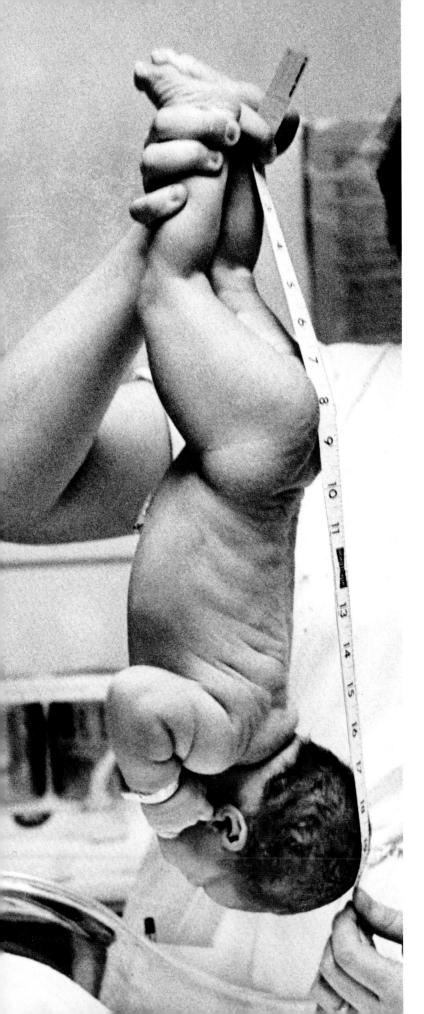

ing room. I was not looking for a Maslovian peak-experience, the kind of epiphany that reputedly accompanies the moment of birth. I was doubtful, not just because of my usual skepticism, but because of my previous career. In medical school, I had assisted at several births, including a couple of Caesareans, and always had trouble seeing the poetry for the blood.

There was little poetry this time either. It was an agonizing hour for her, and for me. (Daniel did very well.) The poetry came afterward, in the recovery room, where I found Daniel asleep in Robyn's arms.

It has been poetry and reverie ever since. Having a child, I discovered, makes you dream again and, at the same time, makes the dreams utterly real. Lately I have been dreaming of the future. I find entirely new meaning in what we in Washington call "out-years." Take 1989, the year the budget deficit comes down to $100 billion. A time far, far away…until I figured it is the year when we retire Daniel's Pampers. A manageable deficit, only a few thousand nappy changes away.

Stranger years, years of exotic immensity, years that till now had meaning to Arthur C. Clarke only, become utterly mundane. 2001, the year of the mystical obelisk, and Daniel should be getting his learner's permit. 2010, the obelisk returns and Daniel is looking for a job. 2050, a year of unimaginable distance: his first Social Security check.

"Checks? Social Security?" my friend Pepe interrupts. "Where's your imagination, man? They'll all be memories. Think big. 2050: the year he takes a sabbatical on Saturn."

I'm thinking small. I gaze at his body, so perfectly formed, so perfectly innocent. It has yet to be written on. I look at his knee and wonder where will be the little mark that records his first too-hard slide into second base. ■

Charles Krauthammer is a senior editor of the New Republic *and a syndicated columnist.*

If you're a single person, watching your friends turn into parents can be unnerving. It's not unlike being in the movie *Invasion of the Body Snatchers* and watching your friends turn into Pod People. The difference is that the Pod People, for all their faults, didn't openly discuss their babies' bowel movements.

New parents do this. You go to visit them, and you find they have suddenly developed a profound interest in the subject. "She had one today," the mother, a stockbroker, will report in the concerned, thoughtful tone that people normally use to discuss the Middle East. "It was runny, and sort of yellow." "Huh!" replies the father, a very creative advertising executive. "I thought it looked a little yellow yesterday, too!"

Having no views on this issue, you feel totally left out. So you stand there, examining a stuffed rabbit—their living room, once the epitome of subdued and tasteful decor, now looks like an illustration for *Bambi*—and you wonder: Is this permanent? Will I ever get them back?

Relax. All will be well. Your friends have not suddenly become stupid. Well, okay, they *have* suddenly become stupid, but it's not permanent. What you're dealing with here is a natural law, one that is little known (because I just made it up), but instantly recognizable as true. It is the Law of Parent-Child IQ Equivalence.

You see, Mother Nature, who is no fool, realizes that if new parents were to remain at their normal level of intelligence after the baby's birth, they would quickly go insane. This is because taking care of a newborn baby means devoting yourself, body and soul, 24 hours a day, seven days a week, to the welfare of someone whose major response, in the way of positive reinforcement, is to throw up on you. So, as a protective mechanism, Mother Nature causes both parents, immediately after the delivery, to secrete vast quantities of IQ-reduction hormones. Mother Nature wants the parents to be just smart enough to feed and change the baby, but also dumb enough to be highly amused if the baby inadvertently makes a noise such as "gwoooossshh." As the baby gets older, the hormones start to wear off, and the parents eventually climb back up to the intelligence level of their friends.

At the beginning, though, you just have to accept new parents as they are. To help you through this trying time, I have drawn on my own experience as a reduced-IQ parent to compile the following helpful guide to proper behavior around new parents and their baby.

HOW TO LOOK AT THE BABY

Looking is mandatory. You must not only look at the baby, but you must also make an appropriate remark. This does not include such offerings as: "Well, I understand they really improve after a couple of months."

Nor should you make the obvious observation that all newborns look like Mr. Potato Head. You must think of something positive. This can be difficult when you're actually looking at a newborn infant, so it's good to memorize your positive statement ahead of time. You might even practice saying it aloud while gazing adoringly at, say, a basket of laundry. Two traditional, appropriate statements are: "Ooohh! She has her mother's eyes!" and "Ooohh! She has her father's mouth!" This is assuming that (a) the baby is a girl, and (b) the father doesn't look like a catfish.

Note: If the baby spends the whole evening screaming loud enough to interfere with commercial aviation, you might throw in an additional remark such as: "Such an *alert* baby!"

HOW TO HOLD THE BABY

I'm afraid this is also mandatory. Say to the parents, with wholeheartedly feigned sincerity: "Oh! Do you think I could hold her?" And the parents, smiling like maniacs to disguise the fact that they're certain you will drop the baby on its head, say, "Ha ha! Of course!" Then, using both hands—you will have to put down your drink—you lift the baby up and clasp it lovingly to your bosom for eight one-millionths of a second, which is how long it will take the baby to develop a lifelong fear of you and raise its voice to a full shriek. Don't worry—at this point the mother will snatch her child away as if you were a mugger and the baby were a Gucci purse.

THREE POPULAR TOPICS OF CONVERSATION WITH NEW PARENTS

1. Their baby. 2. How interesting their baby is. 3. Postmodernistic art, and whether it might scare their baby.

WILL THINGS GET BETTER AS THE BABY GETS OLDER?

Yes and no. The good news is that the parents will, after about six months, reach the point where they can focus their attention on subjects other than their child for spans of up to 30 and even 40 seconds. The bad news is that this will happen just as the child enters the developmental stage where it begins to Explore Its World, by which I mean it crawls around trying to kill itself. So you'll find this is still not the ideal time for confiding those innermost secrets:

You: So I told John that if he wanted to sleep with me, he would...

Parent: Excuse me. Jason! Spit that out! (To you) I'm sorry. What were you saying?

You: I was saying I told John that...

Parent: Jason!! We do *not* put our fingers in that part of the doggy!!

And so on. But trust me, eventually your friends will get back to normal. Give them time. Perhaps it's even a good thing: While they're away, you'll develop new interests, maybe meet some new people. So when your friends return to the Land of Grown-Ups, ready to relate to you again as intellectual equals, you'll have new and exciting concepts to share with them.

Such as that you are pregnant. ∎

Dave Barry is a humor columnist for the Miami Herald.

BEDOUIN MOTHER
NURSES HER CHILD
IN THE SINAI.
NATHAN BENN/
WOODFIN CAMP,
INC.

LIFELINES

How did they clothe you?

In a cap that protected your eyes from the sun

and your soul from evil spirits?

In hand-sewn shoes adorned with colorful beads?

In wraps of sheepskin or linen?

How did they amuse you?

With the jingling

of bells on a rattle?

With playthings of shells,

gourds, or palm leaves?

With a whistle

whose sound

you could mimic?

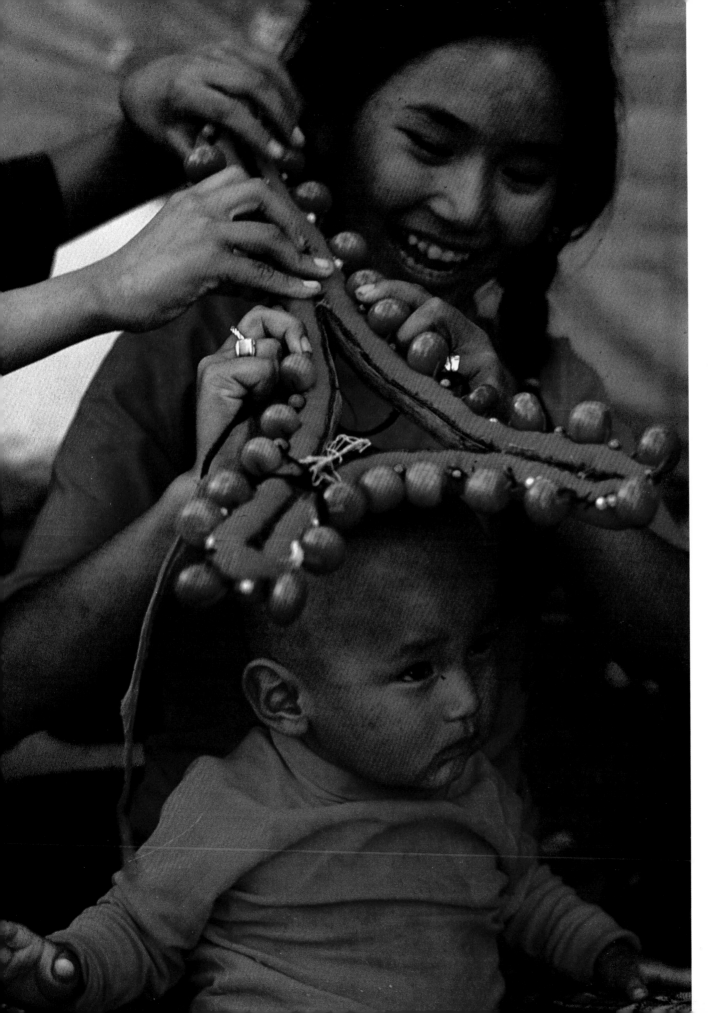

TIBETAN CHILD IS
DRESSED FOR A
FOLK-DANCING
FESTIVAL.
RAGHU-RAI/
MAGNUM

How did they cradle you?

In a sling

that rested on

your father's back?

In a shawl

that wrapped you close

to your mother's side?

In a bed

made to shield you

from outside worlds?

178

Women take the child to be rubbed in salt or oil, have the nose pinched, head pressed, limbs drawn straight and swaddled, shaping their newborn in accord with the culture's standard of beauty and well-being.

Prayers of thanksgiving will be said for a son, others for a daughter. Well-wishers say the child is pretty or strong, sweet or a "real boy," bring gifts that tell what the future holds, of roles that must be filled: toy cart or spinning wheel, knitted booties in pink or blue.

Where envy or the evil eye put a child in danger, where the soul can escape through an open mouth, the newborn is held close, hidden beneath a shawl. No one must notice, no one praise. Where light is thought to harm, the child is kept in darkness. Where abusing spirits threaten entry, a red cap is set on the baby's head and garlic put round her neck.

This child is born not only of one man and one woman. From the moment of birth, they speak of this baby with his uncle's nose, her sister's ears, his grandfather's chin. From the beginning, too, values vital to the culture are transmitted. So skillfully are the lessons taught by everyone around that the newborn sees no other reality. There can be no doubt that this child belongs, to family, to village, to the human community. ■

Sheila Kitzinger

A CHILD IS CARRIED IN AN ORNAMENTAL LEATHER CARRIER, NAMIBIA. ALON REININGER/ WOODFIN CAMP, INC.

EVEN THE SMALLEST
TOYS AND GARMENTS,
LIKE THIS JAPANESE
DRUM RATTLE,
CHINESE TIGER HAT,
AND KOREAN
HEAD ORNAMENT,
BEAR SYMBOLS OF
A CHILD'S ETHNIC
HERITAGE (cats. 157,
159, 215).

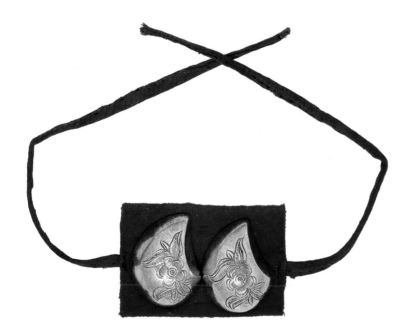

PRISCILLA RACHUN LINN NO OBJECT TOO SMALL: A THOUGHT ON BABIES, THINGS, AND CULTURE

Once, as a fledgling anthropologist, I spent hours in the company of traditional Maya women in San Juan Chamula, Chiapas, Mexico. I laughed at their bawdy jokes, shared the bottles of celebratory rum — and paid no heed whatsoever to their babies. Caught up as I was studying religious ritual where men took the starring roles, I never thought about the cultural influences that might prepare infants to take part in these rituals when they were grown. It never occurred to me that the objects used in tending very young babies had anything to do with the glamorous religious trappings that claimed my rapt attention. I never wondered what baby care had in common with the kinship organization, political systems, or economics that took urgent priority in my research.

Only years later did I realize the magnitude of my oversight. The passing of culture from older to younger generations through the activities of everyday life is a social force with the unfelt impact of gravity. Certainly culture is transmitted through other means that involve formal education, rituals, ceremonies, and so forth. But the remarkable process of an infant's daily enculturation takes place through commonplace objects, routines, and habits.

What do we make of the messages sent by the objects used in child care?

Cribs, cradles, and carriers tell us how the distance between mother (or caretaker) and child is established. Some babies spend their early months wrapped in a shawl or other carrier,

almost always close to another human body. Others lie or sit in cribs, hammocks, or special seats, much of their time spent alone.

As children are getting used to the kind of physical contact accepted in their culture, so they are learning about their environment. Carriers, clothing, toys, and feeders are among the many objects made from plant and animal fibers, wood, metal, or plastic in the child's world. All combine to give the first impressions of the kinds of materials either found, traded, or imported into their surroundings.

And as children learn about their environment, so objects begin to give them a sense of their identity in that environment. Dress and decorative arts as seen in textiles, furniture, and toys become some of the first hallmarks of a child's ethnic heritage and often indicate how the infant is expected to grow into culturally assigned sex roles. We assign pink and blue, and frilly or tailored styles to create distinctly different appearances for girls and boys, while other cultures use hats, shirts, shoes, and adornments to the same end.

Alongside these many differences, however, one consistency of purpose seems to pervade the way artifacts are made and used in rearing infants worldwide.

Almost every object imparts a message concerned with the child's health and well-being. Carriers, clothing, and amulets are usually designed, directly or indirectly, to protect against physical or supernatural harm, to ward off sick-

ness, and to promote health, growth, and luck. Lest we scoff at what appears to be a reliance on magic, think about the advertising of baby products in our country: Is it surprising that a popular brand of children's wear is called Health-Tex or that copy for Ultra-Pampers should read "the only diaper officially accepted by pediatric experts"?

In some cultures, infants are marked with soot or dressed in simple or shabby clothing to make sure that they call no harmful attention to themselves. Elsewhere babies are resplendent in their cleanliness and finery—as if to say that only what is good, right, and moral can be attracted to a baby as well outfitted as this. And if an elegant baby also advertises family status, wealth, and community standing—so much the better. There really is nothing new about designer clothes for babies or strollers whose cost entails a second mortgage on the home.

What interests me about all these objects is the way they offer clues to babies about who will protect them, who has power over them, who they can trust or turn to for help, and who or what is dangerous and to be feared. Seldom have researchers examined how the objects of child care teach children to set up vital relationships with other humans, animals, and the supernatural. Thus object research boils down to basic issues of human fear and trust, power, and dependency—hardly insignificant trifles, and even of major significance in understanding kinship, political systems, and economics. ■

Dr. Priscilla Rachun Linn is a sociocultural anthropologist with a special interest in material culture. She was curator of collections and a member of the curatorial committee for the Smithsonian's Generations *exhibition.*

KOREAN HEAD ORNAMENTS FOR INFANTS WERE VALUED NOT ONLY AS DECORATIVE ITEMS, BUT ALSO BECAUSE THEY WERE THOUGHT TO HAVE PROTECTIVE PROPERTIES (cat. 154).

FINE TURKISH BABY
SHOES WERE FASHIONED
TO RESEMBLE ADULT
FOOTWEAR AND OFTEN
WERE AN IMPORTANT
SYMBOL OF A FAMILY'S
WEALTH AND STATUS
(cat. 184).

WE CAN BE QUITE CER-
TAIN THAT THE BABY
WHO WORE THIS FUR
AVIATOR HAT DID NOT
WANT TO PULL IT OFF.
WARMTH, STURDINESS,
SOFTNESS, AND A SNUG
FIT WERE ESSENTIAL
FOR ALL CLOTHING

WORN BY THE CHILDREN
OF NOMADIC HERDERS,
WHO SCALED BITTER
COLD ALTITUDES ON
THE IRAN-PAKISTAN
BORDER (cat. 153).

Cradles and cribs have been part of Western culture for centuries, surviving changes in design, function, and meaning wrought by the many peoples who have used them. They seem to be universal artifacts of infancy. But beyond the West and its colonial influences, the necessity for a separate—and separating—apparatus to control the infant does not appear to be an idea shared by all.

African and Asian cultures, past and present, have not even used such devices, reflecting their primary concern with nurturing, rather than controlling, the baby. To satisfy the infant's need for security and bonding, the mother or wet nurse carries the baby close or, during the working day, sets him or her nearby. Among nomadic Tibetans, the infant spends most of the day "within the blouse of his mother's sheepskin coat, bare skin next to bare skin."[1]

Although current and latter-day cultures in the Far East and the Americas have restricted infants' movements more than those of Africa and Asia, none of these peoples has relied on the heavy, mechanical apparatus that Europeans and Euro-Americans did (and still do). Non-Western peoples have felt a need for physical closeness with the child, day and night. Even sedentary cultures with spacious housing have seldom set up a nursery to isolate the infant at night.

The crib is more familiar to us today because of Christianity's opening drama: the birth of Jesus in a manger. This "nativity crib" (the original was probably just a recess carved out of the manger's rock wall) very early became the preeminent symbol of protected purity. The first dateable image of the nativity crib appeared around 343 A.D., in a Roman-Christian sarcophagal relief. Some sources claim that, in the 400s, an oratory chapel in Rome's church of Santa Maria Maggiore had a carved-out stone representing Christ's crib, and that *ad Praesepe* ("of the Crib") was added to the church's name at that time. Church documents from the 12th century say that the original crib—constructed of five Levantine sycamore boards—was installed in such a chapel there during the 700s. The crib remained until the 13th century, when Alnolfo di Cambio's splendid marble sculpture replaced it as part of a remodeling.

It was St. Francis of Assisi, however, who popularized the modern image of the nativity crib. The nativity setting that he constructed—a shed roof and manger in Greccio, just outside of Assisi—drew pilgrims from all over the Christian world. As a result, European churches of the 14th century began to display their own nativity cribs, further spreading the image. In the 17th century, the Capuchin Brotherhood promoted use of the crib in the home.[2]

The nativity crib gradually became popular in Protestant homes as well. The simple, raised crib of the nativity may have even provided a model for Victorian forms. The Victorians believed that, through ritual, the ideal of purity could be transferred from the infant Jesus to all newborn infants, who were tainted at birth with original sin. Certainly a crib modeled on a manger fits in well with this belief. But the Victorians also wanted a form to present the infant to "polite society," a desire rooted not in the evolution of the crib,

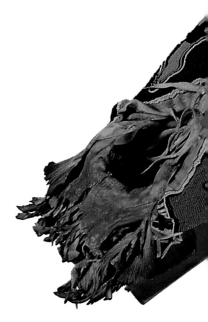

AT AN INFANT'S NAMING CEREMONY, A KIOWA FAMILY PRESENTED THE BABY IN A FINELY DECORATED CRADLEBOARD. ITS QUALITY ILLUSTRATED NOT ONLY THE WEALTH AND GOOD STANDING OF THE FAMILY, BUT ALSO OFTEN THE INFANT'S STATUS AS A FAVORED CHILD OR FUTURE LEADER. KINSWOMEN OF THE NEWBORN—GLAD TO HELP WELCOME A SPECIAL MEMBER OF THE FAMILY—LABORED FOR MANY HOURS ON THE BEADWORK REQUIRED TO MAKE SO ELABORATE AN HEIRLOOM (cat. 119).

but in the evolution of the cradle.

This need to display the infant can be traced back through the notion, prevalent among late medieval Europe's nobility, that the cradle symbolized one's social position, or estate. The idea probably originated before 1300 (though data are scarce) with the king's belief that he, as God's appointed authority, needed a form grander than a meager manger—the apparatus the nobility had likely used before then—to signify his earthly rank. The noble hierarchy picked up the idea, modifying the king's design to signify the lesser status of their infants. This cradle, the "cradle-of-state," became typical of late medieval expression, developing a complex symbolism in its forms and decorations.

By the late 1300s, Europe's rising merchant class, and the force of land reform, challenged the aristocracy's economic and social prerogatives. The great seigniorial houses of the Burgundian empire became less open in form; their owners began to structure the space within so that families were separated from servants and tenants, and rooms took on more specialized use. Aristocratic rights and precedence, more mutable than rank, needed the visual reinforcement provided by sumptuous textiles and furniture.

Descriptions of noble birthing practices by Alienor de Poiters—in her *Les honneurs de la cour,* written between 1484 and 1491—explained the implications of different textiles, furs, and furniture surrounding the infant at birth and baptism. Two cradles were required. The higher, more

TURKEY.
MARC RIBOUD/
MAGNUM

elaborate cradle-of-state remained in the mother's chamber and served to display the noble infant to visitors. Alienor notes that the cradle sat near the fire, resplendent with its damask *celour* (a canopy like those of full-size beds), samite curtains, and coverings of ermine and *crespe* (a fine French silk) that touched the carpet surrounding it. Her accounts of noble birth and baptism practices describe how the infant was brought into the chamber from the nursery and placed for standing viewers in "a high cradle hanging by means of iron rings between two wooden uprights [and] provided with a circular or square pavilion or sparver of silk."[3]

The form and use of medieval cradles evolved with later European and American experience. During the day, the Europeans displayed the infant in a large, elevated cradle-of-state that rocked in place. This daytime cradle, elaborately furnished, continued to connote the importance of the infant's lineage—it was this function, and not just a family's fat purse, that determined its character. At night, a knee-high cradle was used, which allowed servants to attend to the infant from a seated position. This cradle, though, served to further separate child from mother. Historical examples of both day- and nighttime cradles reveal slots along the side for binding tapes to hold the swaddled infant securely in place.

The low-to-the-floor cradle with rockers was introduced in America by upper-class European settlers, sometime before 1650. Its use spread throughout the new world, though few documented examples remain from before 1750. A basic rectangular form with flared sides predominated, despite the addition of hoods, pierced and scrolled sideboards and headboards, and turned posts.

The 19th century saw Americans opening up to the new ideas on childhood and infant care filtering over from the Continent. In Europe before 1700, infancy and childhood had been unrecognized as developmental stages. Infancy was largely an inconvenient time, and the social position of infants was much more important than their "personality development" (as we saw with the cradle-of-state). But the French writers of the Enlightenment changed things. They declared that childhood was not a miniature adulthood, but a separate stage of human development. Europe thus "invented" childhood, and the new invention came to reflect attitudes of the day on education, labor, and religion.[4] So much so that, by the early 1800s, bourgeois opinion had done a complete turnabout. No longer were infants seen as "less than human"—animal-like in their lack of upright posture, speech, and reason. Now they were "more than human"—helpless innocents crying for protection from a corrupt adult world.

Medical specialists added their voices to the chorus. Violent rocking could induce dizziness and stupor, they said, and might even cause brain damage. They also claimed that the cradle's tight lacings, solid sides, and constricting swaddlings restricted natural growth and the flow of air. With precious cargo to protect, the cradle had to go.

To replace the cradle, other devices were quickly designed to protect and please infants and to

CRADLES GENERALLY WERE PLACED IN THE COMMON ROOM OF THE HOUSE, WHERE FAMILY MEMBERS COOKED, ATE, WORKED, AND OFTEN SLEPT. SECURITY AND HEALTH CONCERNS SUSTAINED SOME OF THE CRADLE'S POPULARITY, SINCE THE INFANT COULD BE SHIELDED FROM DIRTY FLOORS, INDOOR DRAFTS, OPEN FIRES, AND OTHER POTENTIAL DANGERS. EVEN WHEN PARENTS COULD NOT AFFORD ELABORATE BABY FURNITURE, THEY SOUGHT TO PROTECT THEIR CHILDREN WITH DURABLE MATERIALS. APART FROM THEIR PROTECTIVE QUALITIES, HOWEVER, CRADLES WERE CHERISHED PERSONAL POSSESSIONS, FOR OFTEN THEY WERE MADE BY THE BABY'S FATHER AND WERE PASSED DOWN WITHIN THE FAMILY. A FAMILY'S GOOD CHARACTERISTICS WERE THOUGHT TO BE INHERITED WITH THE CRADLE (cats. 138, 139).

further their development (the influence of the Enlightenment), while presenting them, in all their purity, to an admiring adult world (the influence of the cradle-of-state). The swing-and-spring "jumper" provided healthier movement than a wildly rocking cradle; the highchair, fitted with its own tray, allowed the child to join the family at mealtime. The perambulator presented the pale-skinned innocent in flattering tones of soft textiles, in an intimate recess as safe as the womb.

It was, however, the crib of wicker—raised to standing height, fully flounced, and renamed the bassinet—that best stated Victorian attitudes about infancy. The bassinet was set out for daytime display in the bedroom or parlor. At night, the infant was removed to the nursery and placed in another crib, which by 1890 was actually a miniature metal bed with high, let-down sides that served the child to the age of three or more. A wide price range of these "little beds" was offered in the 1897 *Sears, Roebuck and Co. Consumers Guide.*

Like the cradle, the crib encouraged the separation of infant from mother. It provided an isolated, individualized space and maintained the middle-class attitude that an infant's innocence required protection from the industrialized, urbanized world of 1900.

It was not until the World War II baby boom, with the advice of Dr. Spock, that many American infants began to enjoy closer contact with parents. Today, slings and pouches hold baby close, recalling the methods used for centuries by less technically developed societies to create bonds between generations. ■

Richard E. Ahlborn is curator of community life in the department of social and cultural history at the National Museum of American History, Smithsonian Institution. He was a member of the curatorial committee for the Smithsonian's Generations *exhibition.*

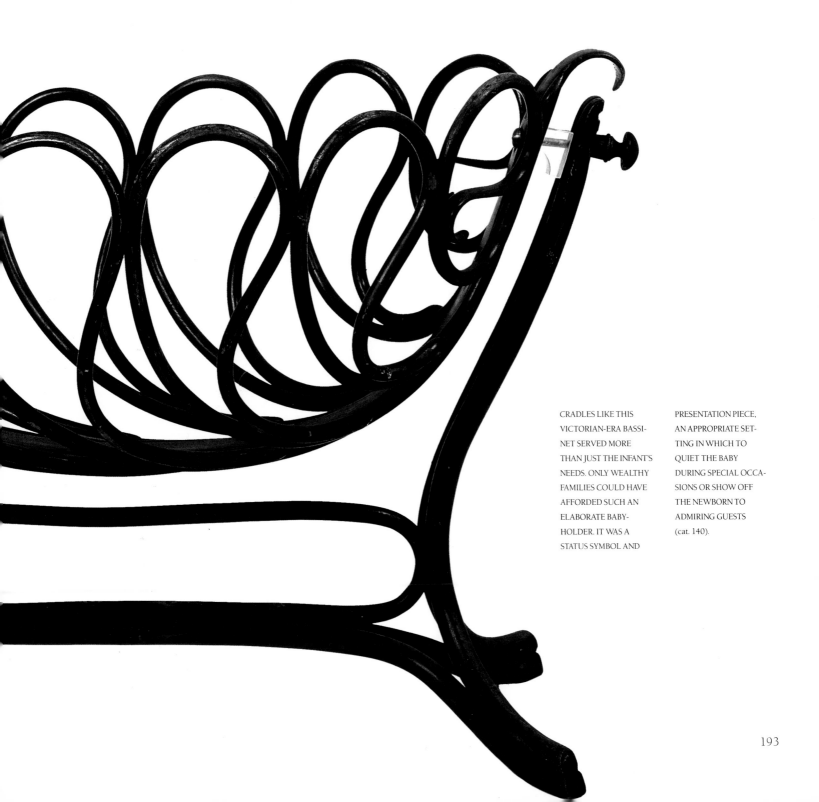

CRADLES LIKE THIS VICTORIAN-ERA BASSINET SERVED MORE THAN JUST THE INFANT'S NEEDS. ONLY WEALTHY FAMILIES COULD HAVE AFFORDED SUCH AN ELABORATE BABY-HOLDER. IT WAS A STATUS SYMBOL AND PRESENTATION PIECE, AN APPROPRIATE SETTING IN WHICH TO QUIET THE BABY DURING SPECIAL OCCASIONS OR SHOW OFF THE NEWBORN TO ADMIRING GUESTS (cat. 140).

RATTLES ENABLE BABIES TO AMUSE AND SOOTHE THEMSELVES. THEY ARE MADE FROM MATERIALS THAT OFTEN PROVIDE IMPORTANT INFORMATION ABOUT CULTURAL ATTITUDES AND ECONOMIC CONDITIONS IN DIFFERENT PARTS OF THE WORLD. A CHILD WHOSE FIRST TOY IS CRAFTED FROM GOURDS AND HEMP, FOR EXAMPLE, WILL BECOME FAMILIAR EARLY ON WITH THE APPEARANCE, FEEL, AND SMELL OF THE SURROUNDING NATURAL ENVIRONMENT. THE FINELY WORKED SILVER RATTLES, WHICH REFLECT POPULAR DECORATIVE ART STYLES, ARE A MEASURE OF THE EXTENT TO WHICH FAMILIES SOUGHT TO MIRROR THEIR OWN SOCIOECONOMIC STATUS THROUGH INFANT ITEMS (cats. 193-228).

195

HMONG FATHER
AND CHILD,
NORTHERN LAOS.
JOEL HALPERN/
ANTHRO-PHOTO

196

**RONALD G. BARR AND
URS A. HUNZIKER**

INFANTS WHO ARE CARRIED
MORE CRY LESS

Crying is one of the enigmas of early infancy. Infants in Western industrialized societies tend to cry in a strikingly consistent pattern. Typically, an infant's crying escalates between birth and the second month of life, then decreases until the fourth month, and stabilizes at that point for the rest of the first year. Over a 24-hour period, the crying does not occur equally, but a baby usually cries more frequently in the evening. Of course, this pattern may be much more marked in any one infant than in another. But in groups of infants, the pattern remains the same, despite differences in how parents care for their babies.

The existence of this pattern reinforces the notion that the way Western babies cry is a normal part of their development. Some experts have even suggested that an infant's crying may be inborn—a behavior intended to capture the attention of adults so as to make sure that baby gets fed and is protected from roving predators. Still, crying often represents a clinical problem in that it can be a source of considerable tension for adults. Crying can even compromise the interaction between parent and infant: It can be the reason for switching from breast feeding to formula feeding and, in extreme cases, the catalyst for child abuse. The dilemma is understanding how behavior that is part of a child's normal development can also be the source of such distress for parents.

A clue to unravelling this mystery comes from observations of infants in other cultures. Westerners returning from non-industrialized societies report that babies there cry less than our own. A notable difference between these cultures and ours is that infants in these societies are carried most of the time. Here in the West, babies are often put out of direct contact with their parents—in cribs, carseats, and playpens.

Controlled experiments suggest that these factors may not be coincidental. Various elements of the act of carrying—motion, contact, warmth, and change in posture—have been demonstrated to soothe crying babies. It seems reasonable to ask whether the amount and/or the pattern of crying among Western infants could be changed by carrying them more than is typical in our society.

In a study carefully designed to answer this question, one group of mothers increased the amount of time spent carrying their babies between the fourth and twelfth weeks of life to 4.4 hours per day on average. Another group carried their infants for 2.7 hours per day. The effects were striking. At six weeks of age, when the amount of crying is generally at its height, the babies in the first group cried 1.2 hours per day compared to the 2.2 hours of the second group—a 43 percent difference. When only evening crying (between 4 P.M. and midnight) was considered, the first group cried 54 percent less than the second.

A MOTHER CARRIES
HER CHILD TO THE
RICE FIELDS, CHINA.
JOHN ISAAC/UNICEF

The study showed that, although the *frequency* of crying was the same for the two groups of babies, the *duration* of crying was impressively reduced when mothers spent more time carrying their infants.

These results provide a clear answer to one question, and have interesting implications for many others. They clearly suggest that, overall, infants who are carried more cry less. Since the frequency of crying did not change, the reduction was due to still-frequent, but shorter, periods of crying. Concerning the question as to how crying can be a normal part of an infant's development while at the same time be so stressful for parents, perhaps frequent but shorter cries function well to assure the baby's nutrition and protection, while it is the longer crying bouts (more typical of our society's babies) that cause parents such distress.

What the results do *not* demonstrate is whether we *should* carry our infants more. Our decisions about infant care must be made in the light of many biological and cultural factors, of which the need to have less fussy babies is only one. But the results do suggest that crying that becomes a serious concern for parents may not necessarily require treatment with medication, or a change in feeding habits. We might instead adopt patterns of interaction between parent and child that are part of the human experience elsewhere in the world. ■

Ronald G. Barr, M.D.C.M., is associate professor of pediatrics at McGill University and Montreal Children's Hospital in Canada. He combines anthropology and pediatrics in his studies of crying and pain syndromes in children. Urs A. Hunziker, M.D., is a staff physician with a specialty in developmental pediatrics at the Kinderspital Hospital in Zurich, Switzerland.

MOTHERS CARRY
THE WEIGHT OF
THEIR CHILDREN
FROM STRAPS
ACROSS THEIR
HEADS, CHINA.
EVE ARNOLD/
MAGNUM

MARJORIE SHOSTAK   EARLIEST MEMORIES: GROWING UP AMONG THE !KUNG

!Kung children spend their first few years in almost constant close contact with their mothers. The !Kung infant has continual access to the mother's breast, day and night, usually for at least three years, and nurses on demand several times an hour. The child sleeps beside the mother at night, and during the day is carried in a sling, skin-to-skin on the mother's hip, wherever the mother goes, at work or at play. When the child is not in the sling, the mother may be amusing him or her—bouncing, singing, or talking. If they are physically separated, it is usually for short periods when the father, siblings, cousins, grandparents, aunts, uncles, or friends of the family are playing with the baby while the mother sits close by. Separation from the mother becomes more frequent after the middle of the second year, but even then it is initiated almost exclusively by the child, who is steadily drawn into the groups of children playing around the village. Still, the mother is usually available whenever needed.

!Kung fathers—indulgent, affectionate, and devoted—also form very intense mutual attachments with their children. Nevertheless, men spend only a small fraction of the time that women do in the company of children, especially infants, and avoid many of the less pleasant tasks of child care, such as toileting, cleaning and bathing, and nose wiping. They are also inclined to hand back crying or fretful babies to the mothers for consolation. Fathers, like mothers, are not viewed as figures of awesome authority, and their relationships with their children are intimate, nurturant, and physically close. Sharing the same living and sleeping space, children have easy access to both parents when they are around. As children—especially boys—get older, fathers spend even more time with them.

Assuming no serious illness, the first real break from the infant's idyll of comfort and security comes with weaning, which typically begins when the child is around three years of age and the mother is pregnant again. Most !Kung believe that it is dangerous for a child to continue to nurse once the mother is pregnant with her next child. They say the milk in the woman's breasts belongs to the fetus; harm could befall either the unborn child or its sibling if the latter were to continue to nurse. It is considered essential to wean quickly, but weaning meets the child's strong resistance and may in fact take a number of months to accomplish.

Within a year of being weaned from the breast the child is "weaned" from the sling as well. !Kung children love to be carried. They love the contact with their mothers, and they love not having to walk under the pressure of keeping up. As their mothers begin

A FAMILY AFFAIR. HERERO FATHERS PROVIDED THE SHEEPSKINS FOR SUCH BABY CARRIERS; MOTHERS SOFTENED AND PREPARED THEM UNTIL THEY COULD BE USED. INFANTS THEN WERE CARRIED ABOUT TO AND FROM DAILY TASKS, GIVING THEM A CLOSE-UP LOOK AT HOW THEIR PARENTS LIVED AND WORKED (cat. 120).

to suggest and then to insist that they walk along beside them, temper tantrums once again erupt: Children refuse to walk, demand to be carried, and will not agree to be left behind in the village while their mothers gather for the day.

!Kung parents are concerned that these events not hit their children too hard, but coming as they do one after the other, these times are difficult at best. The father may try to spend more time with the child, or the child may stay with a devoted grandparent or aunt (who will be sure to spoil her) in a nearby village for a while.

Alternate generations are recognized as having a special relationship, especially when the child is the grandparent's "namesake." Personal and intimate topics not discussed with parents are taken up freely with grandparents, and grandparents often represent a child's interest at the expense of those of the parent. Also, since older people contribute less to subsistence than do younger adults, they have more time to play with their grandchildren. It is not surprising that children are willing to live with them or with other close relatives, especially during times of conflict with parents. As one young girl explained, "When I was a little girl, I lived with my aunt for weeks, sometimes for months at a time. I didn't cry when I lived with her; she was my second mother." ■

Marjorie Shostak is adjunct assistant professor of anthropology at Emory University. During two field trips to study the !Kung San of Botswana, from 1969 to 1971 and again in 1975, she spent hundreds of hours interviewing !Kung women about their lives.

LAURIS McKEE   THE DIETA: POSTPARTUM SECLUSION
IN THE ANDES OF ECUADOR

Birth signals the first separation of a mother from her child. From that moment, their relationship, formerly a biological one, is transformed into a deeply significant social one. The ease or difficulty of the transition and transformation will depend to a great extent on a culture's norms, beliefs, and customs. In the Highland regions of Ecuador, traditions surrounding the postpartum period guide the treatment of new mothers and their infants. The behaviors and attitudes encoded in custom provide for the reordering of social and emotional relationships in the family, and facilitate the integration of the new baby into the group.

During this period, mothers living in rural Highland communities practice seclusion, following a custom known as the *dieta*. The dieta provides a complete "script" for the actions of the immediate family. Moreover, its rules enjoin the collaboration of the mother's female kin and her husband's female kin, whose responsibility is to nurture the new mother and to assume her household tasks, permitting her to turn her full attention to her child. The dieta as described here derives from ethnographic research among mestizo families in Tungurahua and Bolivar provinces, although the practice also plays a part among a small number of Native American groups.[1]

Dieta, literally translated, means "diet," but its customs prescribe far more than a regimen of preferred and tabooed foods. Sexual continence is the rule, and the light of the sun must be avoided by remaining indoors for 42 days (this is the number most frequently mentioned, though variants of 40 and 45 days also have been recorded). This social isolation begins on the day of the birth, and it confers certain benefits: Mothers are freed from the heavy labor of normal work obligations, and they rest in bed, attended by their kin.

Furthermore, women symbolically assume the status of children. For the first three days postpartum, their bodies are tightly wrapped from buttocks to breast, so that they resemble the swaddled infants who lie beside them. This is done in order to "realign their bones" and to strengthen their bodies, which have been weakened by the "opening of the bones" during childbirth. Proper wrapping of the mother is also thought to delay another pregnancy. When the wrapping is removed, women are dressed in heavy clothing and their heads are covered with shawls that can be pulled across their faces. Their kin, especially their mothers- and sisters-in-law, attend to them, cook for them, and bring them gifts of food from their own kitchens.

During this period, the sun is viewed as an active, pathogenic force. For that reason, the room as well as the bodies of mother and child are carefully shielded from its light. Windows are covered, and if possible, a canopy is hung over the bed to prevent the entry of any errant ray. People who have been out-of-doors are discouraged from visiting: The sun's burning power might be transferred from their bodies to those of the secluded pair. Exposure to the sun produces a grippe-like illness in new mothers, whose bodies are viewed as excessively "hot," but its effects are worse for infants. Women say the sun "burns" the milk in their breasts. When the baby suckles the "burned" milk, the infant becomes feverish and (possibly) fatally ill. These effects can be neutralized by expressing some of the breast milk before nursing. Another tactic is used that rarely fails: throwing the expressed milk into the cooking fire to burn. This strategy, however, is said to be exceedingly risky, for the magical effects of the burning are so powerful that they can dry up breast milk completely, or worse: *permanently*, depriving future children of sustenance.[2]

In Ecuadorian ethnomedicine, the humoral theory of "hot and cold" normally governs the treatment of the ill. A person is healthful when these two qualities are in an internal equilibrium, such that the body is in a "neutral" state.[3] In the humoral schema, body states, food, and drink are classified as hot, cold, or neutral (*templado*). These qualities are also ascribed to plants and animals, and when these are eaten, their heat or cold is transferred to the consumer's body. For example, lamb, chicken, beans, and rice are viewed as cold, whereas beef, pork, onions, and grapes are hot.

It is apparent that the qualities hot and cold are not thermal in nature, but are metaphorical.[4] Food items are classified by their perceived effects on the body, and the principle of opposites prevails: In order to reestablish internal balance, if one is cold, one eats hot foods, if one is hot, one eats cold foods. The thermal heat or cold of the ambience also figures in dietary strategies. The body of the parturient at the moment of birth is thought excessively cold, but shortly thereafter, her body becomes hot, and susceptible to infection. So, hot foods are eaten immediately after birth, but for the remaining 42 days, cold or temperate foods are consumed.

Thus, diet is important. Consumption of the appropriate foods returns a new mother to health. Excessive overconsumption of hot foods could lead to death. The dieta prescribes foods in three categories: cold foods, white foods, and soft foods (*comidas suaves*). It is customary that every new mother is given a whole chicken to eat. Chicken is an expensive luxury for the rural poor, and rarely served, but if a husband denies his wife this special food, he invites general condemnation and comments on his stinginess.

MOTHER FEEDS HER BABY IN THE MARKETPLACE AT SAN FRANCISCO EL ALTO, GUATEMALA. ANTOINETTE JONGEN/BLACK STAR

Chicken possesses all three preferred qualities, and chicken soup is considered the most nourishing dieta food. Other preferred foods (note that they are white and soft) are noodles, rice, and thickened beverages (coladas) made with milk (if it is affordable), oatmeal or other cereal flours, and cornstarch. Poor families may have to substitute with coladas made of sugar, water, and cornstarch, and soups of potatoes and noodles.

Some foods, including hot peppers, avocados, limes, oranges, and ground peanuts, are prohibited because they are said to "cut" the blood and to cause blotchy skin, a condition colloquially termed la pana (in U.S. culture, called the "mask of pregnancy"). Foods that are classified as cold, but "irritating" (thought to irritate the digestive tract and exacerbate hidden infection), are avoided as they produce infection. Other foods are avoided for different reasons: Beans and plantains, for example, are said to give the baby colic.

In that mothers are secluded for approximately six weeks, the dieta resembles a custom of the same name practiced in 16th-century Europe and introduced to the Andes by the Spanish invaders. Nonetheless, the symbols and beliefs that provide motivation for the Andean custom differ remarkably from European ones. In the Judeo-Christian tradition of the Europeans, blood shed in childbirth was thought polluting and a potential danger to others. Jewish customary law required postpartum seclusion followed by ritual purification.[5] In Christian

practice, a new mother's failure to be ritually purified before rejoining the society of the faithful was punished by a two-week fast.[6]

In Ecuador, blood-pollution and endangerment of the community are not concerns that motivate seclusion. Instead, women fear the illness and death that the sun can inflict on themselves and their infants. The rationale is especially interesting, because although the sun makes the body (humorally) hot, it also is an ancient Andean deity, masculine in gender, whose power in an equatorial country is felt daily. The moon also is an ancient deity, the wife of the sun, and it is tempting to speculate that the dieta was shortened in Ecuador, from 45 to 42 days, in order to link it more closely to the moon (42 days equals one and a half lunar cycles). Supporting this notion is a description by Ecuadorans of the seclusion's desirable outcome: The faces of the new mothers at the end of the dieta—pale from staying indoors—are said to resemble the moon in beauty and whiteness.

White, as a dieta symbol, figures also in a conceptual equation of sperm and milk. These substances, both life-giving, share qualities of whiteness and ejaculation.[7] In off-color stories and insults, "milk" is euphemistically substituted for "sperm," but the association seems to go beyond mere appearances. Abstinence from sexual relations is thought to ensure a good supply of breast milk: Sex, somehow, reduces the amount of milk. A similar belief was reported for Inca society:

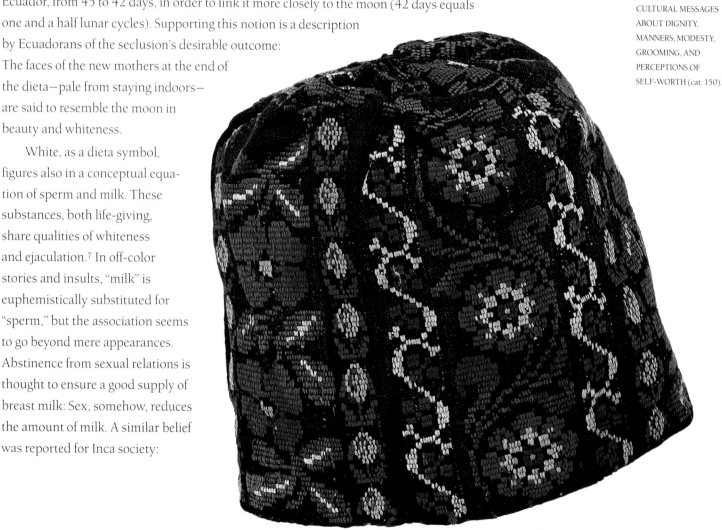

If parents had sexual relations during the two years a child was supposed to be nursed, the child grew sickly, and eventually died. Such a child was called *ayusca*, the identical epithet used for young men who had been deserted by their sweethearts.[8]

At the end of the dieta, women are bathed in water boiled with herbs, perfume, and a cup of milk, or with the petals of three white roses (the bath recipes vary). For mothers of first-borns, this signals their entry into true adult status. But for all mothers, it marks their reintegration into the social world with new tasks and responsibilities to manage.

Today, many women complain that husbands and kinswomen permit them only a "minimum dieta" of eight days. The shorter period is becoming the standard. Today's world is less generous with time, but is the dieta merely time wasted in unproductive ritual?

A pragmatic analysis shows that in rural communities lacking access to modern medicine, seclusion most likely has highly positive effects on a woman's health. In the early postpartum period, strenuous agricultural work can cause hemorrhage. Rural women perform heavy agricultural work, and even domestic tasks such as laundering clothing require lifting the weight of wet linens washed in icy cold mountain water. Traditional women carry their infants virtually constantly, the weight adding to the stress of any task performed. The dieta provides a respite from backbreaking work, and from carrying burdens for long distances, a mobility that is more stressful in a mountainous environment. Most of all, the dieta requires that mothers receive special attention and treatment that otherwise might not be granted.

As for the child, the new infant's exposure to pathogens is reduced by limiting their social and environmental contacts—the identical goals motivating infant isolation in North American hospitals. The 42-day period permits the development of mutually satisfying patterns of interaction between mother and child that lead to a deep emotional attachment. Research shows that by 8 days, mothers and infants have established inter-action "styles" that tend to endure and to color their future relationship.[9] Taking these factors into account, the dieta appears to be not merely a human but a humane tradition that enhances the quality of life of mothers, infants, and, ultimately, Ecuadorian family life. ∎

Dr. Lauris McKee teaches anthropology at Franklin and Marshall College.

AESTHETIC APPEAL AND STATUS SOMETIMES WERE REFLECTED IN INFANT FEEDERS. THE ELABORATENESS OF POSSET POTS AND FOOD WARMERS SUGGESTS THAT APPEARANCE AS A MEASURE OF THE CHILD'S WELL-BEING MAY HAVE BEEN AS IMPORTANT AS FUNCTIONALISM AND DURABILITY. YET DESPITE THEIR ATTRACTIVENESS, SUCH VESSELS OFTEN CLOGGED, WERE DIFFICULT TO CLEAN, AND FOSTERED INFECTIOUS MICRO-ORGANISMS THAT CAUSED ILLNESSES TO THE BABIES WHO USED THEM (cats. 242-247).

NOT ALL BABY BOTTLES ARE MADE FROM TALL PLASTIC CONTAINERS WITH THROWAWAY POUCHES AND SPECIALLY STERILIZED NIPPLES. BEFORE THE 19th CENTURY, PEWTER OFTEN WAS USED FOR INFANT FEEDERS. TODAY WE SURMISE THAT THIS METAL MAY HAVE CONTRIBUTED TO THE HIGH INFANT MORTALITY RATE BECAUSE ITS LEAD CONTENT INDUCED POISONING (cat. 230).

BILL COSBY   HIGH ANXIETY

On a recent cross-country flight, I saw a dramatic example of why being a parent is a harder job than being president of the United States. In fact, the scene I saw could have been a commercial for birth control.

On that flight were a mother and her four-year-old son, whose name was Jeffrey. Everybody on the plane knew his name was Jeffrey because his mother spent a major part of the trip talking to him, generally from a distance:

"Jeffrey, don't *do* that!"

"Jeffrey, will you get *down* from there!"

"Jeffrey, now look what you've done!"

All of the passengers knew not only Jeffrey's name but also his age because, as he merrily ran about kicking their legs, he kept crying, "I'm four years old!" I happened to have been spared his kicking my particular legs. Instead, he merely smeared chocolate on my shirt.

And so, as our terror flight moved west, sleep was made impossible by the counterpoint of the voices of mother and son:

"Jeffrey, get down!"

"I'm four years old!"

"Jeffrey, now *look* what you've done to the man!"

"I'm four years old!"

If the passengers had been given a choice between riding with Jeffrey and riding with a hijacker, I know what their choice would have been. The hijacker might have allowed a few of us to sleep; and even if he hadn't, he certainly would not have kept saying, "I'm twenty-three years old!"

As the plane moved west, the feelings of the passengers toward Jeffrey grew more intense. When we reached the continental divide, one gentleman invited him into the lavatory to play with the blue water.

At last, however, there was mercy and Jeffrey fell asleep—five minutes before we landed. When the plane reached the terminal and the passengers began to leave, a few of them took special pains to wake up Jeffrey and say good-bye. And their hearts went out to his mother, who had aged ten years in five hours. Her hair was disheveled, her mascara had run, and exhaustion had seeped into her face. After every other person had left, she summoned the last traces of her strength, picked up Jeffrey, and carried him off the plane, as if she were taking out the garbage.

And there, at the end of the ramp, was Jeffrey's father. He was smiling, he had a deep tan, and he was wearing a clean white shirt and brightly checkered pants. The mother handed Jeffrey to this man and then quietly told him to go to hell. ■

Bill Cosby, humorist and father of five, holds a doctorate in education.

WOMEN AND
CHILDREN IN AN
EXTENDED FAMILY
VILLAGE,
BANGLADESH.
LUCINDA LEACH

MOTHER AND
CHILD,
BANGLADESH.
KEVIN BUBRISKI

216

REALITIES

Did they say you were born

during hard times?

When there was

famine,

drought,

war,

disease?

When they had no wealth,

no food,

no medicines?

BUNDLING THE
BODIES OF SMALL
CHILDREN WHO
HAVE DIED OF
MALNUTRITION

AND DISEASE, IN AN
ETHIOPIAN RELIEF
CAMP.
MARY ELLEN MARK/
ARCHIVE

Did they say you arrived during good times?

In a world of calm and abundance?

Did they protect you?

Abandon you?

Embrace you?

Neglect you?

Cherish you beyond measure?

CAMBODIAN CHILD
LOOKS AFTER A
YOUNGER SIBLING
AT THE TEMPLES OF
ANGKOR.
JEAN SHOR, © 1960
NATIONAL
GEOGRAPHIC
SOCIETY

CHILD WEARING
U.S. ARMY HELMET
IN THE LAST DAYS
BEFORE THE
KHMER ROUGE
TAKEOVER OF
CAMBODIA, 1975.
MARK GODFREY/
ARCHIVE

A quiet haven, sheltering arms, a mother singing a lullaby as darkness gathers, a father tenderly watching the baby in the crib; playthings in the nursery, music-box, patchwork and rocking-chair—security, peace, love, and space for a child to grow fearless and strong—this is the dream.

High-pitched, repetitive, questioning baby-talk, the beat and rhythm strong, nonsense rhymes, ridiculous words and names and the lilting sing-song that goes on and on, pausing as the child responds with pursed lips, half-formed sounds, eyes direct on yours, tongue-lip protruding; nursery rhymes that capture danger and make it music—this is the dream.

The cry of the child in the rubble of the bomb-wrecked building, the plea of the child with the swollen belly—this is reality.

The child shaped by poverty, born by the river spilling acid foam, home the shell of an old automobile or packing case on the mud by the harbor, or in a shantytown where shacks cling like broken teeth to the hillside above the beautiful city, or the child of the junkie twitching and jerking in an intensive care crib. These children must be quick to scrape a living, grab food, be streetwise, sink or swim. They are the children of violence.

Must this be reality? ∎

Sheila Kitzinger

What does a child's mind make of the world? Every society has its own view of what it means to be human and its way of embedding that sense in its young. Nonetheless, the primary reality of children the world over is being in the power of adults. By both direct and subtle means, children are informed of what and whom they may become, admire, hate, and fear. Children are shaped morally and politically by the strivings, attitudes, and tensions of the adult world. They are stamped with society's vision for the future and charged with the mandate to carry it out. As psychologist Neil Postman remarked, "Children are the living messages we send to a time we will not see."

The lives and thoughts of children tell us much about the societies in which they live. Initially, tribal communities viewed themselves as an integral part of the natural world and as belonging to a complex web of kinship and responsibility. Initiation rites bonded children to the community, preparing them for a life in their culture. Change transpired slowly; reinforcement of the culture's values was the norm.

For both tribal and complex societies, this picture has changed. In both extreme and everyday circumstances, children become separated from the world of their parents. New technologies repeatedly redefine our relationships to the environment and confound easy communication between generations. Children are now subject to multiple or shifting political and cultural contexts, which often disregard or contradict long-standing systems of identity.

The expansion of multinational industry has brought formal education and mass communication to formerly isolated and distinct cultures, redefining their social, economic, and spiritual boundaries. No longer is the oral transmission of knowledge considered sufficient; literacy is seen as the child's key to the future. Yet, oral tradition and written language are conceptually different. And what is learned at school may refute knowledge deeply rooted in the child's community; in the name of assimilation, some children have even been barred from speaking their native language. Only recently have minorities begun to press for education that reinforces the cognitive process shaped by the child's native culture and the constellation of relationships that form the child's perception of the world. Still, for many, education raises expectations that will never be met.

The values of today's world, where innovation is champion and change equals progress, elevate youth to a powerful but precarious position. Children develop their self-identity within a broad context of relationships to authority, in a fragmented and interdependent global environment that provides few guideposts for the future. The goals and values of this increasingly standardized world lure youth away from parents and community. The promise of affluence and the stylized reality manufactured by the media shape the young in much the same way that traditions did in the past.

Exacerbating this social and cultural upheaval are extreme economic and political situations that affect huge populations of children. In the developing countries, nearly half the population is under the

A SMALL CHILD
CARRIES HER
YOUNGER SIBLING,
NEPAL.
KEVIN BUBRISKI

223

age of 15. These children are the most numerous casualties of famine, war, and forced migration. They are the exploited labor, the victims of repression and systematic violence. Governments not only fail to protect the rights of the child, but endanger children to achieve political ends.

Two decades ago, the Chinese cultural revolution recruited a vast youth army to rise up against the Chinese elite and overcome centuries of Chinese heritage held by community elders and educators. It unleashed what amounted to armed intergenerational warfare. In Cambodia, under the Khmer Rouge, children were separated from their parents, and recruited as foot-soldiers in the armies of Pol Pot, now known to have brutally murdered hundreds of thousands of their countrymen and kin. More recently in Uganda, children orphaned by war were absorbed into the fighting forces against Idi Amin. At present, young Iranian zealots are taught to seek martyrdom through death in the fight for Islam.

In South Africa, where black youth are a current target of police and security force repression, inflicted violence and torture are only part of broader systematic oppression that deprives families of adequate food, housing, and health care, and pushes youth into marginal and often dangerous labor. Human rights abuses in Guatemala, Chile, Peru, and El Salvador have taken the lives of thousands of children, while psychologically devastating countless others.

Parallel to the physical maltreatment of children is the emotional trauma triggered by exposure and witness to violence, separation from family and community, and the loss of nurturance necessary for healthy development into adulthood. Repression has repercussions far beyond its immediate victims, and we can only speculate about the kinds of adults these children of "especially difficult circumstances" (in the words of a recent UN conference) will become. Despite examples of extreme courage and moral determination, the information from psychiatric studies is discouraging—that child victims of violence tend to re-enact violence as adults.

International agencies, in conjunction with local governments, have taken impressive strides toward curbing child deaths from dehydration and from disease preventable by innoculation. Yet similar advances in the improvement of the nutrition and human rights of children are slower in coming. During the past decade, developing countries have spent significantly less for health care and education while spending more for the military. In 1985, the United Nations focused international concern on the problem of violence against children. This new movement must address the root causes of violence if recommendations and corrective action are to have more than temporary or local significance. Sociologist Kaspar Naegele once said, "The adult world…sees in youth a special embodiment of its own wider assumptions; that life is open, that there is space for change and betterment, and that the future will improve on the past."

Time will tell. ∎

Jane Cook is a freelance writer and media artist with a background in anthropology.

SAMBURU BABY
EATS FROM A
GOURD CONTAINER,
KENYA.
KEN HEYMAN

One morning, 18-year-old Sherita Dreher said goodbye to her 2-year-old son Marquis and walked through the streets of southeast Washington, D.C., to tell her story of despair to Mayor Marion Barry's blue-ribbon panel on teenage pregnancy.

If she was nervous, she did not show it. She rose to face the crowd of 800 in the Ballou High School auditorium—classmates and friends who remembered when she was a chubby, outwardly hostile 15-year-old—and spoke clearly, directly, with a kind of cynicism and pragmatism often found in teenage mothers.

She began having sex, she said, at the age of 15, succumbing to the advances of her 16-year-old boyfriend. They did not use any kind of birth control because she did not believe she could get pregnant; she blamed her ignorance on her mother, who died of cancer without telling Sherita much about sex or birth control.

That is how she ended up pregnant. "I laid and I paid," Sherita said.

Sherita's story had all the well-known elements of teenage pregnancy, a nationwide social phenomenon that experts say has reached crisis proportions in poor, black communities such as Washington Highlands, where Sherita lives.

But the story she told was not the full story. Sherita, like so many people, had adopted an account of her life—a version she told to friends as well as the Ballou panel—that differed dramatically from reality.

After the Ballou hearing, during a series of lengthy interviews, Sherita gradually discarded parts of this version. Then one day, in answer to a question, the full story tumbled out, unexpectedly, almost before she could stop herself:

Her pregnancy, she said, was no accident. She *wanted* to have that baby, *needed* to have it. She said she had tried to get pregnant, hoping that it might help her hold on to her boyfriend, William Wheeler, the same boyfriend who was her first sex partner—when she was 11 and he was 12.

She was afraid of losing William, she said, and afraid that if she did, she would never get another boyfriend as handsome.

"My girlfriends had a nice little shape and everything," she said. "They don't worry about boys. They knew [that if] one is gone"—she stopped and snapped her fingers—"here come another one. It wouldn't work like that with me because I was so fat. But even though I was real big, I wasn't gonna accept anything that came my way. You had to have some looks, be red [slang for light-skinned] and have pretty hair."

But Sherita did not talk about these motivations when she testified before the experts at Ballou. She did not tell them that her plan did not work, that her boyfriend was furious when he learned that she was pregnant, that he was too busy stealing cars and dealing drugs to help raise Marquis, that he had ended up in prison.

The panel also did not find out that Sherita tried to commit suicide after her mother's death, that she got pregnant nine months later, that her brother hit her after learning she was pregnant, that her family eventually broke apart—and that, finally, she and her baby ended up in a rundown motel as temporary wards of the D.C. government.

The Sherita who appeared before the mayor's panel portrayed herself as a victim, a casualty of seduction and her own ignorance. The Sherita who emerged after months of interviews is tough, sophisticated, and clearly aware of her motivations.

She is not alone.

In Washington Highlands, which is separated from downtown Washington as much by its culture and values as it is by the Anacostia River, many teenagers have sex, often reject birth control, get pregnant, and have children—not because of ignorance, but because they see those actions as ways to keep a relationship alive, or escape their families, or achieve something in a life filled with failure, violence, uncertainty.

The experts describe teenage pregnancy as just one more strand in an intricate, destructive web of poverty, neglect, drug abuse, alcoholism, violence, unemployment, and, sometimes, child abuse. In their view, Sherita Dreher got caught in this web.

But these are the words of experts, not Sherita's words. She does not talk about the poverty and violence around her. Instead, she talks about the people in her life, mostly men, who she says abandoned her—people she calls "triflin'," her word for weak and irresponsible—and left her to face a kind of private hell, alone. ∎

Leon Dash spent a year in Washington Highlands, one of Washington, D.C.'s poorest neighborhoods, examining the problem of teenage pregnancy on assignment for the Washington Post.

UNWED TEENAGE
MOTHER AND BABY,
USA.
POLLY BROWN

MARIAN WRIGHT EDELMAN   TEENAGE PREGNANCY:
AN EPIDEMIC TAKES ITS TOLL

Each day more than 3,000 girls get pregnant and 1,300 give birth. Twenty-six 13- and 14-year-olds have their first child, thirteen 16-year-olds have their second child. Each year, 1.1 million American teenage girls—one in ten—become pregnant.[1] That is more than the entire Massachusetts school enrollment. Over half a million teenage girls have babies, a number nearly equal to the total population of the city of Boston. More disturbing is the pregnancy increase among younger teens. Each year, 125,000 girls 15 and under become pregnant.

According to data from the Alan Guttmacher Institute, the United States leads nearly all developed nations of the world in rates of teenage pregnancy, abortion, and childbearing, even though it has roughly comparable rates of teen sexual activity.[2] The data show that our top-ranked status does not result only from the high rates of pregnancy and parenthood among minority teens. The pregnancy rates for white teenagers are twice as high as those of Canada, France, and England. Moreover, the maximum difference in birthrates occurs among girls under the age of 15, the most vulnerable teenagers.

The costs of adolescent parenthood are enormous—for the teen parents, for their children, and for society.

□ Forty percent of teenage girls who drop out of school do so because of pregnancy or marriage. Only half of the teens who become parents before the age of 18 graduate from high school.

□ A teen parent earns half the lifetime earnings of a woman who waits until age 20 to have her first child.

□ Teen mothers are twice as likely to be poor as are non-teen mothers. Babies born to single mothers are two and a half times more likely to be poor than those born to two-parent families.

□ Only 54 percent of all teen mothers in 1983 began prenatal care in the first three months of pregnancy. Babies of mothers who receive late or no prenatal care are three times more likely to die in their first year of life than those who receive early care.

□ Babies born to teens represented about 14 percent of all births in 1983, but 20 percent of all low-birthweight births. Low-birthweight babies are 20 times more likely to die in the first year of life and special hospital care for low-birthweight babies averages $1,000 a day.

☐ Medicaid pays for 30 percent of all hospital deliveries involving pregnant teens, at an annual cost of about $200 million a year.

☐ In 1985 half a million babies were born to teenage girls. The public cost was $1.4 billion.

The international data make it clear that these costs are not the inevitable outcomes of increased adolescent sexual activity, but of our inability as a society to deal in a preventive way with the implications of that increase: to provide early comprehensive sex and family-life education in our homes, schools, and other institutions and to give sexually active teens access to family planning services and counseling. The United States laments its high numbers of teen pregnancies but winds up providing for large numbers of teen parents and their children because we do not encourage early parental and other appropriate adult communication with children about the consequences of too early sexual activity, and we refuse to give our teens the capacity to delay parenthood, while unsuccessfully imploring too many of them, too late, to delay sexual activity.

The norm in the United States is definitely too little too late. Fewer than one school district in five offers students in-depth discussion of such basic issues as the responsibilities of parenthood, the consequences of teen pregnancy, or how to resist peer pressure for sex, before the ninth grade. And four out of every ten sexually active teens who need contra-ceptive counseling and services are not receiving help from a clinic or private doctor.

Teenage pregnancy is a problem because it very often precludes the completion of education, the securing of employment, and the creation of a stable relationship, and because it makes the completion of each of these transitional steps more difficult. We no longer live in an America in which 18- and 19-year-old men can earn enough to support a family, and we have never had an America in which the average single woman with children could earn a decent wage at any age. Meanwhile, young men, especially young black men, are increasingly unable to fulfill a traditional role as breadwinner and are less willing to accept their responsibilities as fathers. In 1970 three teen births out of ten were to single mothers. In 1983 this number had increased to more than five out of ten.

Contrary to popular perception, the majority of teen parents are white. Poor and minority teens, however, have a disproportionate share of teen births and are disproportionately affected by the social and economic consequences of early parenthood. A black teen is twice as likely to become pregnant as a white teen. A black teen is five times as likely as a white teen to become an unwed parent. This is primarily, albeit not completely, correlated to higher poverty rates among black teens. Nor is teen pregnancy just an urban, big-city problem. The ten worst states for percentage of teen out-of-wedlock births are overwhelmingly southern states that are typically less urbanized.[3]

How to target our efforts to reduce the incidence of teen pregnancies, and to set and track specific percentage goals, is a complicated process. Do we focus on the nine states that produce half of all teen births? Do we pick sites where the problem may be less severe but where chances of initially designing innovative successful remedies are more likely? Do we focus on reducing pregnancy and birthrates among girls 16 and younger? Do we put substantial effort into neglected males or leave that to other groups, such as the Urban League? Do we focus primarily on poor and minority children, or must we develop a more balanced set of overlapping strategies for poor and middle-class youth in order to broaden the political base for change? What kind of non-stifling evaluation procedures do we build into local projects and national policy development? Who should do it?

We must not fear testing a variety of approaches until we hit upon the combination that works. Social-reform strategies are not different from the scientific method; it is trial and error, trial and error. We must avoid unrealistic expectations for ourselves and others. Comprehensive, long-term efforts are essential to recapture the future for today's youth. Few, if any, major social reforms, whether child labor protection or dismantling legally entrenched racial segregation, whether female suffrage or black voting rights, have accrued in the absence of a long and arduous struggle, usually lasting decades.

The pace of American life has quickened, and perhaps social problems develop more quickly than they used to. Certainly public attention is more ephemeral than it used to be. But strengthening families and preventing teen pregnancy requires the same concerted effort over the long term as did earlier struggles for social progress. A setback this month, this year, means little. The struggle will take many years. Nothing less will make a real difference. ■

Marian Wright Edelman is president of the Children's Defense Fund.

ROBERT COLES   BRINGING NEWBORNS INTO THE NUCLEAR THREAT

Rather obviously no newborn child knows what kind of world faces him or her upon birth. Soon enough, though, an infant's body will begin to respond to the world. If there is no steady supply of food, the body knows spells of aching hunger: a gnawing stomach pain, a restlessness and irritability, a panic of the central nervous system, it might be put. Or as a pediatric neurologist, a friend of mine, once phrased it, "a startle, a scream, a discharge of nerve and muscle all over, as if God is being addressed pronto." He was, usually, not given to such literary talk; but he wanted us to realize not only how urgent it is for a baby to eat (we surely knew such to be the case) but how powerfully and pervasively an infant's hunger affects its body—a shock to its entire being.

It is only later in life, with the knowledge that language allows, that boys and girls begin to comprehend what kind of world they inhabit. Well before a child is old enough to enter school, he or she knows a lot about what the world has to offer, in the way of hope and good prospects, or in the form of a fearful, thwarting environment. Chronic hunger, a lack of medical care, faulty housing—all of those "socioeconomic variables" —have their own manner of shaping a child's consciousness, its sense of what life is about, or how life is to be lived.

Even in the comfortable circumstances of America's middle-class world, young children (say, four or five years old) can begin to understand the fearful constraints, the anxious threats of a particular existence. A boy of four told me, years ago, how uniquely in jeopardy our world is: "They have this bomb, and it can wipe out everyone— even you and me!" Those last few words, spoken after a momentary pause, were his way of getting as concrete and specific as possible, in the manner young children aim to be. I am not saying that this boy was already terrorized by a pervasive fear of nuclear war and annihilation. I am simply pointing out that the nuclear threat to all of us is not beyond the appreciation of our children. What matters, for any given child, is the attitude of the adult world to such a state of affairs—the manner in which a mother and father come to terms with *their* knowledge of what a nuclear threat means to this world.

For the first time in history, those who have brought children into this world have had to contemplate the distinct possibility that human life can be virtually destroyed— en masse and abruptly—and thus bring to an end the cycle of renewal and growth, of hope against hope, that childbearing has traditionally meant for all of us. In a sense, then, bringing children into a world in the shadow of the nuclear threat is taking a calculated stance: The parent knows the terrible danger, but also knows how important it is to avoid letting that danger become, ironically, a psychological reality so triumphant that its mere presence does damage enough—never mind the physical damage that the actual event would surely accomplish. I heard this comment years ago from a young mother as she thought about her newborn child and the nuclear arms race, then in full swing:

I wonder whether he [her son, then a month old] *will live to my age—will live to be old enough to go to school, or college. You'd think, coming from this neighborhood, his chances are pretty good. We've got just about everything we want and need here—the best world possible for a baby to have. But I pick up the papers and read what we're doing, and the Russians, and more and more other countries—building those bombs in secret—and I look at my little boy, lying in his crib, sleeping, and I think to myself: My God, we can "blow it." We can end up destroying this planet. My son doesn't know what I'm thinking, of course. How could he? Or does he— I mean, can he sense that we're worried, his father and I, and we look at him sometimes and get even more worried? I'm sure he doesn't know what worries us, but maybe he senses our nervousness. If he doesn't, it won't be long before he does! In just a few years he'll be learning about nuclear bombs and missiles, and he'll know what the score is—that scientists have given us quite a "gift," and we're sure holding onto it, and increasing its numbers! It used to be that parents might worry that their children will grow up and learn some "bad" fact about their family—some "psychological problem." But now, we have to wait for our kids to ask if we think there will be a life ahead for them! That's progress for you!*

So it goes, a moment of ironic reflection on the part of a mother of a newborn; a moment, too, of shrewd and knowing awareness of what now obtains, what may well continue to haunt us for generations to come. ■

Robert Coles is a child psychiatrist who teaches at Harvard University. He has written extensively about children's struggles with moral and political issues.

GUATEMALAN
MOTHER AND
DAUGHTER MOURN
THE DEATH OF A
YOUNGER CHILD.
ANTOINETTE
JONGEN/
BLACK STAR

The drawing is stark and simple, devoid of any details that give a sense of time or place. A nine-year-old Maya Indian, at my urging, has drawn a picture of his homeland. But nowhere in the image are the verdant mountains or the adobe homes of his former village, in Guatemala's highland province of Huehuetenango. Only three black figures are evident on an otherwise blank sheet of paper. Tumbled onto the right half of the page

are a head and an arm, both having been severed by a bayonet-wielding figure on the left. The small, dark-eyed boy told me he was so close to the murder that he heard the gurgles as the victim's throat was cut. As he related this grisly detail, his face flushed and he began to perspire. Then, in a whisper, he recalled: "Both of them were boys not much older than me."

At least 50,000 Maya Indians died in Guatemala between 1981 and 1984, and probably many more. No one knows exactly how many or what percentage of the victims were children. But it is known that children comprised over 60 percent of the populations in villages like Coya, Suntelaj, Finca San Francisco, Santa Teresa, Estancia de la Virgen—where all, or nearly all, the residents were killed.

In one sense, Guatemala is only in part unique. Indeed, the almost unimaginable experience of the young boy, in which the victim, the perpetrator, and the witness of violence were all children, tells us much about war in our age.

Wartime deaths of civilians in general, and of children in particular, have been rising sharply throughout this century. Only about 5 percent of World War I's casualties were civilians. During the Second World War, that figure rose to 50 percent. By the Vietnam War, the civilian death toll reached the 80 percent mark, only to be eclipsed by current-day conflicts, such as in Lebanon, in which 90 percent of the casualties are mothers and children. Today, more children than ever are bombed in their schools, burned alive in their homes, and shot while fleeing down urban alleyways or mountain paths.

Much of this steep increase in civilian casualties is because wars are no longer fought on battlefields between two opposing armies. In what are now largely internal conflicts or civil wars (even though outside forces often intervene), insurgents camouflage themselves within larger populations, and in many cases forcibly recruit children into their cause. Counterinsurgents respond by destroying entire regions of the countryside in an effort to undermine a people's economic base and morale, and to expose and exterminate enemy forces. Rather than attempting to distinguish civilian from combatant, whole villages are massacred and survivors relocated to zones controlled by the military.

But not all of these children are killed as a result of indiscriminate attacks on villages or towns. Or because, at least for older boys, they might someday become insurgents. Children of both sexes and all ages are being methodically maimed or murdered. In Guatemala, parents from seven villages in Huehuetenango told me how children were killed while adults were left unharmed. In Afghanistan, children have lost hands, eyes, and even their lives by picking up booby-trapped miniature airplanes, stuffed animals, or other tempting toys. In El Salvador, Nicaragua, Ethiopia, and elsewhere, children have become the select target of violence. This is how one 24-year-old Guatemalan mother described the military's retaliation against a village suspected of aiding the guerrillas:

[This] time the soldiers said we had to be punished. They pushed five boys forward, made them lie face-down on the ground, and shot them in the back. A baby girl was then pulled from her mother's arms and her skull crushed against the side of a house. The last

death occurred when a soldier cut open the stomach of a pregnant woman, saying that
even our unborn will not be spared.

Why are children, the future of any community if not the world itself, being singled out in today's wars? Paradoxically, it is precisely because they are so precious to us. To destroy what is of highest value to someone is clearly an "effective" form of terrorism; to kill and injure children is to rob a family or an entire group of its future. What better way to undermine popular support for a cause than to attack what we love and value most?

And today, more than ever, children themselves are bearing weapons in armed conflicts. Often, the young recruits undergo heavy indoctrination mixing religious fervor with national pride to intensify the call to duty; schools and media reinforce the message. In Iran, thousands of 10- and 11-year-olds were sent to their deaths carrying keys they were told would ensure their entrance into paradise. Handicapped children were used as human mine detectors to explode mines in the path of advancing tanks.

The lack of food and protection has turned many a child into a soldier. "I have a gun, food, and a place to sleep," one nine-year-old Ugandan recently told a relief worker. "That's more than I had in my village. If I stayed there I'd probably be dead by now."

Children also have been expected to commit violent murders against civilians as a kind of rite of passage into the combat forces. During "la violencia" in Colombia, boys were sometimes forced to kill children their own age to gain entry into paramilitary groups, often their sole protection from the same fate. Most carried out the executions only after they were severely beaten. Indeed, many of these child executioners were reluctant at first but—under the watchful eye of adult overseers—their initial feelings of fear and guilt were transformed into the kind of rage that obliterates all moral sensibility. As one Khmer Rouge leader told me: "It usually takes a little time but the younger ones become the most efficient soldiers of all."

Why have we failed so miserably to protect these children? Not because we lack legislation, it seems, but because we lack the will and the means to implement it. While most countries have signed the Geneva Conventions, few have abided by them when directly involved in war themselves, or when selling arms and providing military aid to other embattled nations. On the other hand, less than 30 countries have formally agreed to uphold the 1977 Geneva Protocols, which set forth the strongest prohibitions against the use of children in armed conflicts. Moreover, a number of these signatories have since recruited and trained underaged children as armed combatants.

And despite all the past tragedies, there is still no viable structure, no Amnesty International for Children so to speak, to safeguard their basic rights. In war and refugee situations, the International Committee of the Red Cross and the United Nations High Commissioner for Refugees have mandates to do so. As United Nations bodies, however, both must function through quiet diplomacy with national governments, whose cooperation is seen as essential, especially when operating in countries that have not ratified the conventions and protocols. Critics suggest that this sometimes leads to silent bargains in which protection issues are neither aggressively pursued nor publicly disclosed. Nongovernmental relief organizations, which often provide assistance directly to children endangered by war and uprooting, also have been caught in this bind. Since they are only "guests" of the governments in most of the countries in which they work, they find that their programs are sometimes shut down and their personnel threatened or expelled when they protest too loudly.

But no one can expect any of these organizations to shoulder the burden alone. Any attempt to realize a moral purpose demands the constant attention of a much broader audience: us. As people and parents, as members of professional and religious groups, and as citizens of nations and the world, the obligation to ensure that children's rights are recognized and protected is ultimately our own. "Why don't more people know who the guns are pointed at?" is the way one Guatemalan mother once put it to me, a question many of our world's children need answered. ■

Neil Boothby, a psychologist who has worked with war refugees in Asia, Africa, and Central America, is a visiting assistant professor of policy studies at Duke University.

A FATHER HOLDS HIS CHILD ABOVE THE RUBBLE IN A BEIRUT, LEBANON, BOMBING.
YAN MORVAN/ SIPA PRESS

GLENN FRANKEL   HUNGER IN SOUTH AFRICA:
APARTHEID'S OTHER FACE

The crudely painted sign over Rhiana Letoaka's hospital crib read "HOPE" but there was precious little of it in this overcrowded children's ward deep in rural Lebowa, one of South Africa's black "homelands."

She had the hollow eyes, graying hair, and swollen belly of malnutrition. She was nearly three years old but, at 16 pounds, she was too weak to move or even cry. She only stared emptily at the wall.

There were 30 small children like her in this ward at Jane Furse Hospital here, northeast of Pretoria, many of them two to a crib. All but two or three had serious nutritional deficiencies.

A few would die; others would gain weight temporarily and be sent home only to come back again in a few months. "We're fighting a losing battle," said Michaeline Mamakoko, a ward nurse. "Some mothers are ignorant, but most just don't have enough food."

It was a scene reminiscent of many an impoverished African country in the recent years of drought and famine. But it was taking place in South Africa, the subcontinent's richest and most powerful nation, one that has long called itself "Africa's breadbasket" and that takes pride in the comparatively high standard of living of its disenfranchised urban blacks.

This, then, is the other face of apartheid.

While many children in South Africa's explosive townships battle the police, those in these remote rural areas face enemies that are equally relentless—hunger, disease, poor sanitation, and overcrowding. Its critics contend South Africa's system of rigid segregation is a prime contributor to these conditions and to the impoverishment of its black rural population.

The result, say doctors, nurses, and relief workers, is a pattern of malnutrition and children's diseases similar to that found in some of Africa's most destitute countries.

The official infant mortality rate for blacks is 80 per 1,000 live births, roughly six times higher than for whites. That puts blacks here on a par with comparatively better-off African countries like Kenya, Ghana, and Zimbabwe.

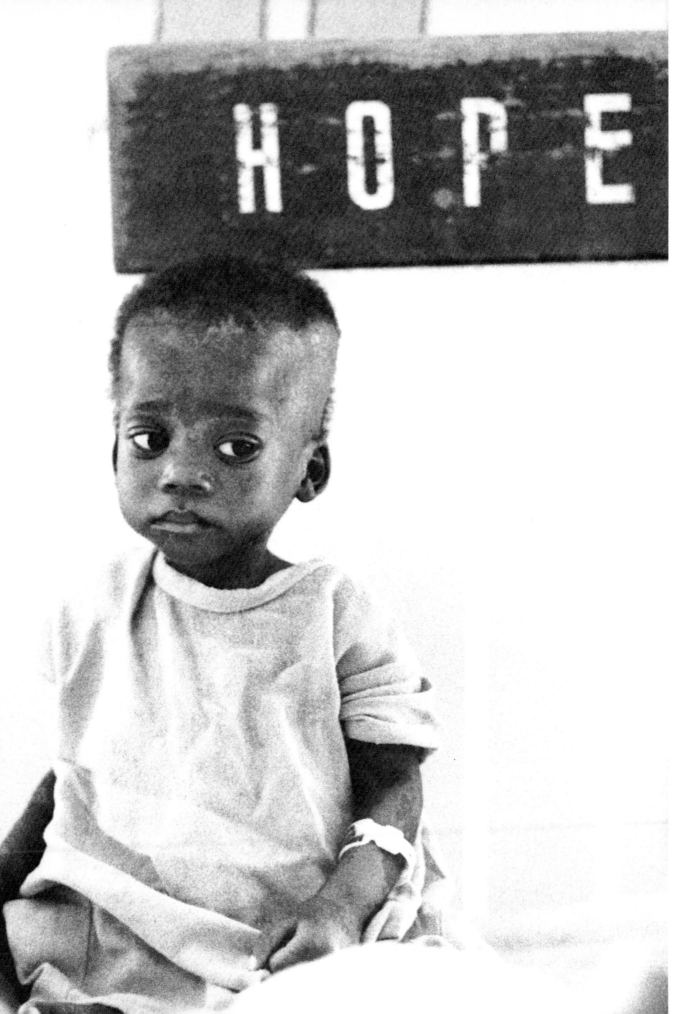

MALNOURISHED
CHILD IN JANE
FURSE HOSPITAL IN
LEBOWA, SOUTH
AFRICA.
GLENN FRANKEL

But that statistic ignores blacks living in the quasi-independent homelands, for whom the rate soars far higher—as high as 190 per 1,000 in parts of Transkei and Ciskei, according to University of Transkei researchers.

While there is virtually no malnutrition among whites, about one-third of South Africa's black children below age 14 are chronically malnourished, according to a 1984 study by University of Witswatersrand researchers. The death rate from malnutrition of black children under age five is 31 times that of whites.

For established black urban dwellers in Johannesburg and Cape Town, South Africa boasts a relatively high level of care. Although it is chronically overcrowded, Baragwanath Hospital in Soweto may be the best-equipped hospital for blacks in all of Africa.

But in the 10 rural homelands, conditions are often dismal. While the doctor-patient ratio for whites is 1 to 600, in the homelands the average is 1 doctor for 40,000 blacks, according to University of Cape Town researchers. In some of the homelands, they say, the proportion of malnourished children exceeds 60 to 70 percent.

If apartheid touches every facet of South African life, it also touches death. Whites die of the diseases of Western affluence, blacks those of Third World poverty. South Africa's whites have one of the highest death rates from heart disease and circulatory ailments in the world; the first heart transplant was performed in Cape Town, in 1968. Meanwhile, the largest killers of blacks are infectious and parasitic diseases—including tuberculosis, typhoid fever, cholera, and measles—that are virtually unknown among whites.

South Africa's poverty stands out in part because it exists alongside such massive affluence. Twenty percent of the population controls 75 percent of the wealth, according to economist Francis Wilson. It also stands out, said Wilson, because "so much of it is a consequence of deliberate government policies."

"The biggest mistake one can make is to blame the drought for all the malnutrition" said Ina Perlman, executive director of Operation Hunger, a volunteer agency still feeding nearly a million persons despite the fact that for most of South Africa, the drought is over.

"It really dates back to the land acts early in the century," Perlman said. "They took the land away from these people and forced them into confined areas with poor soil and water. That's what made them poor and vulnerable, and the policy of restricting people to the homelands keeps them that way. The drought was just the cherry on top."

While most of Africa is seeking ways to improve food production by rural peasants, Perlman said, South Africa has been systematically dismantling its peasant farms.

At the turn of the century at least 80 percent of rural dwellers were subsistence farmers. Perlman estimates the figure is now down to 8 percent.

Those who left the land became seasonal laborers on South Africa's white-owned commercial farms. But the combination of five years of drought and growing mechanization has led to skeletal labor crews. In the corn industry alone, 250,000 workers were laid off, Perlman's group estimates.

The ideologues of apartheid who designed the homelands system contended that the black states would become magnets for separate development of agriculture and industry. But some experts estimate that 70 percent of the supposedly arable land in the homelands is in fact marginal wasteland.

As a result, at least 9 million rural blacks live below the poverty line, and 1.4 million of them have no measurable income at all. Instead of attracting economic growth, the homelands have become human dumping grounds where the risks for children are highest.

In Lebowa, for example, health officials estimate that nearly 50 percent of the homeland's 600,000 children suffer from malnutrition. Jane Furse Hospital lacks many of the basic health programs available in some of Africa's black-ruled states such as Zimbabwe.

Conditions for urban blacks are better. The infant mortality rate at Crossroads, the massive shantytown east of Cape Town, is almost three times lower than in the Transkei and Ciskei homelands that feed it a steady stream of migrants.

Nonetheless, Graham Bresick, a doctor at a Crossroads clinic, says "malnutrition underlies almost all of the problems I see. The diseases that healthy children ward off—measles, diarrhea, just plain colds—can do terrible damage to these children." ∎
Glenn Frankel writes for the Washington Post *foreign service.*

Almost every afternoon at Smyk, a large children's store in downtown Warsaw, a line of pregnant women forms in front of a counter on the second floor where supplies for babies are sold. Each woman shows a clerk a card certifying pregnancy, and in return is handed a red plastic basket containing pajamas, T-shirts, sweaters, bibs, blankets, and small cotton towels. The basket is not a gift. Buying everything in it could cost a prospective mother the equivalent of three or four months of a typical salary.

Nevertheless, these women are enjoying a kind of special treat: for this is their one and only guaranteed opportunity to buy some of the most sought-after goods in Poland, baby clothes, for zlotys. Once they take the items they want from one basket—up to four pajamas, four shirts, two sweaters, and two towels, among other things—their "pregnancy card" is stamped and they are not allowed to purchase the rationed items again.

Unless, of course, they have another child.

The line at Smyk is just one of the peculiar customs pregnant women in Poland have come to accept as normal in recent years. Unlike most of the rest of Europe, this nation of 37 million is experiencing a baby boom, and state-provided services, from maternity wards to bib manufacturing, have not kept up.

The result is not only inconvenience. In the last year, poor hygiene and supplies have caused the deaths of groups of newborn babies in hospital maternity wards at least twice, with a total of 14 dead. Many women complain about less serious infections picked up by their infants at the hospital and about crowded maternity wards where doctors' visits, sanitary materials, and even clean sheets can only be obtained with bribes.

The boom of births began in 1982 and peaked in 1983, when a record 720,000 babies were born. Since then, the numbers have declined, with an estimated 675,000 births in 1985. Demographers, however, said Poland continues to have one of the highest rates of population growth in Europe, trailing only Ireland, Iceland, and Albania.

The high number of births in recent years is an "echo" of the huge baby boom Poland experienced after World War II, culminating in the mid-1950s. Like their parents, the current wave of children will form a "population wave" in society that will soon strain schools, housing, and eventually, the job market.

At the moment, the greatest hardships seem to be borne largely by the mothers of the new generation. For many Polish women, the shortages of goods and services during pregnancy are matched by the regimented procedures of hard-pressed maternity clinics.

For most, the state's role in a baby's birth begins when a doctor, usually the one who confirms the pregnancy, presents a woman with a "Card of Pregnancy in Course," to be carried at all times. This document records a woman's visits to her physician during pregnancy and allows her various privileges, such as the one-time shopping spree at the Smyk store. Pregnancy cards also allow women to move to the head of Poland's ever-present shop lines, but only on weekdays. "At 3 P.M. on Friday I stop being pregnant," one 25-year-old Warsaw woman in her first pregnancy complained. "Maybe the authorities don't think pregnant women should go out on weekends."

The regulations multiply once pregnant women enter the hospital for deliveries. All are required to remain in maternity wards for at least five days, the day of the delivery plus four 24-hour periods afterward, regardless of their condition or wishes. During this time, mothers may see and hold their children only if they are nursing them. Once they agree to nurse, they must do so seven times a day, exactly every three hours, without exception. No flowers, gifts, visitors, or incoming telephone calls are allowed at most clinics.

In theory, at least, fathers may not attend the birth, and must wait four days to see their new child. They may not even learn the baby's sex unless the mother can gain use of a phone or smuggle out a letter, because in some clinics officials will not reveal the sex of newborns to callers in order to avoid embarrassing mistakes.

Predictably, such regulations have encouraged some extraordinary practices that have become part of the custom of childbirths here. When a pregnant woman enters the hospital, for example, families and friends assemble neat, inconspicuous packages of juices, chocolate, and other treats that can be smuggled into wards by porters or nurses who carry out such favors in exchange for tips. Some anxious fathers try to smuggle themselves in for a peek at their babies. Others assemble outside the clinic and attempt to hold shouted conversations with their wives through the windows.

Doctors say the mandatory four-day stays are intended to allow for the treatment of newborns with antibiotics, while other rules are forced by the harried pace and over-crowding of wards. In some clinics, delivery rooms can be packed with six or seven women at a time attended by a single doctor.

Although all maternity services are nominally free, having money to spend on a pregnancy can make an enormous difference. "If you want any service at all, you have to pay," said a 30-year-old Warsaw secretary who recently gave birth in the hospital. "Otherwise you can't even get a clean gown." ∎

Jackson Diehl writes for the Washington Post *foreign service.*

It had to happen sooner or later. Conspicuous consumption has trickled down from parents to teenagers to kids. The little ones are demanding everything from little leather sneakers and bomber jackets to pricey designer labels—burbling the words Benetton and Esprit years before learning how to spell them. Gone are the pastel pinafores and embroidered poodles worn by previous generations; now many kids are running around in scaled-down copies of the sleek, chic clothes first fashioned by Chanel and Azzedine Alaïa.

Retailers attribute the mini-couture boom to the style-conscious '80s. Today's trendy tykes are simply mimicking their equally trendy parents—affluent, two-career couples who put a premium on quality. "These children are a little more fortunate; their parents have thought about them a long time and can afford to give them special things," says Phyllis Pressman of Barneys New York, which features $350 imported party dresses and $120 Burberry raincoats.

ENGLAND.
WILLIAM STRODE/
WOODFIN CAMP,
INC.

Children's boutiques specializing in status apparel are springing up around the country, offering sophisticated styles for the very young—off-the-shoulder dresses, leather skirts, tweed suits, and "Miami Vice"-inspired baggy pants and jackets. There are even baby ball gowns and tuxes for sale at My Movie Star Daughter & Son in Stanford, Connecticut. Instead of wash-and-wear, many of the labels read "Dry Clean Only."

But many adult manufacturers are making huge profits by pleasing parents and kids. Benetton has opened more than 125 of its 012 outlets around the country; in 1985 the children's division accounted for more than $80 million in sales. Esprit recently introduced a new line for two- to six-year-olds, offering funky adult fashions from $10 for a T-shirt to $55 for a sweater. In the past few years leading designers began making children's sportswear, betting that parents would pay the same prices for the same fashions on a smaller scale. "Now that kids don't have to wear pink and blue, kids' fashion is attracting some of the top young designers," says Steven Pickett, whose four Arlequin children's shops in San Francisco carry black clothes in cutting-edge styles for the under-six set. "No one wants to see their baby in last year's line," says Pickett.

Chances are that all the kids really care about is where the new togs will put them among their peers. Influenced by movies, MTV, and sitcoms from "Family Ties" to "The Cosby Show," even toddlers these days are up to date on what's hot and what's not.

Label consciousness is not just a passing phase. The pressure begins in preschool, and it just gets worse as the kids get older. One mother whose daughter transferred from a midwestern school to the San Francisco Day School says her fourth grader was shunned for months. Then a classmate took the outcast aside and whispered, "You'll make more friends if you wear Esprit clothes." The wardrobe change worked wonders. But dressing right can become an obsession. "Some girls measure their worth by the number of Guess jeans they own," said one Boston mother. In an age of up-to-the-minute fashions, hand-me-downs—which smack of past fads such as Izod shirts, Jordache jeans, and neon ensembles—are utterly despised.

Naturally, some experts are inclined to blame the children's excesses on the parents. According to Alison Lurie, the novelist and author of *The Language of Clothes,* it all boils down to parental guilt. "They don't see as much of their children as they ought to, and they tend to overspend, buying expensive lessons, expensive sporting equipment, and expensive clothes," she says. "They don't know what children are like, and it doesn't dawn on them that, for a kid, a pair of jeans that cost $50 is in no way superior to a pair that's $10." ■

Jennet Conant writes for Newsweek. *Barbara Kantrowitz, Jessica Kreimerman, and Nadine Joseph assisted with this article.*

DID CONCERN FOR STYLE OR WELL-BEING DETERMINE THE APPEARANCE OF INFANTS' ITEMS? THESE BONNETS, RATTLES, SHOES, AND BOOTIES WERE MADE AS MUCH TO LOOK IMPRESSIVE AS TO PROTECT AND AMUSE LITTLE BABIES. COSTLY MATERIALS, EXQUISITE ORNAMENTATION, AND PAINSTAKINGLY DETAILED HANDWORK INDICATE THAT NO TROUBLE OR EXPENSE WAS SPARED FOR THE BABIES WHO USED THESE OBJECTS (cats. 145, 147, 175, 179, 201, 217).

BARBARA EHRENREICH AND DAVID NASAW

KIDS AS CONSUMERS AND COMMODITIES

Like other economically nonproductive and socially suspect groups, children in this century have had to find ways to defend their right to subsistence and to maintain a modicum of self-respect. For children the key "strategy" has been consumerism. Ever since the first nickelodeons opened their doors almost 80 years ago, the young have done their part to keep the wheels of commerce turning. Neither recessions nor depressions nor declining fertility rates have slowed the growth of the kiddie markets. According to a survey by the Rand Youth Poll for the National Restaurant Association, while the teenage population declined 6.6 percent between 1975 and 1980, teen spending rose more than 50 percent. Trade journals—with little else to glow about in the depressed early 1980s—reported enthusiastically on the continuing growth of the kiddie markets, accelerated by the volatile commerce in video games.

Children are the last of the big-time spenders. Marketing experts predict that they will not only increase their purchases of toys, games, cosmetics, soft drinks, and designer jeans, tops, and sneakers, but will double their consumption of snacks and become major buyers of big-ticket items like audio and video equipment and home computers. In many households, children are replacing their mothers as chief decision-makers on some purchases. As *Seventeen* magazine reported in a full-page ad in the January 17, 1983, *New York Times*, the child has become the "Speaker of the House." Children play a major, often *the* major, role in choosing their families' foods, appliances, diet sodas, breakfast cereals, toothpaste, and soap. As *Seventeen*'s ad noted, "Last year they personally spent 37 percent of the family food budget, or $13 billion."

For children, the marketplace provides a kind of autonomous zone, which insensitive, interfering, and pushy adults cannot easily enter. By choosing what, where, when, and how to spend, children create their own subculture in opposition to the adult world. In the 1950s, they organized that subculture around comic books and *MAD* magazine (with its vicious satires of the adult-dominated consumer culture). In the early 1960s, preteen girls horrified adults with their frenzied worship of the Beatles and all things Beatle-related; for years rock remained a youth enclave almost impenetrable to adults. In the 1980s, children aggregate around video games and baffle large corporations by unpredictably switching their allegiance from Pac Man and Ms. Pac Man to Donkey Kong and Frogger.

It is as consumers that children have been able to win a supportive constituency among wealthy and powerful adults. Manufacturers of retail goods (and not only those consumed solely by the young) have long promoted the idea that children are worthy of high levels of parental subsidy. Both through their advertising and the TV programs their advertising pays for, they reliably endorse the notion that children are fun to be around and that their needs—whether for Pampers or Pop Rocks—merit serious adult consideration. As Ellen Peck, author of *Pronatalism* and a leading advocate of nonparenthood, observed of some of the more cloying TV commercials, "Frankly, one wonders what is being sold: Pampers? Or babies?...Hershey bars or children's faces?" Thus, by becoming consumers, children came to be promoted as commodities—either indispensable adjuncts to adulthood, as in the fervently pronatalist ideology of the 1950s, or as interesting additions to a household, as they are more likely to be portrayed today.

But the consumerist strategy has its psychological costs. For one thing, it strains whatever affection parents spontaneously feel for their young. Kiddie market manufacturers spend $800 million a year on television ads urging children to wheedle, whine, or harangue their way to new acquisitions. These ads find their way not only to the homes of the upper middle class but to the homes of the unemployed and the chronically hard pressed, where the expense of a single Smurf figure (from "the collectible world of Smurfs") could sabotage a family meal. For the poor as well as the merely thrifty, nothing undermines parental affection more decisively than a trip to the supermarket with a couple of TV-wise junior consumers. Any vestigial sentimentalization evaporates; the kids are revealed as "economic liabilities" or, worse, as the real-life counterparts of the filmic monsters who devour their parents and entire civilizations.

Children themselves pay an immediate psychological price for their dual role as dependent consumers and likable commodities. In the emotional economy of the American family, they are expected to be "cute"; that is what they learn from prime time programming and very often from the adults they encounter in real life. But from a child's vantage point, cuteness involves a performance in which dignity must constantly be sacrificed for attention—a parody of adulthood which exploits the handicaps (small stature, lack of motor coordination, defective pronunciation) of the performer. Toddlers are cute not only because they walk but because they stumble. (And, of course, what is cute one moment, like a chocolate-smeared face, may be punishable the next.) For many children, the strain of being cute leads to a state of perpetual embarrassment, manifested either as a desperate silliness or a guarded withdrawal from adult contact.

Women, finding themselves in a similar role as financial dependents and displayers of obligatory cuteness, took immediate measures to change their situation. Betty Friedan advocated women's return to the workforce because the housewives she surveyed for *The Feminine Mystique* seemed to be losing their sanity and self-respect. The worst she could say about them was that they had been "infantilized," and the best she could suggest was that they grow up and get out of the house. But for children there is no such clear-cut escape. All that remains is to burrow deeper into the consumer culture, while, of course, dipping deeper into their parents' pockets.

Consumerism, whether as acquiescence or escape, is always a limited and risky strategy. While some may cruise the shopping malls with a full deck of credit cards, others must nag their parents or learn to shoplift. In poor neighborhoods, small children hustle pizza parlor patrons for quarters to play video games; some of them will soon be big enough to mug pedestrians for the wherewithal to buy "muscle-builder (radio/tape deck) boxes." Seventy-four years ago, Jane Addams reported from Chicago that much of the "petty pilfering" that went on was a result of the children's need for nickels for the nickel-odeon. In the 1980s, the nickels have become $5 bills and some of the petty pilferers carry guns. So long as children are both financially dependent on their parents and exposed to a spectacle of consumer temptations, the disjunction between their "needs" and their families' incomes will regularly generate child outlaws. As the incidence and intensity of child crime increases, adult sympathy for children as a class declines.

A truly pro-child public policy should be based on the recognition that in many ways the needs of children are like those of any subordinate social group: They need economic security, and they need dignity and respect. If all children had a claim on public services and resources—day care, health services, etc.—no child could be regarded as an economic burden by the very adults he or she must look to for love.

Beyond that, children need some source of dignity other than consumerism. Some countries, like China and Cuba, build children's sense of dignity by enlisting them in a collective enterprise. We who would no doubt reject a U.S. equivalent of the Red Guards or Young Pioneers have left our children to find autonomy and purpose in the hands of Atari, Mattel, and McDonald's. We seem to lack the confidence to treat children as fellow persons; we prefer to see them as cute rather than as competent; we would rather leave their fantasies to the kiddie market than engage them in our own. Our abdication of responsibility reflects our own condition in a society where, as Paul Goodman observed, there is very little work that is worth a man's (or woman's) time. If we cannot collectively give dignity and meaning to childhood, it is perhaps because we have not yet found these things in our adult lives. ■

Barbara Ehrenreich is co-chair of the Democratic Socialists of America and a regular colum-nist for The Nation *and* Ms. *magazine. David Nasaw is a professor of history at the College of Staten Island, City University of New York.*

USA.
ALEXANDRA
DOR-NER

JONAS SALK   ARE WE BEING GOOD ANCESTORS?

Evolution is a process without end. We are not only a product of this process, but we have become instruments of it as well. We are, in effect, energy and matter that have evolved to a form that is now conscious of itself. We have become uniquely endowed with the freedom to choose. We have become the tools and trustees of evolution.

In other forms of life, choice is the province of genes and of the natural process of selection. Humans, through their possession of consciousness, have in a sense escaped genetic control. But they cannot escape the consequences of their choices, about which nature will have the last word.

The human species is, at present, the most actively evolving and the most dominant. This dominance gives rise to both the dangers and the opportunities that confront us. But will we choose the paths of opportunity or of danger? Will we have the wisdom to perceive the long-term as well as the short-term outcomes of our choices? Will future generations speak of the wisdom of their ancestors just as we are inclined to speak of ours?

There is now a need to balance undisciplined growth in quantity with disciplined growth in quality. This change is so unprecedented, though, that the past provides no definitive course. What's more, each day brings a further erosion of the traditions and mores that could help us make the change, and in the process chips away at the cultural foundation essential to building for the future. And as our inherited culture is destroyed, new pathological patterns rush in to fill the void.

There is now a tendency for human beings to become slaves of the machines and of the systems they have created. This course must be reversed if we are to improve the deteriorating quality of life and accommodate the necessities arising in the metamorphosis of our new epoch. The roles we will play and the strategies we will use to do so cannot be the same as those of the past. To understand this will go a long way toward reducing tensions created by clinging to habits just because they are familiar and comfortable.

Today, the planet is so small that the fate of all humankind is intertwined. All wars are now civil wars; there is no such thing as a "local" conflict. Increased international and intercultural relationships—as well as goodwill and friendship among all peoples—have become necessities in our rapidly shrinking world. As individuals we must see ourselves as parts of a single organism.

There is a saying in the West that we cannot choose our parents, but we can choose our ancestors. This means that each generation can choose from the past the models left by those who came before. Of course, we cannot just indiscriminately adopt yesterday's tradi-

WELSH MINER AND
CHILD.
BRUCE DAVIDSON/
MAGNUM

tions; many of them do not speak to our times. But we must reinterpret the customs of the past in the light of today's world, and thereby inherit the wisdom of our own ancestors.

And if we want to be good ancestors ourselves, we must show future generations how well we coped with an age of great change and great crisis. Human history has been distinguished by many moments of great insight and foresight. Each generation should emulate such moments.

I would like to offer my vision of the choices that face all of us—as individuals and as members of different cultures and nations—in an inevitably emerging world culture.

The circumstances of life on this planet have changed dramatically in recent years. To a large extent, today's problems have resulted from our successes, a situation that is itself a product of evolution. Science, in all its forms, theoretical and experimental, has contributed to this. Many of the solutions that science found for yesterday's problems have given birth to our current dilemmas.

So how do we avoid being consumed by our own successes?

COLOMBIA.
KEN HEYMAN

The imminent eradication of smallpox from the face of the earth was possible only through a cooperative worldwide effort. This model can work at the level of human values as well. When the common enemy is identified and made the target of our common concern, incalculable progress can be accomplished by cooperative efforts.

If we become the ancestors to a future world where cooperation is of the highest value, we will be seen as wise forebears. If not, we will be seen as prodigal forebears who, at a decisive moment, dissipated an opportunity by not assuming responsibility for the evolution of our species.

Those who have come before us have left a rich heritage upon which to build. This inheritance can be fortified with the wisdom of all the cultures on our planet today. Thus, we can pass on a vision of a world where understanding and friendship reign.

If we are to be good ancestors, transmitting the possibility of a better life and the joy of living, we have work to do. The first step is to open ourselves to the as yet unrealized possibilities that exist in humankind. Only in the future will it be known whether we have been wise ancestors. But now is the time to accept the challenge. ∎

Dr. Jonas Salk developed the first polio vaccine. He is founding director and distinguished professor in international sciences at the Salk Institute for Biological Studies.

GENERATIONS

THE EXHIBITION

CURIOSITY AND MYSTERY

How did they explain where you came from?

Did they say the stork brought you? Or that you were found in a cabbage patch?

Did they say you were the reincarnation of someone who lived before; perhaps an ancestor from generations ago?

Did they say you emerged from a seed that grew in the womb, from a set of genes shared by your father and mother?

Did they say your flesh and spirit came to your mother as she passed by a stream?

Perhaps you were told something else. In every time and place people have explained birth in ways meaningful to them. Each explanation is an attempt to satisfy our curiosity—a need to know how new generations come into being. The examples ahead illustrate the diversity of our thinking.

1   ATTIC RED-FIGURED *SKYPHOS* (CUP), c. 460 B.C.
Attributed to the Penthesilea Painter
Ancient Greece, Athens or Attica (found at Vico Equense near Sorrento, Italy)
Terra cotta
Boston Museum of Fine Arts (H.L. Pierce Fund, 01.8032)

According to Greek mythology, Aphrodite's birth occurred when the god Kronos castrated his father, Uranos. The severed organ was thrown into the sea, but the foam engendered as it floated in the water coalesced into Aphrodite, the goddess of love. Eventually she landed on the island of Cyprus, which became the major center of her cult. Because Aphrodite was born from the sea foam, depictions of her birth often show her rising from an open seashell. Some depictions also include a figure of Pan, the goat-headed Greek divinity associated with fertility and sexual energy.

This 5th-century B.C. drinking vessel includes a young female, dressed with a *saccos* (a kind of snood or hairnet) and *peplos* (belted dress) rising from the ground. She is flanked by two dancing Pans. Although the original Greek inscriptions that often identify characters are missing from this skyphos, the label "Aphrodite" is inscribed on another Greek vase that illustrates a similar scene. We cannot be certain that this vase illustrates the Goddess of Love, but there is strong evidence to suggest that the rising female figure represents the Penthesilea Painter's version of her birth.

2   ETRUSCAN MIRROR, c. 350-300 B.C.
Palestrina (ancient Praeneste), now Italy
Engraved bronze
The British Museum, Department of Greek and Roman Antiquities (Br. 617)

The birth of Athena is the subject of this ancient Etruscan mirror. The story is identifiable because the artist provided proper attributes and labels for the four characters involved. According to Greek mythology (which the Etruscans knew intimately), Zeus, the king of the gods, impregnated Metis, an obscure goddess of wisdom. Metis, it was prophesied, would bear a goddess first, and then a second child who would rule over all the gods. Disturbed by this potential threat to his supreme power, Zeus eliminated Metis by swallowing her. Later, however, Metis gave birth to a divine child, a woman born fully grown and fully armed, from the head of her father. The "midwife" who enabled the delivery by splitting Zeus' head with an axe was Hephaistos (Vulcan in Roman mythology).

The artisan who engraved this piece depicted Zeus (Tinia in Etruscan mythology) seated at the center of the mirror's disc. In his right hand he holds a stylized thunderbolt, one of his most common attributes. Popping out of his head is the figure of Athena (Menrya in Etruscan mythology) wearing a helmet, aegis, and long, belted dress. She carries a shield and spear, appropriate attributes for the goddess of war.

The Etruscans depicted the story of Athena's birth in versions often very close to original Greek representations. In this mirror, however, some changes were made. Athena here has wings, and Hephaistos is replaced by two winged Etruscan female figures, who attend Zeus, carefully bandaging his head. The inscriptions identify these figures as Ethausva and Thanr, and it is likely that both were Etruscan birth goddesses. Their appearance on an object used mostly by women seems especially fitting.

The Etruscans were the major pre-Roman inhabitants of central and northern Italy. Between around 500 and 100 years before Christ, they produced hundreds of cast bronze mirrors like this one. One side of these objects was polished carefully to reflect the viewer's image; the other side often was engraved with a mythological scene. Handles frequently were made of bone or ivory and attached by means of a tang, as was the case with this mirror before its handle was lost.

3 **CONCEPTION OF THE BUDDHA,** Kushan Period, 2nd-3rd century A.D.
Pakistan, Ancient Gandhara
Gray hornblende schist
Asian Art Museum of San Francisco, The Avery Brundage Collection (B64S5)

Inspecting humanity from *Tusita* (joyful) heaven, the *bodhisattva* (buddha-to-be) chose Māyā, pure and peerless queen of King Śuddhodana, to bear him in his final incarnation. Māyā begged her husband to allow her to lead a chaste and moral life. Accompanied by her woman, she lay herself on a bed high in an isolated palace. Buddha then descended from heaven in the form of a gleaming white elephant, and entered her womb through the right side. Māyā experienced this event as a dream, thus conception occurred simultaneously in mind and body.

Māyā could see the bodhisattva in her womb, clean and radiant, sitting with legs crossed. He caused her no pain in pregnancy or in birth, emerging, as he entered, from her right side. So severed of physiological realities, the process of conception, gestation, and birth of Śakyamuni, the historical Buddha, becomes analogous to the manifestation of absolute reality in the illusory or created world. In Sanskrit, that world is called *māyā*.

4 **BOOK OF HOURS,** c. 1500
Flanders
Illuminated miniature painted on thin fine vellum
The Library of Congress, Rare Book and Special Collections Division
    (The Warburg Hours)

5 **BOOK OF HOURS AND PRAYER BOOK,** c. 1420
Attributed to workshop of the Boucicaut Master
France, Paris
Painted miniature on fine vellum
The Library of Congress, Rare Book and Special Collections Division
    (De Ricci #92)

The representation of the Nativity in the "Warburg" miniature emphasizes the humility of the birth of Jesus Christ. The Virgin Mary kneels in the foreground, protected only by her mantle, and the tiny Christ Child lies nearby. Saint Joseph, Mary's husband, kneels to the right. In the background is a sheaf of grain that refers to ideas associated with the birthplace of Christ. That city's name, Bethlehem, means "house of bread," alluding to the two sacred mysteries of the Christian religion, the Incarnation and Holy Eucharist.

The Nativity also is the culmination of events in the life of Mary. She bore the son of God sheltered only by an open stable. The "De Ricci" miniature depicts the newborn Christ Child, lying on a bed covered by a rich scarlet-and-gold cloth, extending his hand in a blessing, as Mary and Joseph kneel in prayer. The open book resting on the bed symbolizes the Word of God.

The "Warburg" book was produced in a 15th-century school of manuscript illumination that flourished in the Flemish cities of Ghent and Bruges. Characterized by a multilayered representation of space, the works by Flemish miniaturists of this period were "framed" like windows through which exquisitely detailed, brilliantly colored images appeared to be seen on a plane of vision different from that of the spectator.

The "De Ricci" miniature is believed to have been produced in a 15th-century Paris workshop directed by the Boucicaut Master. The hallmarks of this artist—an understanding of space and perspective, the placement of harmoniously grouped figures, and the application of detailed naturalistic elements and clear, luminous colors—may be identified here.

The *Book of Hours* was a personal prayer book and the most popular religious volume of the late medieval period. Religious practices required that daily prayers be recited at seven particular times or canonical hours, and the basic text consisted of devotions to the Virgin Mary. Hour Books often were privately commissioned, which explains why the format and decoration of each reflects the individual taste, status, and wealth of its owner.

6 *DER SWANGERN FRAUWEN UND HEBAMMEN ROSENGARTEN (THE ROSE GARDEN OF PREGNANT WOMEN AND MIDWIVES),* 1522
Eucharius Roeslin, author
France, Strasbourg
Woodcut
The National Library of Medicine, Bethesda, Maryland

Early 16th-century obstetrical knowledge was limited at best. These woodcuts illustrate the strange unreality that often dominated anatomical descriptions of the fetus *in utero*. The puppet-like fetus is shown as a fully-grown figure with a head of hair, no apparent umbilical connection, and ample room to stretch out in the flask-shaped uterus. There is no proportional relationship between fetus and uterus, and the acrobatic postures indicate that problematic fetal positions are not understood.

Although these woodcuts first were published in 1513, they may be traced directly to a 6th-century manuscript by Moschion who, in turn, had written a revised 2nd-century obstetrical catechism by Soranus of Ephesus. Thus, when the 16th century began, knowledge was being used that had not been improved or embellished upon for over 1,500 years. Perhaps this explains why these illustrations were used not only for diagnostic purposes, but also for technical information, since they were accompanied by texts that explained how to remedy problem positions of the fetus *in utero*.

7 DE CONCEPTU ET GENERATIONE HOMINIS (ON THE CONCEPTION AND BIRTH OF MANKIND), 1554

Jakob Rueff, author
Zurich
Woodcut on vellum
The National Library of Medicine, Bethesda, Maryland

Aristotle's theories of fetal development formed the basis of most embryological thought for 2,000 years. His description of the mysteries of human generation is shown here, illustrated by a later Renaissance interpreter. Aristotle did not believe that a fetus was perfectly formed from the beginning, but held instead to the theory of epigenesis, saying that it began as an undifferentiated mass and went through various developmental stages, or steps. In this process, the role of the female was a passive one, offering mainly the nutritive principle of "matter" to the male's more important contribution of "form," soul, or life principle. In Aristotle's view, then, the woman provided only the proper environment for the fetus to grow—as though she were soil to the male's seed, which contained all the intrinsic determinants of human life. Such a belief only reinforced the minor role of women in medieval and Renaissance society.

These woodcuts show Aristotle's concept of the seven stages of fetal development. Since he studied primarily the chick egg, the uterus is depicted as egg-shaped. The first stage involves the blending of semen and menstrual blood in the uterus. By the fourth stage, blood vessels are apparent. By the last stage, the fully formed fetus sits in the uterus, as was believed, with its face toward the mother's back. Just before birth, the fetus supposedly turned itself toward the mother's navel, thus assisting in its own delivery.

8 KITÁB ITMÁN AL-NI'MAH AL-KUBRA'ALA'ÁL-ALAM BI-MAWLID SAYYID WULD ÁDAM, 1505-1506

Ahmad [ibn-Muhammad ibn-'Ali] ibn-Hajar al - Haythami, author
Arabic-speaking area
Ink on glazed oriental paper; in Nashki with catchwords, headings, and
    entries in red; blind-stamped and tooled oriental leather binding
The Library, Princeton University, Garrett Collection of Arabic Manuscripts

Mohammed, the originator and the Prophet of Islam, was born around 570 A.D. in the oasis town of Mecca in the Arabian Peninsula. We know the names of his parents, Abdallah ibn Abd-al-Muttalib and Amina, and the nomadic tribe to which they belonged. We also know much about his humble beginnings, including the death of his father when Mohammed was only six.

In deference to the Prophet's sacredness and Islam's commitment to modesty and humility, representational images depicting Mohammed's birth are rare. There is, however, an extensive body of written commentaries on his life. This 16th-century volume discusses the history and significance of the Prophet's birth and is interspersed with special prayers. The book's title translates as "The Book of the Consummation of the Greatest Blessing to the World Through the Birth of the Lord of the Children of Adam." Written more than eight centuries after Mohammed's death, it is a measure of the Prophet's lasting and powerful influence on the spiritual lives of his followers.

9 DE FORMATO FOETU (ON THE FORMATION OF THE FETUS), 1627

Adriaan van der Spiegel, author
Italy, Padua
Copperplate engraving
The National Library of Medicine, Bethesda, Maryland

This is how a 17th-century anatomist described the near-term fetus *in utero*. Anatomically the drawing is correct, showing the umbilical cord and placenta, as well as a properly positioned fetus. These details are presented in a tastefully arranged scene that imbues the pregnant woman with an air of romantic elegance even as it displays anatomical realism with a high degree of technical sophistication. The care and delicacy with which this illustration is executed is due partly to the use of copperplate engraving, which lends itself to representations far more precise than woodcuts.

The depiction exhibited here is one of a series of plates entitled "Eviscerated Beauties." The text for this work was written by Adriaan Spiegel and was published after his death. The illustrations, which detail the pregnant uterus, placenta, and the fetus, were prepared by Spiegel's master and predecessor in the Chair of Anatomy at Padua, Giulio Casserio. Although Casserio died before he could use the drawings in his own publication, the beauty and accuracy of his engravings encouraged others to abandon the medium of woodcut in anatomical illustrations.

10 PREGNANT ANATOMICAL FIGURE, 17th-18th century

Germany
Ivory
Trent Collection in the History of Medicine, Duke University Medical
    Center Library

During the 17th and 18th centuries, dolls like this one helped to explain the complexities of human reproduction. Doctors and other types of healers sometimes used such figures during their consultations with female patients. Women thus were able to indicate their symptoms or clarify anatomical details without compromising their modesty by revealing their own bodies. In turn, physicians and healers could provide specific information about the pregnant woman's condition and what she might expect as she brought the baby to term.

11 NANCY STUART WILSON WITH HER DAUGHTERS, 1792
William Clarke, artist
USA
Oil on canvas
Collection of Major General and Mrs. George Fergusson, Los Angeles

This woman would not have known about the complex biological processes that lead to multiple births. Yet the safe arrival of her twin daughters undoubtedly was an exciting and joyous occasion, for it would have marked the end of a period of uncertainty and concern. Multiple births were—and still remain—unusual events that often excite curiosity, awe, or fear. Cultural groups worldwide ascribe different meanings to twins. Some consider them a source of good fortune; others regard them as unnatural or dangerous.

For Nancy Stuart Wilson, the wife of an 18th-century Maryland doctor, twins were a source of great pride. In this portrait, she cradles her young daughters protectively. The girls appear to be secure, happy, and content, perhaps in response to their mother's special love and devotion.

12 STORK DELIVERING THE NEWBORN, 1907
USA
Stereograph
Collections of the Margaret Woodbury Strong Museum, Rochester, New York

13 BABY HATCHING FROM EGG CANDY CONTAINER,
1885-1890
France
Wax composition
Collections of the Margaret Woodbury Strong Museum, Rochester, New York

In many Western cultures, alternative explanations of birth were popular even as scientific advancements were beginning to clarify the biological processes of conception. During the Victorian era and into the beginning of the 20th century, for example, popular beliefs attributed babies to the work of the stork. Such lore was rooted in earlier German and Scandinavian folk traditions, which understood the long-legged, powerfully winged bird as an omen of good fortune, especially for those desiring children. The stork thus was encouraged to build its platform nests on the housetops of young couples. Legend had it that when the egg hatched, the bird would deliver a blanket-wrapped newborn in its beak. Other popular notions maintained that babies were hatched from egg shells or were found in cabbage patches and rose bushes.

14 PREGNANT WOMAN; original wax executed 1896-1911;
cast posthumously, c. 1919-1924
Edgar Degas (1834-1917)
France
Bronze
Smithsonian Institution, Hirshhorn Museum and Sculpture Garden
(86.1415)

Intimacy and mystery characterize Degas' view of this woman in an advanced stage of pregnancy. Looking down towards her protruding belly, the mother-to-be—apparently feeling signs of life from her unborn child—touches her abdomen. Birth seems imminent, for the woman bends her knees slightly to retain her balance against the weight of the baby, which pulls her body forward. Degas was a careful and exacting observer. Toward the end of his life, partially blind and voluntarily reclusive, he focused on images of nude adult women, ritualizing and immortalizing their daily routines of bathing, dressing, and combing their hair. Combining his skill for anatomical observation with an understanding of the psychological mood of his subject, Degas achieved with this figure a true-to-life yet universal image of pregnancy.

15 VIDEO SEGMENTS OF EGG-PRODUCING CELLS, 1985
Lennart Nilsson, filmmaker
Sweden, Stockholm

Science understands conception and birth as intricate, complex biological processes. Women are fertile between their teens and the time they stop menstruating. During these years, at four-week intervals, females undergo a "follicle maturation" cycle whereby the uterine lining is rebuilt, ovulation occurs, and the body prepares to receive the ovum, or egg-producing cell. On or around the fourteenth day of this ever-repeating cycle, the ovum enters a woman's oviduct and begins its passage through that tube. It is here that the egg-producing cell may be fertilized. Millions of male sperm travel towards the oviduct in an effort to attach themselves to the ovum. Yet only one sperm actually may fuse with the egg-producing cell. Conception occurs when that fusion takes place.

INTENT

What does an old wives' tale about hanging garlic on the doorknob have to do with having children?

A good suggestion?
An odd prescription?
Something you might do yourself?

And why so much advice? Why so much concern?

Because for many, new generations hold the promise of…
carrying on the family line,
herding the flocks,
inheriting the land,
fishing the seas,
hunting the forests,
running the business.

For others, new generations would strain…
an overcrowded world,
the well-being of a family,
the rations of bread.

Throughout time people have sought to influence fertility. Some have followed advice like that above. Others have used prayers, rites, and medicines to prevent or overcome barrenness, influence the sex of a child, and regulate the size of the family. Ancestors, deities, votive figures, health practitioners, and others often are called upon to assist.

16   NANDĪ, c. 1200 A.D.
India, Tamilnadu
Granite
Lent anonymously

Nandī (giving delight) is the name of the god Śiva's sacred white zebu bull, his *vahana* (conveyance) on which he rides and by which his presence is announced. Images of Nandī appear in temples of Śiva throughout India but are particularly prevalent in the south. Nandī in the form of a couchant bull can reside in several parts of the temple, although he is found most

often outside of the front hall facing the *garbhagrha* (inner sanctum). Before approaching the sanctum, the worshipper circles around Nandī, reverently touching the nose and horns of the bull. A barren woman who desires children also may touch the bull's testicles, which sometimes are exposed prominently, for as an image of virility Nandī can aid fertility. Nandī is the very embodiment of sexual potency and has been depicted throughout India's many millennia of artistic production. In mastering the bull, the god Śiva, the great ascetic, also masters lust and taps the power of generation.

17   STATUETTE OF ARTEMIS EPHESIA, c. 200 A.D.
Probably from Roman Asia Minor
Marble
Indiana University Art Museum, Bloomington (81.59.4)

Artemis (or Diana) of the Ephesians is a later Graeco-Roman manifestation of the early Anatolian fertility deity, the Great Goddess. Worship of that goddess, which took place at ancient Anatolian sites (now modern Turkey) from around 8500 B.C. on, was connected with the rise of agriculture and the need to ritualize the processes of regeneration and growth in the natural world.

Artemis' association with fertility was symbolized by her rows of pendulous breasts, and by the honeybees and flowers on her garment. She also was revered as the protectress of children and young animals. The stiff, hieratic pose of this figure conforms with the attributes of ancient cult statues. Although the original cult statue of Artemis Ephesia from the Temple of Artemis is lost, scores of copies survive. Many of these are large and probably were worshipped as cult statues in other temples. The numerous small-scale copies like the example in the exhibition suggest that this fertility goddess also was worshipped by individuals in the privacy of their own homes.

18   ŚIVA LIṄGA, 7th-13th century A.D.
Cambodia, People's Republic of Kampuchea (Khmer)
Buff sandstone
The David and Alfred Smart Gallery, the University of Chicago
   (Gift of Gaylord Donnelley, 1982.20)

The earliest Indian depictions of the *liṅga* (mark or emblem) of the god Śiva are naturalistic representations of the human phallus. Over the centuries, the form of the liṅga became standardized and abstracted, all details and measurements textually prescribed. Mythological explanations of liṅga worship stress the ambiguity of this image in terms of procreation. It is the generative organ of the god yet it is erect, the seed drawn up and contained, as is appropriate for Śiva, the great ascetic who also is the creator.

Only the circular upper third of the liṅga would have been visible to the worshipper, the lower segments encased within the stone slabs of a round pedestal. Texts prescribe that the liṅga be made of male-stone, the pedestal of female. The combination of liṅga and pedestal, the latter called *yoni* (vulva) in certain instances, is a symbolic as well as visual depiction of coitus, further emphasizing Śiva's dual nature.

The liṅga, image of harnessed generative power, stands alone in the *garbhagṛha* (inner sanctum, literally "embryo-house") of the majority of Śiva temples throughout the Hindu world. In the Khmer kingdom of Cambodia and northern Thailand, the liṅga came to embody the king as well as the god. It became the source of all power, temporal and divine. The Khmer kings placed liṅgas in the uppermost shrine of their palace-temples. These multistoried structures symbolized the mountain home of the gods, center and axis of the universe, like the liṅga itself.

19   **SPOON**, 20th century
Africa, Liberia
Dan people
Wood, metal, nails
Smithsonian Institution, National Museum of African Art (Bequest of
   Samuel Rubin, 79-16-28)

Among many cultures, fertility is sign of abundance and well-being. It is part of a healthy growth-process and an important measure of one's accomplishments. Fertility also is linked to other sources of achievement associated with fullness and abundance, such as success in agricultural pursuits and food preparations, personal generosity, hospitality, and physical energy. This spoon is a mark of distinction for women who are especially accomplished in these areas.

The spoon on exhibition is an emblem of the *wakede*, or the woman who distinguishes herself most as a special provider within her town quarter. The wakede is responsible for preparing foods not only for her extended family, but also for larger groups at special festivals. At the major feast, all wakede in the town must appear and dance in order to demonstrate that they are more generous and hospitable than other wakedes from rival towns. The wakede's spirit of nurturing and giving is thought to grow as her success grows. Decorative spoons are given to the wakede to acknowledge and symbolize her many accomplishments.

The bowl of this spoon forms a belly that is said to be "pregnant with rice." It is desirable for this "belly" always to be full. Since the spoon also embodies the power vested in the wakede, it is thought to enable her to perform her duties well. Sometimes spoons like these also are incised with chameleon-lizards, creatures that are regarded as intermediaries to aid in one's request for fertility.

20   **KUAN YIN STATUE**, late 7th century (T'ang Dynasty)
China, Honan Province
Limestone with traces of polychrome painting
Smithsonian Institution, National Museum of Natural History,
   Department of Anthropology (448104)

See cat. 22

21   **KUAN YIN STATUE**, 19th-20th century
China
Ivory
Smithsonian Institution, National Museum of Natural History,
   Department of Anthropology (415843)

See cat. 22

22   **KUAN YIN STATUE**, 18th century
China
Blanc de chine ceramic
The Nathan Aronson Collection

Kuan Yin is a Buddhist deity associated with mercy. Kuan Yin is a *bodhisattva*, a being who chooses a life dedicated to saving all humans before becoming a buddha. The words *Kuan Yin* mean "hear the cries," a reference to the deity's willingness to help those in distress by taking any appropriate physical form. Early representations of Kuan Yin, like the 7th-century example in the exhibition, often show a male form with many heads and arms, emphasizing this ability to reshape appearance. In later Chinese popular religion, however, Kuan Yin developed into a female figure, becoming one of the most popular of Chinese deities.

Kuan Yin's willingness to help the needy and to change form as required resulted in a goddess often associated with childbirth. The Buddhist idea of mercy expanded into an emphasis on nurturance, motherhood, and purity. The statues emphasize female nurturance. The seven swallows rising on a cloud from the vase of the ivory figure in the exhibition, for example, evoke images of springtime, a symbolic reference to regeneration and reproduction.

Popular tales of Kuan Yin's origin depict a pious daughter who chose the Buddhist faith and its requirement of celibacy against the will of a domineering father. Later she sacrificed part of her body (eyes in some stories, limbs in others) to save her father's life, and then went on to save ghosts suffering in the underworld. Kuan Yin retains the Buddhist idea of saving all beings before she herself chooses to enter *Nirvana*. As a nurturing virgin, she represents all that is positive in Chinese ideas of motherhood—saving and answering prayers while avoiding the perils of sexual danger, birth pollution, and family quarrels.

23 SAINT ANTHONY WITH THE CHRIST CHILD *BULTO*,
first half of 19th century
Attributed to Santo Niño
USA, northern New Mexico
Spanish Colonial community
Polychrome wood
International Folk Art Foundation Collections, Museum of International
   Folk Art, a unit of the Museum of New Mexico, Santa Fe (FA.79.64-113)

Scattered settlement and frontier conditions in New Mexico during the
1830s and 1840s made pregnancy and childbirth more hazardous than
usual. Diaries kept by frontier women describe the fear and danger that
preoccupied expectant mothers living in isolation, often without the social
or medical resources available in the urban environment. Under these
conditions, the Roman Catholic population turned to the saints with special prayers for protection and good health. Saint Anthony of Padua was an
especially important source of spiritual support, for he was revered as the
patron of women in confinement. This figure of Saint Anthony with the
Christ Child probably was created for a family devotional in a chapel or
small church.

24 FIGURE, 20th century
Africa, Ghana
Ashanti people
Wood
The Marcia and Irwin Hersey Collection

This small figure is called *akua ba,* or "Akua's child," in reference to an Ashanti
story about a barren woman named Akua. Akua consulted a priest, who
told her to have carved a small figure of a beautiful child that she could
carry on her back as she would a real infant. Friends laughed at her, calling
on everyone to see "Akua's child." But when Akua bore a beautiful daughter, other Ashanti women adopted the practice as a cure for barrenness.

This akua ba bears the marks of beauty esteemed by the Ashanti. Her
elegant, high, glossy-black brow, and the rings of fat around her neck, are
indications of health and well-being. The fact that this piece is a double
figure, with a second, smaller form seated back-to-back with the larger
doll, is unusual. The presence of two figures—one much smaller than the
other—may refer to the owner's desire to bear two children, rather than
twins. The sex of the doll is irrelevant, however, for female dolls signal the
desire for both male and female babies.

25 FIGURE, 19th century
Africa, Zaire
Bembe people
Wood and beads
Smithsonian Institution, National Museum of Natural History,
   Department of Anthropology (399499)

A female figure like this one was thought to have had the power to bring
children to its owner, and then to protect that person from death by witchcraft after the birth. The figure was carved by a Bembe ritual specialist
who, with magical force, would place a magical substance—especially white
clay, or *mukuya,* that represented the bones of the ancestors—into a small
hole between the buttocks of the form. Women then would wear the figure
suspended from their necks by a string that had been passed through holes
pierced under the wooden arms.

The scarification patterns on the torso of this figure represent accurately
the scars worn by the ancestor whose spirit was embodied in the form. To
make the scars visible, the magical substance on this figure was applied
only to the anal orifice. Among other peoples living along the lower Zaire
River, however, the special potion often covered the entire figure from head
to toe.

26 FIGURE, 19th century
Africa, Liberia
Dan people
Wood of raffia palm and vegetable fiber
The Marcia and Irwin Hersey Collection

Figures like this one were carried about by young Dan girls during the
period when they were secluded in a forest clearing for their initiation into
womanhood. Here they received instruction about their roles as adults,
especially in matters of sex education, childbirth, and infant care. During
this training period, they also were subjected to excision, which marked
their transition from early adolescence to female adulthood.

Such figures are among the simplest of all African dolls. They are columnar
forms, shaped like torsos, which are carved from a short section of the
mid-rib of a raffia palm and decorated with carved geometric patterns.
Vegetable fiber is added, plaited into the form of a hairstyle.

27 FIGURE FOR FATTENING HOUSE, early 20th century
Africa, Nigeria
Ibibio people of southern Nigeria
Wood
The Marcia and Irwin Hersey Collection

See cat. 28

28   FIGURE FOR FATTENING HOUSE, early 20th century
Africa, Nigeria
Ibibio people of southern Nigeria
Wood
The Marcia and Irwin Hersey Collection

Wooden figures like this one and cat. 27, which represent symbolically the ideal female Ibibio physique, are used by young Ibibio girls when they are being prepared for marriage and life as adult women. Such figures are given to them during their long period of seclusion in "fattening houses," where they are fed large amounts of rich foods, especially yams and palm oil, until they develop rolls of fat, which signify health, well-being, and fertility. During seclusion they are given lessons in the skills they will need as married women, especially in matters of sex, childbearing and child-rearing, and cooking. Other kinds of work are not done, and the adolescent girls are not permitted to leave the enclosure in which the "fattening house" is located. When the period of seclusion is over, however, the young women emerge with their bodies oiled, dressed in beads and brass jewelry. Admiring suitors offer the parents a dowry, and marriage soon follows.

29   FIGURE, 20th century
South Africa
Sotho (Suthu) people
Gourds, beads, metal, cloth
The Marcia and Irwin Hersey Collection

A Sotho woman may carry a figure like this one from the time she is betrothed until she becomes pregnant with her first child. Young Sotho girls carry small figures on their backs just as their mothers carry babies. Women who have difficulty conceiving carry similar figures, called *ngoana*, or "child," as fertility aids. The bases of these figures, made from gourds, often are filled with clay until they have the weight of real infants.

Such figures are dressed to reflect local fashion, thus representing their owner's ideas of the way they would like to look when they are grown. The example here shows the heavy accumulation of bright, primary-colored beads favored by Sotho women, as well as an elaborate hairstyle and a short skirt of locally woven, striped fabric.

30   TWIN FIGURE, late 19th century
Africa, Ghana
Fante people
Wood
The Marcia and Irwin Hersey Collection

This looks like a single figure, but in fact it is a representation of twin dolls, mounted on a common base. Their elongated, rectangular heads are characteristic of the style of the Fante, who live near the Guinea Coast. The woman who owned these figures probably wanted to bear twins, which among the Fante are thought to bring good luck.

Such figures are carried by Fante women for a period of time designated by a priest. Often they are decorated with earrings, beads, and other small bits of jewelry, and they may even be "nursed" and put to sleep beneath warm covers in their owner's bed, with the hope that they will promote the birth of beautiful children. After the birth, the figures may be placed on a shrine to the gods that provides special blessings. Similar figures also are specially prepared by priests to help women who have children, but who experienced difficulties during their delivery.

31   DOLL, 20th century
Africa, Kenya
Turkana people
Doum-palm fruit, animal hide, mammal hooves, bottle caps, wild-banana
    seed, cowrie shells, ostrich eggshell-beads, vegetable fiber
Smithsonian Institution, National Museum of African Art (Gift of Daniel
    Collier, 75-34-5)

When Turkana women marry, they relinquish the adornment they wore as young girls to put on adornment symbolic of their married status. Yet there is one item—a fertility doll—that Turkana women usually do not give up. Dolls like the one on exhibition are cherished personal possessions. They are made for little girls by their mothers, and they serve not only as fertility symbols, but also as items associated with one's future role as a mother. Turkana girls play with these dolls as toys and care for them as they would a baby. Often they wear the dolls or carry them about until the birth of their first child. The dolls then are passed down to younger, unmarried female relatives.

Although this doll was made for a young girl, it wears the clothing and adornment of one who is married, and it reflects the fashion and headdress favored by Turkana women. For the pastoral Turkana, adornment symbolizes personal identity, affluence, and status within the group. Children at very young ages thus are given beads by their parents and other relatives. The doll here is adorned with precious ostrich eggshell-beads, strands of multi-colored beads, and pubic aprons. The bottle caps and little horn pendants attached to the strands of beads are thought to reinforce the sounds and motion of dance.

32 MAIDEN SPIRIT MASK, 20th century
Africa, Nigeria
Igbo people
Polychrome-wood, fabric, buttons, metal, hair, thread
Smithsonian Institution, National Museum of African Art (Gift of Robert
 and Nancy Nooter, 83-14-2)

The Igbo regard masks as spirits or incarnate dead who guide, protect, and
influence life on earth. Such spirits may increase or decrease human and
agricultural fertility, depending on whether someone deserves reward or
punishment for wrongdoing. Masking ceremonies are divided into three
groups. Younger men carry out certain traditions, middle-age men others,
and elders still others. Maiden spirit masks like this one are used by the
middle group during elaborate masquerade performances in the annual
cycle of agricultural festivals, which honor ancestors and celebrate motherhood, as well as human and agricultural fertility.

Although maiden masks are used only by men, they represent the ideals of
feminine beauty and inner purity and morality. Those qualities are expressed
here by an intricate, crested hairstyle and refined features, including an
elegant facial tatoo, and dark lines along the nose and mouth. The light
complexion is equally prized, for it symbolizes moral purity, obedience,
generosity, and spiritual beauty.

33 *QLĀDET'ANBAR* OR *'AQD'ANBAR* AMULET, c. 1900
Palestine/Transjordan
Palestinian people
Polished amber
International Folk Art Foundation Collections, The Museum of International
 Folk Art, a unit of the Museum of New Mexico, Santa Fe (FA.73.11-1)

See cats. 34, 35

34, 35 AMULET NECKLACES, 20th century
Africa, North Somalia
Silver, ornamented with filigree silver; amber beads; string
Smithsonian Institution, National Museum of African Art (Gift of John
 and Kathy Loughran, 76-16-3)

To our eyes, adornment is the primary function of polished jewelry like
this. But in the villages where such necklaces are made, jewelry often
serves a more important purpose, for it is believed to have preventive
powers against the effects of the Evil Eye. Protection against all forms of
danger, even envious glances, is regarded as crucial for women who wish
not only to conceive, but also to deliver healthy children. By carefully
safeguarding her own welfare, a woman even might attain the honor of
bearing a son, thus contributing to the prosperity and influence of the
household.

Virtually every aspect of the decoration on these necklaces involves an
amuletic formula to protect the wearer. Amber, for example, is deemed
capable of deflecting the Evil Eye. Abstract representations of the Eye are
included in the raised nodules on the case attached to one necklace. To
ensure that the Eye's wicked effects are kept at bay, these nodules are
grouped as a threesome, forming an odd number thought to have special
protective powers. On the other necklace, each amber cylinder is separated
by a group of seven silver beads. Seven is an odd number also thought to
sustain good fortune.

The hollow tube and case were intended to hold small scrolls inscribed
with protective religious formulas or personal prayers. To augment the
potency of such blessings, both necklaces include a group of five short
chains from which bells are suspended. These form a paradigmatic *khamsa,*
or "sign of the hand," which protects one from a host of potential dangers.

36 *KHIYĀR* AMULET, c. 1900
Palestine
Palestinian people
Silver with glass beads
International Folk Art Foundation Collections, Museum of International
 Folk Art, a unit of the Museum of New Mexico, Santa Fe (FA.72.25-1n)

In many parts of the world, fulfilling one's hope of ensuring fertility or
influencing the sex of a child is carried out symbolically through amuletic
devices, which are thought to ensure one's self-protection and well-being.
This cylindrical silver amulet, called a *khiyār,* often is worn by traditional
Muslim women. It contains a hollow tube that serves as a case for small
scrolls inscribed with prayers. This khiyār also combines two other powerful
amulets. The five short chains suspended from the tube form a *khamsa,* or
"sign of the hand," and the *kharazeh zarqa,* or "blue bead," safeguards against
the effects of the Evil Eye, which in many eastern Mediterranean cultures
is thought to be responsible for the death of one-half of humankind. These
symbolic, protective motifs are repeated here in the groups of coins and
beads on either side of the chain to which the khiyār is attached.

37 *SAMAK,* c. 1910
Palestine/Transjordan
Palestinian people
Niello-decorated silver
International Folk Art Foundation Collections, The Museum of International
 Folk Art, a unit of the Museum of New Mexico, Santa Fe (FA.72.25-53)

The *samak,* or "sign of the fish," is an ancient Mediterranean symbol of life
and fertility, and also an important charm against the malevolent forces of
the Evil Eye. This silver samak, created for a married woman, served the
double function of encouraging fecundity and warding off evil. The eye of

the fish refers to divine watchfulness, and the five Ottoman coins symbolically form a *khamsa,* or "sign of the hand," a crucial source of protection.

38   *QAMĒʿA* AMULET, early 20th century

Iraqi Kurdistan
Jewish people
Silver with beaded edge
The Museum of International Folk Art, a unit of the Museum of New
   Mexico, Santa Fe (3146)

This amulet, called a *qamēʿa,* belonged to a Jewish woman, Masʿuda, whose name is inscribed on the piece. Also inscribed are the names of holy angels, summoned here to "perform [their] action so the bearer of this amulet will become pregnant." According to custom, Masʿuda would have slung the silver chain over her right shoulder and the amulet would have rested against her right flank.

The complexity of this amulet suggests the importance attached to childbearing among Kurdish Jews. The Hebrew text, which begins with the word "Lord," also includes kabbalistic names of God, references to angels with special powers against the demon Lilith, and formulas consisting of the first and last letters of biblical verses and prayers from the Jewish liturgy.

39   *MĀSKEH* AMULET, c. 1900

Palestine/Transjordan
Palestinian people
Niello-decorated silver
International Folk Art Foundation Collections, The Museum of International
   Folk Art, a unit of the Museum of New Mexico, Santa Fe (FA.72.25-54)

In our culture, a woman who wishes to conceive and bear a healthy child often charts the course of ovulation in her menstrual cycle, and then subscribes to a special diet and forms of exercise that will keep her in good condition during pregnancy. Other cultures also regard self-protection as being critical to the health and well-being of a prospective mother. This pear-shaped amulet, called a *māskeh,* is among the devices that an eastern Mediterranean woman might employ to safeguard her welfare while carrying a child to term. The pendant includes a crescent and five-pointed star, Ottoman symbols that also are ancient amuletic signs against the the Evil Eye. The central inscription, "what God wills," is a phrase that is used often to negate the dangerous power of envy.

40, 41   CHARMS, c. 1914

Indonesia, Sulawesi, Kulawi
Cast brass
Smithsonian Institution, National Museum of Natural History,
   Department of Anthropology (304202, 301403)

In the region of Kulawi, the magical power of metals was summoned to enhance fertility. Exactly how these male and female charms were used, however, remains a mystery to us. There are reports of young women who did not become pregnant soon after marriage and so carried these brass images about as conception charms. Other accounts describe newly married couples, who brought the naked pair, along with an equally small, brass buffalo charm, to their new home to promote the growth of the family and the cattle. These figures apparently also were valued items in marriage negotiations. Their strong magical properties were thought to deflect evil, thus protecting a union whose future success would be measured by fertility and prosperity.

42   PREGNANCY CALENDAR, 19th century

England, York
Boxwood, ebony, ivory
Collections of the Wellcome Museum for the History of Medicine,
   The Science Museum, London (A 626822)

Often commensurate with one's intent to bear children is an effort to monitor the time of conception and the growth of the fetus. Rotating calendars like these were used to estimate the time of parturition when the date of conception already was known. The central disc could be moved in relation to the outer scale, which had units that were numbered from one to ten. Conception matched up with point zero. The inscriptions on this calendar tell us that the pregnant woman first noticed movements from her baby at point four, that the fetus was deemed viable at point seven, and that parturition took place at point ten, 280 days after conception.

43   DIAGNOSTIC VAGINAL SPECULUM, 1500-1700

Europe
Steel
Collections of the Wellcome Museum for the History of Medicine,
   The Science Museum, London (A 121424)

See cat. 47

44 ALBARELLO PHARMACY VASE WITH PORTRAIT OF HORATIO, 1530-1590
Italy, Faenza
Polychrome, tin-glazed earthenware
Collections of the Wellcome Museum for the History of Medicine,
    The Science Museum, London (A 240205)

See cat. 47

45 PHARMACY JAR FOR MYRTLE SYRUP, 1585
Italy
Glazed, inscribed pottery
Collections of the Wellcome Museum for the History of Medicine,
    The Science Museum, London (A 164837)

See cat. 47

46 PHARMACY PITCHER FOR WILD CELERY WATER,
c. 1550
Italy, Faenza
Glazed pottery
Collections of the Wellcome Museum for the History of Medicine,
    The Science Museum, London (1985 2262)

See cat. 47

47 OVUM FORCEPS, 1401-1600
Europe
Iron
Collections of the Wellcome Museum for the History of Medicine,
    The Science Museum, London (A 121507)

Is fertility primarily a female issue? Rarely. The lengths to which Henry VIII, King of England between 1509 and 1547, went to produce an heir is but one example of man's concern for perpetuating his lineage through offspring.

Henry had six wives during his lifetime. Although political alliances played a role in his choice of mate, the stability of his marriages depended largely on the success of a particular wife to bear a male heir to the throne.

Henry divorced his first wife, Katherine of Aragon, because among six children she bore no male heir. His next wife, Anne Boleyn, gave birth to Elizabeth I, but also failed to produce a male heir. She was beheaded in 1536. The King's third wife, Jane Seymour, delivered Edward, the cherished son who eventually succeeded his father. Only twelve days after

Edward's birth, however, Jane died. Henry's next marriage to Anne of Cleves lasted a matter of months, and his fifth wife, Catherine Howard, was beheaded. In 1543, four years before his death, the ill and aging king married Catherine Parr. The two had no children.

The exhibition includes apothecaries and obstetrical instruments contemporaneous with King Henry's reign. Artifacts like these were used by the Court physicians during examinations and to remedy maladies associated with pregnancy and childbirth.

48 *DE CONCEPTU ET GENERATIONE HOMINIS (ON THE CONCEPTION AND BIRTH OF MANKIND),* 1580
Jakob Rueff, author
Germany, Frankfurt
Woodcut on vellum
National Library of Medicine, Bethesda, Maryland

What determines a newborn's future? For the 16th-century German, character and fortune were thought to be influenced largely by the positions at birth of the sun, moon, and planets. The presence in this illustration of two astrologers—observing the night sky and preparing to cast a new baby's horoscope—tells us about the importance ascribed to life-predictions based on the exact time and place of birth. Even medical practitioners sought to establish a direct relationship between the patterns of the stars and human anatomy.

This elaborate delivery room scene also is rich in information about the customs and dress of late Renaissance German women. A stout, almost relaxed looking mother-to-be is seated on a birthing chair. Her apparent complacency is belied by the firm grip she has on her chair. She seems about to deliver. The tub of water in the right foreground will be used to wash the baby, and its presence suggests that birth may be imminent. On the table are scissors and twine that will be used to cut the umbilical cord. The empty plate and stein nearby indicate that the expectant woman has taken nourishment during her labor.

The midwife sits on her own stool between the expectant woman's legs, apparently assisting the birth-in-progress. Two other women—neighbors, relatives, or assistants—offer comfort and support. The sumptuous bed is surprising, for it contradicts other bits of evidence in this illustration. The well-separated, large toe of the laboring mother, for example, suggests that she seldom wore shoes and probably was a peasant woman.

49 (a-j)   **TAROT CARDS,** second half of 18th century
Italy, Bologna
Woodblock print with stencil coloring
Smithsonian Institution, National Museum of American History,
   Division of Community Life (63.244)

"Rich man? Poor man?…" People in many parts of the world try to predict
their child's sex, future occupation, or prospects for success. Prediction
may be part of religious life for those who believe that one's fate is pre-
determined. In Western cultures, making predictions traditionally has
involved lighthearted entertainment, as well as serious decisions about a
specific course of action. These 18th-century Italian cards were adapted to
an intricate fortune-telling system intended for games that employed trumps
in different orders and numbers to yield specific information about the
future. Such games often were used to predict one's chances for fertility,
condition during pregnancy, and the birth of a healthy child.

50   **DE ANGELIS EFFERVESCENT MAGNESIUM CITRATE,**
c. 1904
USA, Rhode Island, Providence
Ink on tin
Smithsonian Institution, National Museum of American History,
   Division of Medical Sciences (1984.0782.007)

See cat. 61

51   **THE J.V. HALE NEURO-PHOSPHATES,** early 20th century
USA, Massachusetts, Boston
Printed paper on glass; liquid medicine
Smithsonian Institution, National Museum of American History,
   Division of Medical Sciences (1984.0782.132)

See cat. 61

52   **RUDOLF'S KOLA-CARDINETTE,** 1898
USA
Printed paper on glass; liquid medicine
Smithsonian Institution, National Museum of American History,
   Division of Medical Sciences (M-7250)

See cat. 61

53   **McELREE'S WINE OF CARDUI,** 1906
USA, Tennessee, Chattanooga
Printed paper on glass; cork
Smithsonian Institution, National Museum of American History,
   Division of Medical Sciences (1928.0235.274)

See cat. 61

54   **DROMGOOLES BITTERS,** 1939
USA, Indiana, Lawrenceberg
Printed paper
Smithsonian Institution, National Museum of American History,
   Division of Medical Sciences (M 10,426)

See cat. 61

55   **STELLA VITAE WOMAN'S RELIEF,** early 20th century
USA, Tennessee, Chattanooga
Printed paper on glass; cork
Smithsonian Institution, National Museum of American History,
   Division of Medical Sciences (M 9912)

See cat. 61

56   **IMPERIAL GRANUM UNSWEETENED WHEAT FOOD,**
early 20th century
USA, Connecticut, New Haven
Printed paper on tin
Smithsonian Institution, National Museum of American History,
   Division of Medical Sciences (310901)

See cat. 61

57   **DR. JOHN HOOPER'S FEMALE PILLS,** patented 1744
USA
Printed paper on wood; pills
Smithsonian Institution, National Museum of American History,
   Division of Medical Sciences (1984.0782.089)

See cat. 61

58   **PINEOLEUM CHEMICAL IRON TABLETS,** early
20th century
USA
Printed paper on tin; pills
Smithsonian Institution, National Museum of American History,
   Division of Medical Sciences (M-10257)

See cat. 61

59   **MUNYON'S FEMALE CURE,** late 19th century
USA
Printed paper on glass; tin
Smithsonian Institution, National Museum of American History,
   Division of Medical Sciences (815 06 V05)

See cat. 61

60 ANTIKAMNIA TABLETS, early 20th century
England, London
Ink on tin
Smithsonian Institution, National Museum of American History,
   Division of Medical Sciences (1924.0351.109)

See cat. 61

61 DE ANGELIS GRANULAR MAGNESIUM CITRATE, c. 1904
USA, Rhode Island, Providence
Printed paper on glass
Smithsonian Institution, National Museum of American History,
   Division of Medical Sciences (1984.0782.005)

Women always have taken special measures to influence not only their physical and emotional condition during pregnancy, but also their chances for delivering a healthy baby. In the 19th century, gynecological and obstetrical concerns provided an enormous market for patent medicine makers. Since medical theory at the time linked the nervous and reproductive systems, women were thought to be governed by their generative organs and susceptible especially to hysteria and fatigue. Such conditions were thought to increase dramatically during periods of pregnancy and confinement.

The patent medicines here are but a small sampling of the extensive array of "home remedies" developed under the rubric of "ladies' disorders." Included are tonics and other concoctions for "nervousness," "run-down conditions," "hemorrhages of the womb," "backaches," "dragging of the hips," "uterine spasms," and "pure extracts for expectant mothers…and invalids." Although the scientific value of these medicinals is questionable, they probably provided some measure of relief, since their relatively high alcohol content was especially soothing. Patent medicines also spared pregnant women the embarrassment of sharing their ailments directly with a physician, for treatments could be acquired easily from peddlers and local pharmacists.

62 (a-e) EFFIGY FIGURINES, second half of 14th century to beginning of 16th century
Kingdom of Sukothai, Sawankhalok (now Thailand)
Clay fired with celadon glaze
The Nathan Aronson Collection

Fertility is only one aspect of the intent to bear a child, for conception means little unless it is followed by a healthy delivery for both mother and infant. Some scholars speculate that in the ancient Kingdom of Sukothai, pregnant women used effigy figurines to effect a magical transfer of the dangers of childbirth onto inanimate objects. To accomplish such a transfer, women are thought to have decapitated the figures just before the onset of labor. Perhaps this explains why the neck areas of the figurines appear to have been broken off and subsequently repaired or replaced entirely. Among the many small celedon effigies of diverse human and animal forms that have been found at sites in northern Thailand, only the female figurines show evidence of decapitation.

TRAVAIL

Uncertainty circles the expectant mother and child.
Hope and fear accompany the nine-month wait…

Will we lull the child to sleep with song,
or mourn beside an empty cradle?

Will the child be born an heir, a keeper of the family name?

Will the mother's body be strong enough for both of them?
Will she be able to endure the pain?

Will the child be graced with eyes that see;
with strong and sturdy limbs?

Will this waiting ever be over?

The physical and social changes surrounding pregnancy and birth are filled with risks and uncertainties. People respond to these conditions in different ways. Some use humor—poking fun, for example, at the nervousness of expectant fathers—to ease the tension caused by the unpredictable consequences of giving birth. Others isolate pregnant women based on the belief that the blood shed at birth might endanger the entire community. Still others attempt to combat potential complications during labor by using special tools. These are but a few of the techniques and ritual practices that have been created to help mother, baby, and those around them surmount the fear associated with birth, one of life's most important transitions.

63   **WOMAN GIVING BIRTH,** 18th century A.D.
India, Tamilnadu
Wood
Philadelphia Museum of Art (63-36-2)

Nude but for her ornaments, feet planted firmly apart, this delivering mother is like the immovable earth. Attendant women support her on either side. Dressed in flounced saris, they carry flasks most likely containing oil to massage the mother's body. Crouching below is the figure of a midwife, catching the newborn as it drops from its mother's womb. The small size of the midwife in relation to the other figures nearby is explained by the fact that traditional Indian midwives come from the caste of Barbers,

whose status is relatively low. Although the faces of the mother and attendants are serene, the difficulty of childbirth is illustrated by their intertwined supporting arms.

This carving once adorned a *ratha,* or temple chariot. Multitiered and covered by figural carvings, these carts represent the royal chariot of the deity. On special festival days in south India, the bronze sculpture in which the deity resides is placed on the flat top of the cart beneath an elaborate, cloth-covered pavilion, and paraded about town. Although we do not know the original location of this carving, such depictions of birth, rare in the Indian context, often are found interspersed with erotic scenes on the chariot.

64 (a,b)   **PLACENTA BURIAL JARS,** 15th century
Korea
White porcelain
The Horim Museum, Seoul

See cat. 65

65 (a-c)   **PLACENTA BURIAL JARS AND PLATE,** 1627
Korea, Kyonggi Province, Koyang County
Porcelain
The National Museum of Korea, Seoul

Rituals for disposing of the placenta are as complex as rituals for the birth event itself. In many cultures the placenta represents good fortune; often it is buried in the earth so that those who step on or near the burial spot may be graced with fertility. Among others, however, the placenta is a powerful symbol of birth pollution whose potential dangers must be disposed of quickly.

Among the royalty and nobility of Korea, special areas for placenta burial were designated in the royal cemeteries. The placenta was placed in the smaller jar, which in turn was put in the larger container. Although this custom was widespread, only two sets of porcelain containers like these have been found in all Korea. The 17th-century plate from this set bears an inscription stating that the placenta belonged to the illegitimate Prince Inhung, a son of the king and one of his many concubines.

Modern scholars do not know exactly how royal Korean placenta burial took place, and for how many years it was practiced. Men almost certainly removed the containers to the mountain cemetery. Enclosing the placenta in double jars underscored the reverence and value placed on the owner of the contents. Such positive associations also may be discerned from the jar's knobs, which resemble lotus pods and symbolized creative power and purity amid adverse surroundings.

66, 67   LANTERNS, late 19th century
Korea
Painted and lacquered paper; metal holder for wax candle
Peabody Museum of Salem

Before electricity, these lanterns may have illuminated a darkened chamber in which a Korean woman was giving birth. Probably they were held by female relatives who, along with the midwife, assisted during the delivery. Although this type of lantern was used most commonly by night watchmen, the presence of a bat—a symbol associated with furnishings in the women's quarters—suggests that the examples here were created for a birth setting. The bat, which connotes blessings and happiness, together with the lantern's written characters, which mean "long life," promote an auspicious future for the woman in labor.

68, 69   SCULPTURES OF BIRTH SCENES, 19th century
Indonesia, Bali
Polychrome-wood
Collections of the Museum für Völkerkunde, Staatliche Museen Preussischer Kulturbesitz, Berlin (IC 45,084; IC 45,085)

The risks and uncertainties associated with labor and childbirth are illustrated in this wood sculpture. In traditional Balinese culture, expectant mothers undergo labor on a cot-like, bamboo bed. Just before delivery, they move onto a floor-mat that includes a rolled pillow or brick on which they may rest their legs. Often this mat is placed against a support pillar or near a doorpost so that the laboring woman may bear down by bracing herself against a hard surface with her feet or her back. A *manale*, or midwife, usually is called in to assist.

Childbirth is regarded as a time when the newborn is especially vulnerable physically, and the mother experiences tremendous emotional stress. In one scene, the baby is just emerging from the birth canal, uttering the first cry. Wrapped around the upper part of the mother's still-protruding belly is a binder that periodically has been tightened to assist her with pushing. To her right is an older child, presumably about one year, for his hair has been cut in the traditional single lock atop an otherwise fully-shaven head. Aware that he is about to be weaned from his mother's breast to accomodate a newborn sibling, the older child grasps his mother's nipple. Although a snake-wrapped medicine-man sits to the left, offering a potion-filled vessel to the parturient, the mother cannot be distracted from the demon nearby. This creature, a *leyak*, is thought to frequent birthing rooms, waiting for the opportunity to devour a baby as soon as the child is fully born.

In the other scene, the mother-to-be is in an advanced stage of labor. To ease the process, her husband massages her stomach. Although the expectant woman devotes her full energy to the impending birth, her husband experiences an additional concern. To his left, a male assistant wrestles to contain a leyak, but it is not certain whether the demon will be kept away successfully once the baby emerges.

70   *ACCOUCHMENT* BOWL AND PLATTER, 16th century
Italy, Urbino
Tin-glazed earthenware
Collections of the Wellcome Museum for the History of Medicine, The Science Museum, London (A 642932)

This ornate bowl with matching platter was part of a set of vessels that the *accoucher,* or midwife, used in the birthing room during labor and delivery. The complete set would have included plates, pitchers, and a broth bowl from which the laboring woman could take nourishment.

Scenes of childbirth and infancy dominated the decoration of these vessels, and often they provide rich information about period styles and customs. The central medallion on the upper side of this vessel, for example, depicts a mother with her tightly swaddled newborn. Inside the bowl, two women—presumably assistants or relatives—are shown washing the baby, while another brings broth to the bed-ridden parturient.

71   VESSEL WITH BIRTHING SCENE, 200-700 A.D.
Pre-Columbian, Moche people
Slip-painted ceramic
Collections of the Museum für Völkerkunde, Staatliche Museen Preussischer Kulturbesitz, Berlin (VA 47912)

How much have birthing practices changed? Surprisingly little, if we may judge from the delivery scene on this ancient South American pot. It was made by the Moche, inhabitants until the 8th century of Peru's northern coastal plain.

The Moche had no written language, but they left a vivid record of their culture through modeled and engraved sculptures depicting various activities of everyday life. The carefully rendered, highly personalized vessel in the exhibition is especially important because intimate, ethnographic descriptions of childbirth are rare even in illustrations produced today.

There is no question but that the mother-to-be is the most important figure in this scene. She is the largest of the participants, and compositionally is the one who occupies the central place. Squatting on a low-lying birthing stool, she appears to bear down, thrusting the weight of her body backwards by arching her head and back, and pushing the newborn down from her bulbous belly into the birth canal. Although she uses her feet to anchor herself, the position she needs to assume under the strain of labor is helped along by an assistant, who acts as a brace. By grasping the expectant mother from behind, she enables her to push yet harder. The laboring woman's posture is awkward but not undignified, for the artist took care to drape those parts of her body that would not need to be exposed during the delivery.

Below, seated between the mother's legs, is the midwife, who prepares to catch the baby as it emerges. The lowly status of this practitioner is suggested by her small size and simple garb and features in relation to the other figures nearby.

72, 73 PARTURITION CHAIRS, 1901-1930
Egypt, El Lahem, Fayum
Painted pine
Collections of the Wellcome Museum for the History of Medicine,
  The Science Museum, London (A 602122, A 60841)

Squatting is among the most ancient and widely used birthing positions.
In some societies, women squat suspended by ropes or straps that allow
gravity to assist in the delivery. Birthing stools, like these examples from
Egypt, provided more rigid support for the mother-to-be. Sitting on the
chair and supported by its frame, a delivering woman could labor to push
out the baby. A midwife would crouch in front of the chair, catching the
infant through the opening in the seat as it was born. Birthing stools still
are used in many world cultures. In America, squatting positions often are
recommended to ease the labor process, and specially constructed birthing
chairs sometimes are used in both home and hospital deliveries.

74(a-d) SHINTO CHARMS FOR EASY CHILDBIRTH,
early 20th century
Japan, Chikuzen Province, Island of Kyushu; Nagoya; Kyoto
Paper and ink
Smithsonian Institution, National Museum of Natural History,
  Department of Anthropology (310916, 311140, 310925, 311128)

Japanese worshippers receive *mamori*, or charms, like these at local temples or on pilgrimages. Many include only the name of the temple, serve for
general spiritual protection (or just as souvenirs), and are placed at home
on *kamidana*, or spirit shelves mounted high on the wall in the front room.
Others are worn as amulets.

These examples are from Shinto temples, whose gods often are asked for
help in worldly concerns, including childbirth. Two of the charms invoke
Empress Jingo Kogo, said to have revenged her husband's death in a battle
with Korea, and then to have subjugated Korea while pregnant. Legend
tells that she delayed birth by wrapping a tight abdominal binder around
her, providing an origin for a practice that continues to serve as a way of
keeping the baby from moving around too much and from becoming too
large and thus causing a difficult birth, and keeping the mother's abdomen
warm. Sometimes these charms are worn inside the binders.

75 EMA FOR EASY CHILDBIRTH, 1870
Japan
Ink on wood
Peabody Museum of Salem (E18,479)

An *ema* is another kind of religious request for aid. Supplicants who want
favors from particular gods hang plaques like this one next to the altars of
appropriate shrines. The plaques are requests for favors, usually with the
promise of doing something in return for the shrine. Unlike the paper
charms (cat. 74 a-d), which temples reproduce in standardized forms, an
ema is individualized.

The large characters in the center of this plaque form the name of the
shrine—in this case a small one whose name implies a specialty in helping
with problems of childbirth. The other information includes the name of
the village and its location, and the name of the father of the family making
the request. Probably he was asking for the birth of a son. His success is
shown on the far left, where the characters indicate the delivery of a child
in 1870 on the seventh day of the eleventh lunar month.

76 *HIJĀB* AMULET, early 20th century
Palestine
Palestinian people
Silver; Ottoman Turkish coins
International Folk Art Foundation Collections, Museum of International
  Folk Art, a unit of the Museum of New Mexico, Santa Fe (FA.72.25-3J)

77 *KETĀB* AMULET, early 20th century
Morocco or Algeria
Silver; semi-precious stone
The Museum of International Folk Art, a unit of the Museum of
  New Mexico, Santa Fe (3147)

78 *KHARAZEH ZARQA*, 20th century
Syria or Palestine
Glass
The Museum of International Folk Art, a unit of the Museum of
  New Mexico, Santa Fe (3983)

Adornment and presenting one's wealth and status are among the functions of Near Eastern jewelry like this. But the fanciful shapes and colors
of these necklaces have an additional, and perhaps even more important,
purpose. They are thought to protect people from the omnipresent dangers
of the Evil Eye, which in many eastern Mediterranean cultures is believed
to be responsible for many extreme dangers.

The Palestinian *hijāb*, for example, would have been considered especially
helpful during the stress of labor and delivery, when the risk to both
mother and child is greatest. *Hijāb* means "that which protects," and the
very shape of this piece adds to its efficacy, for the triangle is based on an
odd number. Three, five, seven, nine, and eleven are regarded as being
especially potent sources of protection. The symbolic power of this amulet
further is enhanced by the raised silver nodules that form a smaller inner
triangle, and by the short chains to which Ottoman Turkish coins are
attached. These five pendants are a paradigmatic *khamsa*, or "sign of the
hand," which also is a protective symbol.

North African *ketāb*, meaning "something written," often are inscribed with special prayers or blessings. In the center of the ketāb in the exhibit is a khamsa, which would have protected the wearer against danger or death. During childbirth, a woman might have sought to safeguard her own welfare with a charm like this. After delivery, however, she would have seen to it that a smaller version of the pendant was placed on her newborn as well.

Babies are considered to be especially vulnerable to the Evil Eye. The glass representation of an eye, called "the blue bead," is regarded as a powerful counter-force to the dangerous effects of the Eye. Small beads often are pinned or sewn into the blanket wraps or swaddling clothes of newborns, since the "blue bead" is thought to be an especially strong protector of infants.

79 SANKA TANGAN ZUSHIKI (ILLUSTRATED MANUAL ON USE OF INSTRUMENTS IN OBSTETRICS), 1837

Gihaku, Sansetsu, or Yoshihiro Mizuhara, author (1782-1864)
Japan, Tokyo
Woodblock-printed rice paper, bound with thread and double-folded
Collection of Dr. Gordon Mestler

See cat. 83

80 SANIKU ZENSHO (COMPLETE INSTRUCTIONS ON OBSTETRICS), 1850

Gihaku, Sansetsu, or Yoshihiro Mizuhara, author (1782-1864)
Japan, Kyoto
Woodblock-printed rice paper, bound with thread and double-folded
Collection of Dr. Gordon Mestler

See cat. 83

81 SAN-RON YOKU (CONTINUATION AND EXPLANATION OF OBSTETRICS), 1775

Genteki Kagawa, author (1739-1779)
Japan
Woodblock-printed rice paper, bound with thread and double-folded
Collection of Dr. Gordon Mestler

See cat. 83

82 SANKA SHINRON (NEW TREATISE ON OBSTETRICS), 1820

Ryutei or Tatsusada Tatsuno, author
Japan, Tokyo
Woodblock-printed rice paper, bound with thread and double-folded
Collection of Dr. Gordon Mestler

See cat. 83

83 TASSEI ZUSETSU (PICTURES EXPLAINING THE GIVING OF BIRTH), 1858

Naoyoshi or Taizo Kondo, author (1814-1861)
Japan
Woodblock-printed rice paper, bound with thread and double-folded
Collection of Dr. Gordon Mestler

The first Japanese obstetrical books were published in the 16th century, but an outpouring of manuals like these began only in the mid-1700s, as physicians began to move in on a field previously dominated by midwives. These books were influenced at first by Chinese works. Later they were based on European examples. Genteki Kagawa, who came from a long family line of obstetricians famous for their techniques in forced deliveries, illustrated the treatment of difficult births in book number 81. The plate displayed in the exhibition shows the correct positioning of the fetus in a cut-away view of the abdomen. Despite the stylistic delicacy of such woodcuts, the Kagawas promoted the use during difficult labors of iron hooks to pull the fetus piecemeal from the womb, a practice intended to save the life of the mother.

The leg and foot presentation in cat. 82 is part of a series by Tatsuno illustrating unusual delivery positions. Showing doctors how to invert the fetus in order to avoid such difficult breech positions is explained in the manual by Kondo.

Although these texts were prepared by male obstetricians based partly on theories and methods developed by Westerners, the emphasis in Japanese practice was on the woman. The value placed on the lives of women, especially during reproductive age, is a hallmark of medical illustrations like these, which include many techniques designed to assist or save the mother at the expense of the child.

84 LA COMMARE O RICCOGLITRICE (THE MIDWIFE WHO CATCHES THE NEWBORN), 1601
Girolamo Mercurio, author
Italy, Venice
Woodcut on vellum
The National Library of Medicine, Bethesda, Maryland

Girolamo Mercurio prepared this Roman-dialect volume expressly for Italian midwives. It is divided into three parts: the first deals with natural labor and care of the mother and child, the second with abnormal presentations and difficult births, and the third with diseases complicating pregnancy and affecting the newborn. Mercurio began his career as a Dominican monk. After leaving the priesthood, he taught many things that placed him well ahead of his time, the most dramatic being his advocacy of performing the Caesarean section on a living patient. Although he recommended the sitting position for normal deliveries, he espoused prone posture for the physically exhausted or overweight woman.

This woodcut illustration shows the "hanging legs" position for delivery in cases of a contracted pelvis. The parturient lies on a huge canopied bed, her head supported by one large pillow and her buttocks raised higher by three more. Her legs thus are separated widely, and a midwife kneels between them. This position came to be known as the "Walcher position" after G.A. Walcher proposed it in 1899 as something entirely new. In fact, however, it was described first during the 12th century by an Arab physician.

Mercurio's work was the first Italian book on obstetrics. Eventually it became one of the most famous and popular medical volumes of the Renaissance, being republished and used into the 18th century.

85 NEU ERÖFFNETE HEB-AMMEN-SCHUL (A NEWLY OPENED SCHOOL FOR MIDWIVES), 1679 ·
Christoph Volter, author
Germany, Stuttgart
Woodcut on vellum
The National Library of Medicine, Bethesda, Maryland

This illustration from a textbook for midwives is entitled "How a dead fetus should be delivered, with skill, to preserve the life of the mother." Commensurate with the emergency at hand, the unused birthing chair has been abandoned, and the swaddling clothes basket forgotten. In their place is a male physician, who bends his knees in seeming exertion at the foot of the patient's bed. The presence nearby of a praying priest indicates that the woman's life is in danger.

Given the medical orientation of this book—which offered relatively plausible representations of surgical interventions—and the cutting tools placed on the low table to the left of the doctor, it is likely that the physician is attempting a surgical extraction of the dead fetus. In the 17th century, the presence of a male doctor or of any men during delivery usually was allowed by midwives only when they believed they could do no more. Just how much valuable assistance doctors actually could offer in such dangerous situations, however, is questionable. Here, for example, the physician probably intends to pull the fetus piecemeal from the womb with iron hooks, since he is working not on the patient's abdomen, but rather between her legs. The notion that women were inferior subjects permeated the Western medical establishment at the time this volume was written. This attitude fostered indifference and often an acceptance of the hazards of pregnancy and childbirth regarding miscarriage, hemorrhage, infection, and even death as the price of sexual activity.

86 LES OEUVRES DE M. AMBROISE PARÉ (THE WORKS OF M. ABROISE PARÉ), 1575
Ambroise Pare, author
France, Paris
Woodcut on vellum
The National Library of Medicine, Bethesda, Maryland

This illustration depicts a story told by Mirandula about Dorothie, an Italian woman who supposedly delivered twenty children in only two separate births. An accompanying inscription indicates that Dorothie was so big during her pregnancy that "she was forced to bear up her belly, which lay upon her knees, with a large scarf tied about her neck...." Such descriptions satisfied an appetite for the sensational. Even the most serious 16th-century medical and natural history books contained sections on monsters, deformities, or fantastic abnormalities.

Dorothie's story is recounted in Ambroise Pare's collected works, in a section entitled "Of Monsters and Prodigies." Although this chapter is filled with information about bizarre and unreal creatures, Pare was regarded as a serious physician. As one of the founders of modern obstetrics, he is credited with putting into practice the "podalic technique" (turning the fetus by the feet *in utero*) and with demonstrating how to induce labor in the case of a uterine hemorrhage. Yet Pare's contributions were not restricted to technical matters alone, for as a famous, well-respected surgeon, he gave the field of obstetrics a new level of professional credibility and dignity.

87 *EIN SCHÖN LUSTIG TROSTBÜCHLE VON DEM EMPFENGKNUSSEN UND GEBURTEN DER MENSCHEN (A VERY CAREFUL BOOKLET OF ENCOURAGEMENT CONCERNING THE CONCEPTION AND BIRTH OF MANKIND),* 1554
Jakob Rueff, author
Zurich
Woodcut
The National Library of Medicine, Bethesda, Maryland

In this lying-in chamber, the mother-to-be sits on a birthing chair, looking distressed. The midwife is positioned at her feet and is assisted by two women, one of whom appears to be smiling and offering encouragement, while the other provides support from the rear. On the table nearby are scissors for cutting the umbilical cord and twine for tying it.

This volume, written in German especially for midwives, became the standard text for instruction and examination of midwives in Zurich. It was the first practical manual of its kind since classical antiquity, and it was accepted widely as an authoritative guide. Yet despite its popularity, few if any small-town or country midwives received formal instruction or sound medical information—often to the mother's detriment.

88 *DER SWANGERN FRAUWEN UND HEBAMMEN ROSENGARTEN (THE ROSE GARDEN OF PREGNANT WOMEN AND MIDWIVES),* 1513
Eucharius Roeslin, author
France, Strasbourg
Woodcut
The National Library of Medicine, Bethesda, Maryland

This is the first printed work written especially for midwives. Its text was little more than a compilation of Greek and Roman works, but it was an important codification of "facts" about childbirth since it pulled together obstetrical information from many different sources. It also was written in German rather than Latin, which made the text more accessible to the local midwife community. Its author, Eucharius Roeslin, was the town physician of Frankfurt, a city that by 1491 was regulating the practice of midwifery.

This woodcut is the first known illustration of the lying-in chamber. Looking almost doleful, an expectant mother is attended by two women, one of whom supports her under the arms. The other, the midwife, extends her hands and arms beneath the parturient's ample dress, probably examining her. The mother-to-be sits on the birthing chair, or birth stool, a labor device mentioned in the Old Testament. The only obstetric tools in this spare scene are those in the midwife's bag or purse hanging from her belt.

89 **OUR LADY OF SORROWS** *RETABLO,* early 19th century
Jose Rafael Aragon, artist
USA, northern New Mexico,
Spanish Colonial community
Gesso and paint on pine panel
The Museum of International Folk Art, a unit of the Museum of
    New Mexico, Santa Fe (A.8.59-23)

See cat. 90

90 **OUR LADY OF THE SLEEVES** *RETABLO,* early 19th century
Attributed to Pedro Antonio Fresquis (The Truchas Master)
USA, northern New Mexico,
Spanish Colonial community
Gesso and tempera on pine panel
The Museum of International Folk Art, a unit of the Museum of
    New Mexico, Santa Fe (L.5.85-30)

Women preparing for childbirth on the frontier confronted dangers both real and perceived. The remote villages and outposts in which they lived offered few, if any, of the medical resources available to women in urban areas. Often their feelings of fear and isolation were compounded by the absence of other female family members nearby, who would have been on hand under more normal circumstances to offer personal support and to assist with labor and delivery. Frontier diaries and letters from the 19th century are filled with poignant descriptions of the longing these women had during childbirth to be near their mothers or sisters.

Under such conditions, New Mexico's Spanish Colonial population often turned to the saints with special prayers for guidance and protection. Votive paintings like this *retablo,* created by folk artists, were used for prayer services in small family chapels. This depiction of Mary—the most venerated of saints in the Roman Catholic pantheon—emphasizes her compassion for the sufferings of her son. In her dual role as mother and sufferer, Mary was a primary source of supplication not only for women in confinement, but also for prospective fathers as they faced the uncertainties and potential complications of childbirth in a new environment.

91 (a,b) **FEMALE TWIN FIGURES,** early 20th century
Africa, Nigeria
Yoruba people of Ilorin or Ogbomosho
Wood, indigo, cowries, beads, red powder
Lent by Pace Primitive, New York (7868)

See cat. 92

92 (a, b) **IMAGE OF TWINS, *ERE IBEJI*,** early 20th century
Africa, Nigeria
Yoruba people of Oshogbo
Wood, indigo, beads, red powder
Lent by Robert V. Berg (7810)

The birth of twins among the Yoruba of southeast Nigeria usually is a joyous occasion. At times, however, it also is cause for concern, for twins are regarded as spiritual beings who can bring their parents bad luck as well as good fortune. Twins at birth often are more frail than single infants. They also have a higher mortality rate. Among the Yoruba, if one twin dies, the mother commissions the carving of a single wooden figure called *ere ibeji,* or "image of twins." The figure bears the same sex and lineage face-marks as the dead child. Two figures are carved if both twins die. These figures then are cared for as the real infants would have been treated had they lived, with the hope that they will bring good fortune to their parents.

The faces of these male and female figures have been worn almost smooth by frequent applications of the twins' favorite foods, beans and palm oil, followed by vigorous washing. Their bodies have been smeared with red cosmetic powder mixed with oil, and their hair has been dyed with indigo to a beautiful blue-black. At night their mother may have wrapped them tenderly in small blankets and put them to bed in the corner of her own room, just as she would have with her living children.

The following instruments, detailed in cat. 118, are from the Smithsonian Institution's National Museum of American History, Division of Medical Sciences:

93 **SMELLIE'S CRANIOTOMY SCISSORS,** c. 1900
USA, New York
Steel (316358.73)

94 **IMPROVED SMELLIE'S CRANIOTOMY SCISSORS,** c. 1900
German, based on French design
Steel (316358.74)

95 **ELLIOT FORCEPS,** c. 1880
USA
Steel blade

96 **HALES SHORT FORCEPS,** c. 1880
USA
Steel with hard-rubber handle coverings (316358.9)

97 **NEVILLE FORCEPS,** c. 1896
Ireland, Dublin
Steel (316358.82)

98 **NEVILLE FORCEPS,** c. 1896
Ireland, Dublin
Steel (316358.54)

99 **HODGE FORCEPS,** c. 1850-1875
German
Steel (316358.13)

100 **KJELLAND FORCEPS,** 1915
Norway
Steel (316358.39)

101 **NAEGELE FORCEPS,** c. 1896
German
Steel (316358.36)

102 **COLLINS FORCEPS,** 1830
Ireland, Dublin
Steel blades with rosewood handles (316358.07)

103 **McLANE'S FORCEPS,** c. 1920
USA, New York
Steel blades with hard-rubber handles (316358.25)

104 **PETZALOZZI FORCEPS,** 1915
Italy, Rome
Steel (315358.35)

105 **DU THOLEN FORCEPS,** 1940
Belgium
Steel (316358.33)

106 **OBSTETRICAL HOOK,** 19th century
USA
Steel (1977 0808 60)

107 **BLUNT HOOK,** c. 1870-1890
USA
Steel and wood (316358.66)

108 **OBSTETRICAL SCALE,** early 20th century
USA
Steel with spring balance (M 7916)

109 **OBSTETRICAL SCALE,** early 20th century
USA
Steel with spring balance (302606.243)

110 **VAGINAL SPECULUM,** 19th century
USA
Steel (M 4323)

111 **VAGINAL SPECULUM,** 19th century
USA
Steel (RSN 83521 T41)

112 **AUVARD'S VAGINAL SPECULUM,** late 19th century
Europe
Steel (1977 0808.05)

113 **SPECULUM DIALATOR,** 19th century
USA
Wood and metal (M 7415)

114 **NOEGGERATH'S UTERINE ELEVATOR,** 19th century
USA
Steel with wooden handle (302606.126)

115 **UTERINE ELEVATOR,** 19th century
USA
Steel with wooden handle (302606.407)

116 **NOTT'S UTERINE DIALATOR,** 19th century
USA
Steel (1977 0808 75)

117 **PLACENTA SPIRAL CURETTE,** 19th century
Europe
Steel (1977 0808 13)

118 **BAKER'S VAGIOMETER,** 19th century
USA
Steel with spring balance (M 14 116)

Western obstetrical instruments look forbidding. Yet often they have been helpful either in easing the delivery process or resolving complications during labor.

Each of these items has a complicated history that cannot be covered here in depth. Briefly, however, their purposes are as follows:

Craniotomy scissors were used when a baby's head became lodged in the birth canal, thereby preventing even the insertion of forceps. In difficult cases like this, the child was sacrificed in order to save the mother.

Forceps in different configurations have been used since ancient times to remove an infant from the birth canal during difficult labors. Their looped blades were intended to conform to the structure of the baby's head so as to avoid crushing or compressing it.

Hooks also were employed in the ancient world. Not until the 19th century, however, were they used to assist in breech deliveries or with the extraction of an infant without regard to its mutilation. Thus hooks were used mainly as a measure to save the mother's life at the expense of the child.

Obstetrical scales were created to weigh newborns and infants. Their simple spring balances made them easy to carry from place to place in hospitals and during home visits.

The placenta spiral curette was invented to remove any afterbirth that remained in the uterus following delivery. It could be rotated through the cervical os and then turned to entrap and extract the placental material.

Speculae, diagnostic tools used to examine the cervix and vaginal walls, go back thousands of years but came into widespread use only during the 19th century, when gynecology emerged as a medical speciality.

Uterine elevators were used most often to alter the position of the uterus if it was retroflexed.

Uterine dialators enabled medicaments to be introduced into the uterus. Dialators were used to alleviate dysmenorrhea, to induce abortion, and to provide general access to the uterus.

Vagiometers measured the diameter of the birth canal.

WELCOMINGS

How did they greet your arrival?

Did they tell you that you would till the fields? Hunt for food?
  Mind the store?

Did they offer you special gifts if you slept? If you ate well?
  If you smiled?

Did they assure you that you had inherited your father's eyes? Your
  grandmother's hands? The musical talents of a distant relative?

Did they say that goblins would take you if you cried through
  the night?

Did they promise you success if you sought the wisdom of your
  ancestors? The patience of the saints? The bravery of your village
  leader?

What did you learn as they rocked you to sleep?

Lullabies, blessings, and proverbs welcome the newborn into
a community and a way of life. Often the values, hopes, and
dreams that caretakers share with the infant shape future expectations and behavior. The sound stations in the exhibition
contain some of the many messages that different cultural
groups impart to their children.

LIFELINES

How did they clothe you?

> *In a cap that protected your eyes from the sun and your soul*
> *from evil spirits?*
> *In hand-sewn shoes adorned with colorful beads?*
> *In wraps of sheepskin or linen?*

How did they amuse you?
> *With the jingling of bells on a rattle?*
> *With playthings of shells, gourds, or palm leaves?*
> *With a whistle whose sound you could mimic?*

How did they cradle you?
> *In a sling that rested on your father's back?*
> *In a shawl that wrapped you close to your mother's side?*
> *In a bed made to shield you from outside worlds?*

Protecting and nurturing the newborn are universal concerns. Yet every culture creates its own means of providing for the child. In some places, for example, an infant nearly always is carried— to the fields, to the market, to the stream. Elsewhere, the newborn is placed in a bed separate from the caretaker's activities. These different ways of handling infants affect the emotional character of relationships between children and those who look after them. At the same time, newborns begin to learn about the behavior and expectations of others around them.

All of the objects ahead pertain to the nurturing of infants. At first glance, they may seem familiar. But a closer look at each illustrates the many social, economic, and environmental influences that shape children in different world cultures.

HOLDERS AND CARRIERS

People reveal some of the most unguarded information about themselves and their cultures in the way they hold and carry their babies. Infants have little choice about where they are placed, what kind of closeness their caretaker establishes with them, and how their demanding survival needs for food, protection, and stimulation are met. Babies uncomfortable in their carriers may cry, but people interpret and answer that cry in different ways depending on diverse cultural and personal attitudes.

Many people around the world wrap, tie, or seat babies on their backs. They undertake daily chores knowing that the child is secure, safe, and usually easily fed. The everyday movement of a mother or grandmother to and from the market or field becomes part of the child's daily rhythm. Scheduled feedings, naps, playtime, and bedtime seldom are known to children raised this way.

Might babies, even in their first year of life, absorb ethnic and personal identities from the way they are held, carried, or rocked? Perhaps. Many of the infant holders on exhibit are made of materials readily obtained from nature, trade, or commerce. Thus from the carrier itself children might learn the feel, sight, and smell of natural or handcrafted items in the environment around them. Most likely, too, it is within their carrier or wrap that babies grow accustomed to the climate of their homeland.

The idea of movement appears closely linked with entertaining or soothing babies no matter where the culture. This, we surmise, is why many carriers like cradles and chairs, which keep the child physically separate from a caretaker, often are designed to rock, shake, swing, sway, or bounce.

Some carriers are meant exclusively for babies. Others, such as shawls, serve more than one purpose. The expectations of infants surrounded by material objects created for their use alone thus may be different from the expectations of babies for whom little is earmarked.

Many of the carriers you see here are meant to make babies highly visible. Yet others shield and perhaps even hide the infant. How differently will the small child who is admired and displayed feel towards people than the young one who is sheltered? And how do babies who have been stimulated by a full view of events around them evaluate the world, in contrast to infants whose early glimpses of activities and color are snatched from the folds of a cloth or the top of a crib?

These carriers only hint at the range of artistry and imagination babies may absorb from their material surroundings. Whether plain and sturdy, or highly embellished, infants take from these items their first lessons in design, creativity, and technology. And perhaps most important, it is the interaction not only between babies and their caretakers, but also between babies and the objects of child-rearing, that shapes the first formative social relationships human beings have with each other.

119 CRADLEBOARD, c. 1876

USA, Oklahoma, near Fort Still
Kiowa people
Glass-beaded cotton canvas; pigment-covered skin; stitched tassels; calico
  lining; thread; cradle decorated with metal bells and affixed to pierced
  wooden and painted frame; skin ties throughout
Smithsonian Institution, National Museum of Natural History,
  Department of Anthropology (270042)

For the naming of an infant—and other ceremonial events that brought the
Kiowa together—families presented babies in finely decorated cradleboards
like this one. Less ornamental carriers served everyday use, especially
during the hot Oklahoma summers. Babies were placed in cradleboards
until they could walk. Within these holders, they were sheltered from
many dangers—fire, dogs, bad weather, and falls from horses.

The quality of a cradleboard illustrated not only the wealth and good
standing of the family who owned it, but often the status of an infant as
favored child or future leader. At times such roles were determined even
before birth, and the chosen boy or girl was expected accordingly to show
exemplary behavior. The child in return received many gifts throughout
life, and an elaborate cradleboard usually was among the first.

Several kinswomen of the newborn, glad to help welcome a special member of the family, would undertake the many hours of beadwork required
to make this kind of heirloom. The cradleboard combined beaded symbols
of a family's past feats and honors, together with the hope of proud continuity inspired by the birth of an heir.

120 BABY CARRIER, c. 1961

Botswana, Tsau Village
Herero people
Sheepskin with sinew-sewn leather straps
Smithsonian Institution, National Museum of Natural History,
  Department of Anthropology (407686)

Wrapped in the soft-hair side of this carrier, a Herero baby would have
rested against the back of his or her mother or another kinswoman. Infants
grew accustomed to sitting on the rolled head end of the skin, since wearing the head end up was considered to be a bad omen. The father would
provide the skin from sheep in his herd, and the mother would soften and
prepare it for use by her children.

Today, cloth shawls largely have replaced these more traditional leather
carriers. But while the materials have changed, Herero babies still are
carried about from one daily task to another. They accompany their mothers and watch first-hand the milking of animals, the gathering of wild
plants, and the tending of maize and millet crops.

121 KANTHA, late 19th century

India (Bengal), or Bangladesh
Quilted and embroidered cotton; dye
Museum of International Folk Art, a unit of the Museum of New Mexico,
  Santa Fe (A 80.1-699)

Only with humility and reservation would Bengali or Bangladeshi women
have begun to stitch a quilted *kantha* before the birth of a child. But once a
healthy baby arrived, the kantha provided a perfect gift for the new mother.
Births were among the many festive occasions on which women traditionally exchanged finely handcrafted kantha, which means "a patched cloth
made of rags and embroideries."

Babies were placed on kantha like this one in the morning sun after they
had been bathed and their clothes had been changed. Mothers regarded
morning heat as being especially beneficial for strengthening a newborn's
body and bones during the first month of life. Naturally, infants were too
young to understand that the kantha's central lotus pattern symbolized
cosmic order and the fish, fertility and life. With time, however, children
would learn to appreciate the softness of worn cotton against their skin,
and the intricate patterns embroidered from old sari threads. Still later,
they would come to realize how garment shreds could be remade into
powerful symbols of wholeness and renewal.

122 BABY MAT, c. 1928-1935

Samoa
Woven pandanus, fiber, dye
Smithsonian Institution, National Museum of Natural History,
  Department of Anthropology (396022)

Samoans hold special admiration for skilled and inventive weaves. Dex-
trous patterns and borders especially are prized in baby mats, which offer
a mother or grandmother the chance to show their high regard for a newborn. Early in life babies sleep and play on such mats, often at their
mothers' side.

123 **KILIM HAMMOCK CRADLE,** c. 1920
Iran, Fars area
Possibly Lori or Qashqa'i people
Flat-woven wool; dye
The Textile Museum, Washington, D.C. (L1978.5.71)

This flat-woven Iranian cradle could be suspended, enabling a baby to be swung back and forth in the home setting or transported from place to place. Probably the infant who used this hammock was a child of nomadic herders. Such babies were kept with their mothers in the female side of the tent, which also was the center of domestic activity. Women perpetuated cultural traditions not only in cooking and child-rearing, but also by spinning, dyeing, and weaving woolen textiles like this. The rhythmical geometric shapes woven into this cradle were based on designs passed down from generation to generation.

124 **CARRIER CRADLE,** c. 1896
USA, California, Mendocino County, Russian River area
Shanel people, central Pomoan linguistic group
Willow rods decorated with glass beads and shell; tied with twine and string
Smithsonian Institution, National Museum of Natural History,
    Department of Anthropology (203527)

From birth, Pomoan babies would have been propped upright or carried against their mothers' backs in basketry cradles made by their parents. The gathering of grass and fibers and the patient coiling or twining required to make such holders and other, more elaborate baskets, would have been among a child's earliest observations. To delight the infant's eye, flowers and miniature baskets often were hung at the cradle top.

125 **BABY SLING,** c. 1902
Indonesia, Simeulue Island
Woven rattan with attached cord
Smithsonian Institution, National Museum of Natural History,
    Department of Anthropology (216294)

In the tropical climate where they lived, mothers who crafted slings like this one needed scant clothing for themselves or their babies. Smooth rattan was an abundant resource in the tropics, and an ideal material for baby-holders that would minimize the chafing of mother and child. Soft or smooth surfaces designed to protect a baby's delicate skin still are a common feature of infant carriers around the world.

126 **BABY STRAP,** c. 1912
Paraguay, Upper Parana area
Guayaki people
Woven philodendron bast
Smithsonian Institution, National Museum of Natural History,
    Department of Anthropology (276583)

Guayaki babies would have sat securely in the wide end of this strap as it hung from a woman's shoulder. This carrier is woven simply and is less ornamental than many of the pieces in the exhibition. Such simple objects remind us that, in many parts of the world, child care items are made to be tough, sturdy, and durable. Carriers that babies have used over and over again often are too worn for display. The more decorative pieces in the exhibition probably were created for special occasions or privileged groups rather than for practical infant care among the common people.

127 **BABY CARRIER,** 20th century
Africa, Liberia or Guinea
Toma people
Wood, reed, and fiber twining
Harrison Eiteljorg Collection, Indianapolis, Indiana (46208)

As a respite from agricultural tasks, villagers craft baby carriers like this one using resources from the natural environment. Infants spend time strapped close to their mothers' backs in such holders, which offer strong support for children as they are carried about to everyday activities.

128 **CRADLECOVER,** undated
Sweden, Rattvik, Dalarna
Sheepskin and woven wool
International Folk Art Foundation Collections, Museum of International
    Folk Art, a unit of the Museum of New Mexico, Santa Fe (4125)

Snuggled under a fleece blanket inside a wooden cradle, Swedish babies spent long, cold, dark northern winters with their families in the main room of their village houses. Swedes called the weave on cradle covers like this one "rosepath," in reference to flowers whose patterns could be transformed into thick fabrics practical for use in winter coverlets.

129 CARRYING CLOTH, c. 1966
Guatemala, Palin, Escuintla
Maya people, Pocomam central speakers
Cotton, brocaded with cotton thread; dye
Smithsonian Institution, National Museum of Natural History,
    Department of Anthropology (404456)

A Maya mother might have used this cloth to cover her head, carry a
basket of fruit, or cradle her baby. But when entrusted with an infant, she
would have taken special care to wrap the child as a protection against
potential harm.

Even with babies strapped to their backs, Guatemalan weavers were able
to produce spectacular textile designs. Traditional motifs such as birds and
other native animals often were transformed by village artisans into symbols of ethnic identity that could be passed on from generation to generation.

130 BABY TIE, 1971
Nigeria, Ibadan
Yoruba people
Woven cotton and ramie
Lent by Joanne B. Eicher

When Yoruba infants are secured to their mothers' backs, the pile of the
baby tie faces outward. The fabric thus adds to the decorative presence of
both mother and child. Because good appearance is vital to Yoruba pride
and self-worth, high value is placed on all cloth and clothing worn in social
and ceremonial life. Fine carriers like this baby tie enhance the status of
infants, whose self-esteem and sense of well-being will be represented in
textiles they wear throughout their lives.

131 CARRYING CLOTH, c. 1952
Peru, Callejon de Huaylas, Ancash
Quechua people
Striped-cotton flat weave, brocaded and embroidered with cotton; dye
Smithsonian Institution, National Museum of Natural History,
    Department of Anthropology (392282)

What kind of life did the Quechua mother who carried her baby in this cloth
lead? Was she from an Andean village passable only by foot or on horse-
back? Did her family eke out a meager living from an economy based on
llamas, potatoes, and corn? The careful, elegant weave of this fabric suggests that she was raised in a relatively well-to-do home, but fine textiles
like this one are found in even the poorest, most remote regions of Peru.

Quechua babies are tightly swaddled, then wrapped in carriers that shelter
them from the extremes of Andean climate. As they grow, their lungs adapt
to the thin Andean air, which ensures their survival at some of the highest
altitudes in the world.

132 TUMPLINE CRADLE, c. 1977
Colombia, Prosperidad
Ika (Bintuka) people
Striped-cotton-and-wool flat weave; thread
Smithsonian Institution, National Museum of Natural History,
    Department of Anthropology (421991)

Land shortage on the slopes of Colombia's Sierra Nevada forces the Ika to
travel among widely scattered farm plots and grazing lands. Since a larger
kin group means more agricultural outposts, the more times a cradle is
used for new family members, the better. Among the Ika all textiles, including cradles, are produced by males, who interpret weaving as a symbolic
construction of the placenta. This craft thus promotes fertility, which in
turn eases the strain on a people who must subsist in a demanding
environment.

133 CARRYING CLOTH, c. 1945
Bolivia, La Paz area
Aymara people
Woven alpaca yarn; dye
Smithsonian Institution, National Museum of Natural History,
    Department of Anthropology (387650)

In the first months after birth, an Aymara baby would have felt snug in a
swaddling band wrapped tightly against the skin. Carriers like this one
would have formed yet another layer of protection, shielding both the child
and caretaker against high-altitude sun, cold, and rain. Such protective
cloths also would have been understood to be helpful in preventing sudden
fright, which could cause the loss of one's soul and lead to illness or death.

A wide variety of items—not only babies—were carried in these cloths.
Because infants were transported in them during festivals and on visits to
the farm and marketplace, however, such carriers became an important
part of a child's early ethnic awareness. Symbols woven into the fabric
conveyed the mother's membership in a particular political or ethnic unit,
as well as characteristics of the surrounding environment. Thus, through
cloth and clothing, parents imparted to their children reverence for the
spiritual and physical life around them.

134 BOX CRADLE, 20th century
Indonesia, Sulawesi
Wood
Smithsonian Institution, National Museum of Natural History,
    Department of Anthropology (304268)

A Western observer easily might mistake this baby-holder for a sled. Yet it
is a type of cradle found in Indonesia, and it is intended to be swung from
ropes hung from the rafters of a house.

135 CRADLE, 19th century
Finland (now USSR), district of Antrea, southern Karelia
Wood
Smithsonian Institution, National Museum of American History,
    Division of Community Life (617.899)

In Finland, on Europe's Atlantic fringe, rocker cradles like this example replaced simpler splint baskets. This cradle was a cherished personal possession, for such items usually were made by the baby's father and were passed down within the family. A family's good characteristics were thought to be inherited with the cradle. To enhance these positive attributes, magical charms thought to promote hunting, spinning, and other adult skills were placed in the cradle. Objects intended to discourage supernatural causes of crying also were included.

The responsibility of rocking the baby to soothe it or lull it to sleep often fell to a sibling. Lullabies not only alleviated the tedium of this chore, which could go on for hours, but also imparted to the infant information about the family and the natural environment. This traditional lullaby comes from the area in which this cradle was made and used:

> Sleep, sleep, meadowbird,
> Drowse, drowse, wagtail,
> Make your nest in the field,
> Your mansion on the mountain,
> Your palace on the pine branch,
> Your home on the birch branch!

136 THE FULLER CRADLE, 1660-1690
USA, Massachusetts, probably Duxbury
Maple and white pine
The Pilgrim Society, Plymouth, Massachusetts

Cradles were important family heirlooms. This early American example descended through the Fuller family and ultimately probably belonged to the son of a Pilgrim, Dr. Samuel Fuller (1580-1633).

Commensurate with the important role of this cradle in the Fuller household, it was custom built with special features that probably enhanced not only its appearance, but also the lives of the infant and caretakers. The spindles on three sides of the hood, for example, offered the child more light, visibility, and access to sounds coming from nearby activities. For adults, these openings made it possible to carry out everyday tasks and still maintain a watchful eye over the baby's movement and moods.

137 BABY CARRIAGE, early 20th century
USA
Rattan and iron
Smithsonian Institution, National Museum of American History,
    Division of Domestic Life (67.882)

Baby carriages and strollers developed and grew in importance and elaborateness in America after the 1850s. Landscaped parks and suburbs with paved sidewalks made the family promenade a popular activity. Walking the baby thus gave middle-class parents an opportunity to show off the newborn in the company of loving relatives. During this period, the infant faced away from the carriage-pusher and toward its admiring public. By the early 20th century, however, ornate perambulators were replaced by simpler carriages like this one. Here, babies faced their caretakers, emphasizing the bond between the two.

138 CRADLE, 19th century
USA
Tin and wood
Smithsonian Institution, National Museum of American History,
    Division of Domestic Life (389.124)

See cat. 139

139 TRESTLE CRADLE WITH TAMBOUR TOP, early 19th century
USA, possibly New England
Wood with cotton netting
Smithsonian Institution, National Museum of American History,
    Division of Domestic Life (388.082)

Cradles were used in Europe from the Middle Ages until the mid-19th century. In America they were used until the late 1850s. Generally they were placed in the common room of the house, where family members cooked, ate, worked, and often slept. Security and health concerns sustained some of the cradle's popularity, since the infant could be shielded from dirty floors, indoor drafts, open fires, and other potential dangers. Even when parents could not afford elaborate baby furniture, they sought to protect their children with durable materials. Many child-care experts believed that rocking the cradle provided infants with healthy exercise. Such motion, however, probably was more effective in curbing upset from colic, especially for babies whose diets consisted of flour-and-water pap, a substance that resembled wallpaper paste.

140 SWINGING CRADLE OR BASSINET, c. 1900
Possibly Austria
Bentwood
Smithsonian Institution, National Museum of American History,
  Division of Domestic Life (65.22)

Cradles like this Victorian-era bassinet served more than just the infant's needs. Only wealthy families could have afforded such an elaborate baby-holder. It was a status symbol and presentation piece, an appropriate setting in which to quiet the baby during special occasions or show off the newborn to admiring guests.

Urbanization and the emergence of the middle class promoted the switch from cradles to cribs. Cribs were thought to offer even an infant the assets of modern life—greater independence, a space of one's own, greater room in which to play and sleep. Many believed that cribs also alleviated some of the burdens of child care, since physically they isolated babies further from their caretakers.

CLOTHING

141 BOY'S HAT, c. 1975
Laos, Louang Phrabang Province or Sayaboury tradition
White Hmong people
Cotton and silk fabric, hand-stitched and knotted with applique, reverse applique, and embroidery; French Indochinese coins; silver disc; glass beads; dye; thread
Smithsonian Institution, National Museum of Natural History,
  Department of Anthropology (417655)

See cat. 144

142 HOOD, c. 1975
India, Kutch, Gujarat
Cotton, embroidered with cotton and inset with mirrors; metallic cloth trim with tassels; dye; thread
International Folk Art Foundation Collections, Museum of International Folk Art, a unit of the Museum of New Mexico, Santa Fe (FA.78.60-17)

See cat. 144

143 HAT, c. 1900
China, probably central or lower Yangtze River region
Resist-dyed cotton
Museum of International Folk Art, a unit of the Museum of New Mexico
  Santa Fe (3315 FE)

See cat. 144

144 HAT, 1964
Taiwan, I-liao Village, Pingtung Province
Paiwan and Rukai peoples
Cotton and velvet, decorated with bands of wool-yarn embroidery, aluminum, and plastic discs; wool-yarn tassel trim, braided chin cord; dye; thread
Smithsonian Institution, National Museum of Natural History,
  Department of Anthropology (410240)

If the sole purpose of hats was to protect babies from the sun, cold, and rain, a simple cloth would do. The painstaking handwork and complex patterns and designs on the headwear here suggest that more sophisticated concepts played a role in the fashioning of these tiny garments.

The Chinese cap, for example, includes symbols of long life and happiness. The Taiwanese ceremonial hat is of a type originally created for sons born into the chiefly class. Only social change allowed babies from a "common" heritage to wear such finery. Similarly, the elephants on the Kutch hat from India refer to the power and glory of royal palaces in times past.

The Hmong hat is especially rich with symbolism. It is an excellent example of this people's pride in intricate sewing and fine clothing. Attached to it are coins and a silver disc, symbols of wealth and family status. These ornaments and the fanciful needlework are intended to attract friendly spirits towards the baby. Each applique pattern has a name such as "snail," "vegetable flower," and "tunneling worm," illustrating how the boy for whom this hat was made fit into his father's clan. Traditionally, such hats were given to daughters-in-law, who later made funeral trappings using the same motifs when their mothers-in-law died. Thus these caps emphasized clan ties throughout life and were important items of exchange from one generation to the next.

145 CAP, 18th century
Italy
Embroidered silk, decorated with sequins; lace trim; silk ribbons
B'nai B'rith Klutznick Museum, Washington, D.C.

See cat. 148

146 CAP, c. 1854
USA
Cotton, embroidered with cotton thread
Smithsonian Institution, National Museum of American History,
  Division of Costume (220965.26)

See cat. 148

147   BONNET, c. 1800-1900
Probably USA
Lace-trimmed cotton; thread; silk ribbons
Smithsonian Institution, National Museum of American History,
    Division of Costume (80592Z09)

See cat. 148

148   BONNET, c. 1890
USA, North Dakota
Sioux people
Cotton cloth, woolen stroud cloth, buckskin, dentalium shell, dye, thread
Smithsonian Institution, National Museum of Natural History,
    Department of Anthropology (338902)

Often it is impossible to tell whether concern for style or for health determined the appearance of infant's caps and bonnets. Some early literature
about headwear for babies includes arguments on the relative merits of
fabrics. Lace, for example, frequently was condemned for being too scratchy
and offering poor shade from the sun. Muslin was favored by many physicians, who believed that the primary purpose of an infant's cap was to keep
the head cool so as to avoid "over-excitement in the brain."

These hats were made as much to look impressive as to protect little heads.
Costly fabrics, exquisite ornamentation, and painstakingly detailed needlework indicate that no trouble or expense was spared for the babies who
wore them.

The Sioux cap includes symbols suggesting that headwear involved spiritual,
as well as physical, concerns. The circle, for example, referred to the continuity of life, and the shells to the life-giving qualities of water. These symbols
enhance the cap's elegance, which underscores parental pride in the baby's
appearance. To create a cap like this, a family would have needed to trade
for shells and to have invested hours applying them onto the fabric.

149   CAP, c. 1975
Mexico, Magdalenas, Chiapas
Maya people, Tzotzil speakers
Cotton, brocaded with wool; vegetable dyes; cotton thread
Lent by Priscilla Rachun Linn

See cat. 151

150   CAP, c. 1940-1950
Guatemala, San Antonio Aguas Calientes, Sacatapequez
Maya people, Cakchiquel speakers
Cotton, brocaded with cotton; dye; thread
Smithsonian Institution, National Museum of Natural History,
    Department of Anthropology (406334)

See cat. 151

151   HAT, c. 1940
Peru, Qota, District of Chucuito, Puno
Aymara people
Knitted-wool yarn with purled border; dye
Smithsonian Institution, National Museum of Natural History,
    Department of Anthropology (382182)

In Central and South America, hats and carrying shawls protect small
babies from the cold, rain, and sun of high altitudes. Yet hats woven by
mothers in Central America or knitted by fathers in the Andean regions
provide more than physical protection. In these areas, babies are taught
from birth that when a soul separates from a body, witches or evil spirits
may strike the person with illness or death. Infants' souls are believed to be
especially weak and easily jarred by a sudden fright or fall. Hats thus help
to shelter these fragile souls, hiding babies from the sight of demons.
Among the Aymara people, hats waved over a frightened child even may
coax the dislodged soul back into the body.

The colors and symbols on headwear like this reinforce a baby's ethnic
belonging, and establish an early sense of identity about his or her sex, age,
and social position. Such headcoverings also convey subtle cultural messages about dignity, manners, modesty, grooming, and perceptions of
self-worth.

152   HAT, c. 1912
Alaska, St. Lawrence Island
Yuit people, central Siberian Yupik speakers
Skin, ornamented with glass beads, travertine marble; button, and ivory;
    cotton thread
Smithsonian Institution, National Museum of Natural History,
    Department of Anthropology (280142)

See cat. 153

153   HAT, c. 1966
Pakistan, Baluchistan, Nok Kundi
Probably Baluchi people
Wool-lined leather; metal buckle; thread; dye
Smithsonian Institution, National Museum of Natural History,
    Department of Anthropology (405872)

From looking at these fleece and fur hats designed for severely cold cli-
mates, we can be quite certain that the babies who wore them did not pull
them off their heads. What mattered was warmth, sturdiness, and softness.
The aviator cap, while not indigenous to Baluchi culture, offered a snug fit
perfectly suited to the needs of nomadic herders who scaled bitterly cold
altitudes on the Iran-Pakistan border. For Yuit children, a fur hat ornamented with ivory carvings that probably represent a polar bear and its cub underscored the importance of hunting as key to survival in the Alaskan tundra.
Until the child learned to hunt, however, the glass-and-marble amuletic
beads would have protected his health and welfare.

154 **GIRL'S AMULETIC HEAD ORNAMENT,** 19th century
Korea
Fabric and silver; dye
Collection of Chang Suk-hwan, Seoul

See cat. 157

155 **GIRL'S AMULETIC HEAD ORNAMENT,** 19th century
Korea
Fabric and silver; dye
Collection of Chang Suk-hwan, Seoul

See cat. 157

156 **GIRL'S AMULETIC HEAD ORNAMENTS WITH TASSLE,**
19th century
Korea
Fabric and silver; dye
Collection of Chang Suk-hwan, Seoul

See cat. 157

157 **GIRL'S AMULETIC HEAD ORNAMENTS WITH
MEDALLION,** 19th century
Korea
Fabric and silver; dye
Collection of Chang Suk-hwan, Seoul

Korean baby girls received their first lessons in the art of feminine adornment when head ornaments like these were braided into their hair. The
leaf and flower forms on such headwear were not only decorative ornaments; they also symbolized feminine beauty. Only the affluent could
afford floral motifs worked in gold, silver, or enamelware for their children.
Others used more common metals like brass. Yet the past generations of
grandmothers and aunts who provided such finery were concerned with
more than appearance. The ornaments here were thought to have amuletic
properties capable of deflecting evil spirits that might cause illness. Perhaps
this is why the metal decorations were worn in a highly visible manner,
placed just where the center part began on a baby's forehead.

158 **TORAH BINDER,** 1731
Germany, Halberstadt
Undyed linen, embroidered with polychrome silk thread
Hebrew Union College Skirball Museum, Los Angeles (56.1)

This linen band, or wimpel, is an example of the transformation of a
simple article of infant's clothing into an important birth record and personal religious item. During the 16th century, a folk custom originated
among Jews from southern Germany in which the swaddling cloth used
during the circumcision ceremony of an eight-day-old infant boy was con-
verted into a binder for the *Torah* (Judaism's sacred scroll containing the

first five books of the Bible). The cloth was cut into four sections, which
were stitched together to form a long band. This band then was embroidered or painted, usually by the mother or grandmother, with the child's
name, date of birth, and a special prayer that he grow to learn Torah, to be
married, and to carry out a life of good deeds.

This wimpel was made for Eliakum, son of Joel of Halberstadt, born on
Wednesday, the 27th of *Adar* (Hebrew month), 1731. Eliakum's zodiac
sign is depicted, as are a Torah scroll, marriage canopy, and symbols that
identify his parents' personal hopes for him. A verse from the *Ethics of the
Fathers* also is included. It calls on Eliakum to be "daring as a leopard, light
as an eagle, fleet as a deer, and strong as a lion [to do God's will]."

A wimpel generally was dedicated on the child's first visit to the syna-
gogue, where it then was kept as a birth record. It was used again to wrap
the Torah on the boy's Bar Mitzvah at age 13, and on the Sabbath before his
wedding, thus literally "binding" the stages of his life to Judaism.

159 **BOY'S TIGER HAT,** c. 1900
China
Silk
American Museum of Natural History, New York (70/1562)

See cat. 160

160 **HAT,** 20th century
Israel
Bedouin people
Embroidered cotton
Lent anonymously

What hats reveal about cultures goes beyond issues of style, status, and
climate. Hats also illustrate many of the expectations peoples have for their
babies. The Bedouin hat, for example, enabled even an infant to observe
the traditional practice of covering the head as a sign of modesty and
respect. Ethnic affiliation also is a hallmark of Chinese tiger hats. Created
especially for children, these fanciful items helped to convey deeply rooted
ideas about evil spirits and self-protection. The tiger, a fierce and powerful
beast and mount of the benevolent gods, guarded children from supernatural harm.

161 **BOY'S ROBE AND BREASTPLATE,** c. 1892
USA, Oklahoma
Kiowa people
Fringed buckskin colored with yellow pigment and embroidered with glass
beads; sinew; bones strung with cotton thread to rawhide strips colored
with red pigment
Smithsonian Institution, National Museum of Natural History,
Department of Anthropology (152847)

See cat. 162

162 SWEATER, 20th century

Sweden
Knitted wool yarn
Lent anonymously

Babies born among nomadic plains Kiowa and homebound Swedish villagers would have experienced widely contrasting lifestyles. But when children received clothing like the pieces shown here, they were participating in a similar tradition of fine handwork. In both cultures, women took great pride and gained status from their babies' appearance.

Despite the differences between open plains and forested farmlands, the makers of these clothes each drew inspiration from nature's colors, shapes, and movements, to create garments that might evoke hope for the long and healthy lives of their children. In the Kiowa robe, for example, fringes were used to signify movement and spiritual wholeness. Yellow pigment represented life and light. The Scandinavian sweater included native plants and animals, as well as tree and leaf motifs symbolizing life and growth.

163 BLOUSE FOR BABY GIRL, 1976

Mexico, San Andres Larrainzar, Chiapas
Maya people, Tzotzil speakers
Cotton, brocaded with cotton; dye
Smithsonian Institution, National Museum of Natural History,
    Department of Anthropology (419534)

See cat. 164

164 CARRYING CLOTH, c. 1960

Guatemala, Santa Maria de Jesus, Sacatepequez
Maya people, Cakchiquel speakers
Plain-weave cotton, brocaded and stitched with cotton; dye
International Folk Art Foundation Collections, Museum of International
    Folk Art, a unit of the Museum of New Mexico, Santa Fe (FA.1984.318-2)

Clothing helps to establish the cultural identity of traditional Maya peoples, who most often wrap their babies in handwoven carrying cloths like the one exhibited here. Such carriers protect not only against sun, rain, and the cold night air, but also against fright, soul loss, and witchcraft. Babies, it is thought, easily lose their souls, and evil-hearted jealous people may harm a family, or redress an earlier wrong, by causing infants to become sick or die.

Fear of witchcraft also makes it likely that the handsomely brocaded shirt displayed here was made by a Maya woman for the trade market. A fine garment like this would cause unwelcome attention to a vulnerable baby. To avoid such danger, the highland Maya of Mexico tend to dress their children in modest, well-worn clothing that will not inspire jealousy.

The designs on these textiles reflect a common heritage, yet each bears different ethnic and regional symbols. The Chiapas shirt includes animal forms—such as the wavy "path of the snake"—that probably refer to earth dieties. The abstract linear patterns woven into the Guatemalan carrying cloth depict birds and squirrels indigenous to the Sacatepequez region. These animals take on personalities in myths integral to the cultural heritage of the Maya.

165 CHEMISE, 1832

USA
Linen, decorated with handmade lace; thread
Smithsonian Institution, National Museum of American History,
    Division of Costume (38358)

See cat. 166

166 SHIRT, c. 1850-1900

USA
Linen, decorated with lace; thread
Smithsonian Institution, National Museum of American History,
    Division of Costume (217021.13c)

These baby shirts date from the American Victorian period. What does the color, style, and stiching of these garments tell us about the world of infants during this time?

The white of the shirts hints at the angelic purity Victorian parents attached to babyhood. From the early 1800s on, religious leaders no longer viewed babies as wicked miniature adults doomed by original sin. Instead, childhood was considered to be a time of innocence and simplicity. The color white emphasized this special status. Infants were sexless, sinless creatures, set apart from the complex, competitive lives of adults around them.

Writers on child care in the 1800s often deplored the use of the baby as a tiny showpiece of family fortune. Even underclothes were made of costly fabrics with expensive trim. Right from the start, then, infants from affluent homes were brought up to understand that how they looked could be as important as how they felt.

One Victorian author condemned "cold linen" shirts such as these. As an alternative, she urged mothers to ensure babies' health with undergarments of warm cotton flannel or wool. Another admonished lace by sympathizing with babies who might suffer chafing and scratching from its prickly surface.

The fine stiching on these shirts indicates that time, as well as newfound financial resources, existed for women in the family either to make or buy high-quality baby clothes. Ruffles, lace, and adornment everywhere around the newborn proclaimed the status of a mother with enough leisure time to excel at domestic skills such as fancy needlework.

167 (a,b) SNOWSUIT AND DIAPER, c. 1912
Alaska, St. Lawrence Island
Yuit people, central Siberian Yupik speakers
Fur-trimmed deerskin; sinew; dye; moss-lined deerskin and sinew
Smithsonian Institution, National Museum of Natural History,
    Department of Anthropology (280115, 280141)

Yuit babies of St. Lawrence Island were carried on their mothers' shoulders rather than inside the parka or hood, as was common among other Arctic peoples. Their snowsuits were made especially well because even a small opening could lead to severe frostbite. Garments like this one provided warmth yet were designed to enable children to explore the rugged environment that one day they would need to master.

Another practical feature of this snowsuit is its diaper. Absorbent moss was placed on the piece of hide and was discarded as necessary. The disposable diaper may have revolutionized infant care in this country, but Arctic peoples long have known about the merits of throwaway moss.

168 (a,b) INFANT'S SHIRT AND TROUSERS, 1910
Korea
Cotton
Sŏk Chu-sŏn Memorial Museum of Ethnology, Seoul

All Korean babies, no matter what their class, wore handsome garments like these until they were about one year old. The practical trousers were left open at the bottom for easy access. During the hot summer, infants would have kept cool in the lightweight fabric of the item in the exhibit. When the season changed, however, they would have worn heavier clothing in the same style.

169 UNDERCOAT, 20th century
China
Cotton, resist-dyed with indigo
The Museum of International Folk Art, a unit of the Museum of New
    Mexico, Santa Fe (3312-b)

The Chinese usually dress their babies in clothing that is more colorful and fancifully ornamented than adult-wear. This jacket with butterfly and frog motifs was made by resist-dying, a popular folk technique in central China and the poorer areas of southwest China. Patterns are made from a parchment stencil to which a paste of lime and bean flower has been applied. All treated areas then remain white after the cloth is dipped into vats of indigo dye.

170 MOCCASINS, c. 1860-1915
USA, Minnesota
Probably Ojibwa people
Buckskin and cotton, decorated with glass beads; dye; thread
Smithsonian Institution, National Museum of Natural History,
    Department of Anthropology (307103)

See cat. 172

171 BOY'S MOCCASINS, c. 1890
USA, Oklahoma
Arapaho or Cheyenne people (used by Kiowa people)
Buckskin, decorated with glass beads; rawhide soles; sinew; thread
Smithsonian Institution, National Museum of Natural History,
    Department of Anthropology (152847)

See cat. 172

172 **BOOTS,** c. 1866
Canada, Northwest Territory, Mackenzie River Delta
Inupiaq people
Whaleskin; birdskin; sinew
Smithsonian Institution, National Museum of Natural History,
    Department of Anthropology (1720)

Moccasins for Native American babies closely resembled styles worn by
adults. Parents clad in fine clothes on dress occasions were proud to show
off their babies in beaded and well-sewn footwear like these moccasins.

Styles of moccasins differed widely across North America. Each style marked
tribal identity and was adapted to fit the needs of a specific climate and
terrain. Footwear and clothing, whether decorated or plain for everyday
use like the summer boots for native babies of the Arctic's Mackenzie Delta
region, helped small children learn to distinguish their people from other
native peoples and from whites.

The making of moccasins also helped teach babies how men and women
divided labor to ensure survival. Traditionally men hunted animals, which
provided skins for moccasins. Women usually tanned the hides and stitched
them with sinew or thread. Decorative cloth and beads introduced babies
to items obtained through trading with the outside world.

By the late 1800s, shoes had begun to replace moccasins for everyday
wear. Today the traditional dress of Native Americans, including moccasins, has become a visible means of preserving a living heritage. Only the
small Canadian boots here bear witness to a vanished people. Ironically,
neither cold nor the tundra's barrenness, but rather epidemics and contact
with whites and the Alaskan Inuit, caused the demise of the Mackenzie
Delta's earliest inhabitants.

173 **SHOES,** c. 1817-1830
England
Silk, embroidered with silk and metal thread; silk ribbon; leather;
    thread; dye
Smithsonian Institution, National Museum of American History,
    Division of Costume (311503.39)

See cat. 175

174 **SHOES,** c. 1850-1900
England or USA
Silk, machine-stitched to leather soles; satin ribbon trim; metal button
Smithsonian Institution, National Museum of American History,
    Division of Costume (58698)

See cat. 175

175 **SHOES,** c. 1720-1780
France
Stitched silk-damask and leather; metal buckles; dye
Smithsonian Institution, National Museum of American History,
    Division of Costume (311503.32)

During the late 1700s and early 1800s, boys and girls from wealthier
families spent much of their infancy in long petticoats and gowns. Such
garments trailed well over their feet, usually covering beautifully crafted
shoes like these. Merely owning a pair of such elaborate shoes, however,
was more important than being able to see the luxurious fabrics and
buckle ornaments from which they were made. Americans who could
afford these items took pride in being able to keep up with European
fashions, outfitting their children in scaled-down versions of adult styles.

176 **BOY'S SHOES,** c. 1730
France
Dyed leather, hand-stitched with cotton cord
Smithsonian Institution, National Museum of American History,
    Division of Costume (311503.28)

See cat. 178

177 **SHOES,** c. 1735
France
Dyed silk, hand-stitched to leather; satin ribbon; kid trim
Smithsonian Institution, National Museum of American History,
    Division of Costume (311503.25)

See cat. 178

178 **BOY'S SHOES,** c. 1802
USA, Vermont, Hardwick
Stitched and dyed leather
Smithsonian Institution, National Museum of American History,
    Division of Costume (313212.1)

Were this an exhibit about shoes worn by infants of the poor, the display cases would be bare. Around the time these shoes were made, many families in Europe and the United States did not have the means to cover fast-growing babies' feet. Yet these items reflect more than socioeconomic conditions. They also reveal the way parents encouraged their babies to move.

During the 18th and early 19th centuries, small children wore grown-up styles to create the appearance of adult maturity. Protestant thinking of the day taught parents that babies were miniature flawed adults, tarnished by original sin. Only reason, it was thought, could improve their inherently base human nature at birth. There was little tolerance for babyish ways. Crawling, for example, was regarded as demeaning, animalistic behavior, and even the very young were made to sit straight or stand in chairs or walkers so that they would be "upright" in both posture and behavior. Well-constructed footwear in adult styles emphasized walking and the eventual attainment of "rational" adulthood.

179 **BOY'S LAYETTE BOOTIES,** 1884-1885
USA
Knitted silk
Smithsonian Institution, National Museum of American History,
    Division of Costume (233475.1A)

See cat. 180

180 **GIRL'S SHOES,** 1900
USA, Washington, D.C.
Dyed leather, machine-stitched with cotton thread; cotton cord laced
    through metal eyelets, trimmed with blue silk tassle and stitching; thread
Smithsonian Institution, National Museum of American History,
    Division of Costume (1978.0583.15)

Both the styles and materials of shoes changed dramatically in the later part of the 19th century. The softness and flexibility of these two pairs paralleled a new attitude towards child-rearing. Infants were to be given the freedom to crawl and play, and parents admired baby antics as innocent and joyful. As the infant mortality rate began to decline, early childhood came to be regarded as a treasured time. Dressing infants in soft shoes was a way to emphasize babyhood, and a sign of the value placed on fleeting tender years.

181 **BABY SOCKS,** c. 1932
Korea
Quilted cotton with silk tassel; ribbon ties; embroidery; dye; cotton thread
Smithsonian Institution, National Museum of Natural History,
    Department of Anthropology (363286)

See cat. 183

182 **GIRL'S ANKLE-STRAP SHOES,** c. 1925
China
Embroidered silk; rattan soles lined with red paper; dye; thread
Smithsonian Institution, National Museum of Natural History,
    Department of Anthropology (329731)

See cat. 183

183 **SHOES,** c. 1896-1900
China
Silk, decorated with silk thread and tassel; dye
Smithsonian Institution, National Museum of Natural History,
    Department of Anthropology (422219)

Though different in style and design, these baby shoes and socks reflect the same parental concern—that a child might thrive and someday walk into healthy adulthood. A Chinese baby might have delighted in the fanciful colors and shape of the tiger's face, but he also would have learned that the beast ruled the animal kingdom, was bearer of the male principle, and was a powerful protector against demons. So too, the owner of the blue shoes would have understood that red paper tucked into the soles was talismanic, for red protected, gave life, and brought good fortune. And while a Korean child might not have remembered the celebratory occasion on which he wore the booties shown here, eventually he would have understood that the size of his first shoes—too large for small feet—symbolized growth and long life.

184 **SHOES,** c. 1885-1929
Turkey
Dyed leather; wool yarn; metal; thread
Smithsonian Institution, National Museum of Natural History,
    Department of Anthropology (419103)

See cat. 185

185 **GIRL'S SHOES,** c. 1885
Syria, Damascus
Bedouin people
Dyed leather, embroidered with gold thread; cotton thread
Smithsonian Institution, National Museum of Natural History,
    Department of Anthropology (129410)

Modern footwear largely has replaced the examples of Turkish shoes on exhibit. The red and gold pair from Syria, however, still are worn today by Bedouins. Shoe styles in these countries often are the same for babies and adults. Why would parents in a desert environment invest in such elaborate footwear for their children? Because clothing is a symbol of wealth and family status, and an important factor in creating a sense of tribal identity. A costume replete with fine shoes helps to establish a child's ethnic roots, especially among groups where struggles for territory and autonomy prevail. Often a child's first lessons about the allocation of wealth in the family and the wider community come from the quality and appearance of even the smallest articles of clothing, like the footwear in the exhibition.

186 **ANKLETS,** undated
Nepal, Patan Village
Newari people, Kusle caste
Silver with cotton cord
Smithsonian Institution, National Museum of Natural History,
    Department of Anthropology (406527)

See cat. 188

187 **ANKLETS,** 1964
Burma, Mudon Province
Silver
Smithsonian Institution, National Museum of Natural History,
    Department of Anthropology (408408)

See cat. 188

188 **ANKLETS,** 20th century
Middle East
Palestinian people
Silver
International Folk Art Foundation Collections, Museum of International
    Folk Art, a unit of the Museum of New Mexico, Santa Fe (FA.78.48-69x)

Metals have been thought to hold magical and protective properties since ores first were used thousands of years ago. For centuries, parents have placed silver amuletic anklets like these on babies to help thwart evil

forces and promote good fortune. The Nepalese pair, for example, probably was passed down for generations as a family heirloom. It is impossible even to date these anklets since the pendants on them have not changed for centuries.

Most children, it would seem, might be curious about jewelry like this, and perhaps try to play with it or remove it. Yet by ensuring that their infants wear such anklets, parents are able to convey cultural attitudes about potential sources of supernatural danger. These simple ornaments thus become powerful early symbols of the parental role in shielding children from harm.

INFANT BATHING

189 **CHILD'S BATHTUB,** c. 1880-1900
USA
Painted tin
The Margaret Woodbury Strong Museum, Rochester, New York

See cat. 192

190 **WASHING BASKET,** c. 1900
USA, California
Pomoan people
One rod-willow foundation coiled with roots of sedge grass and bullrush
Smithsonian Institution, National Museum of Natural History,
    Department of Anthropology (327989)

See cat. 192

191 **WASHING BASIN,** c. 1920
Korea, Seoul area
Hand-hammered brass
Smithsonian Institution, National Museum of Natural History,
    Department of Anthropology

See cat. 192

192 WATER VESSEL, c. 1975
Brazil, Sardinha Village, Maranhao
Ramkokamekra-Canels people
Vertical cross section of gourd decorated with strings of glass beads, metal
     medallion, toe tips of deer, twine
Smithsonian Institution, National Museum of Natural History,
     Department of Anthropology (421735)

Definitions about dirt and pollution vary from culture to culture, so that
what appears clean to one people may seem unclean to another. No matter
how cleanliness is defined, however, it is regarded universally as an appropriate condition. Dirt, on the other hand, usually is associated with antiso-
cial behavior, as well as with bad upbringing, character, and morals. Thus
babies from non-Western cultures, like their counterparts in Europe and
the United States, learn early in life that bathing has as much to do with
ideas of health, growth, and civility as it does with removing bodily waste
or grime.

The basin, gourd, and basket here illustrate the range of vessels used for
infant baths. Associated with each are bathing rituals that help us understand that in most parts of the world, taking a bath involves more than a
simple splash or rinse.

At the time the Korean brass basin was used, for example, infant bathing
was linked to concepts of growth. Three days after birth, newborns were
sponged toe to head one day and head to toe the next, until all parts of the
body were conditioned to grow at a balanced rate.

Traditional Pomoan Indians associated baths with a reaffirmation of kin
ties within the extended family. Newborns were given finely made, water-
tight baskets like that shown here by their grandmothers or paternal aunts.
During infancy, children were bathed in them mornings and evenings. The
baskets then became lifelong treasures and visible ties to the kinswomen
who had offered baths of welcome.

Canela Indians understand water as a source of strength and growth. They
bathe daily in a river near their village. At times, however, bad weather
precludes washing a small infant out-of-doors. When this happens, mothers
may fill a large gourd with water to ensure that their babies will continue to
be strengthened.

In our own culture, bathing has been thought to affect an infant's growth,
health, and personality. During the Middle Ages people used bathing to
increase beauty, mold character, and provide stimulation. By the 17th century, however, most advocated waters "lukewarm and mild" to help prevent
disease. Still later, philosophers like Jean-Jacques Rousseau called for "icy
water" in winter or summer. Cold baths were thought to create hardy
children of nature, not only robust and resistant to illness, but also obedi-
ent to parental will. Yet by 1900, families who could afford a tub like the
one exhibited here probably prepared baths to provide their infants with
warm, leisurely, and sensual experiences. Today pediatricians offer surprisingly similar advice—noting that "face to face interaction and stroking with
a wash cloth" helps to "satisfy the baby's sensory needs."

RATTLES
The following items are detailed in cat. 228:

193 WHISTLE RATTLE, c. 18th century
England, Birmingham
Silver and coral
Smithsonian Institution, National Museum of American History,
     Division of Domestic Life (55589.1)

194 WHISTLE RATTLE, c. 18th century
Probably England
Silver and coral
Smithsonian Institution, National Museum of American History,
     Division of Domestic Life (259418)

195 TEETHING RATTLE, 19th century
Origin unknown
Silver and mother-of-pearl
Smithsonian Institution, National Museum of American History,
     Division of Domestic Life (1978.379.1)

196 TEETHING WHISTLE RATTLE, late 19th century
Origin unknown
Silver and mother-of-pearl
Smithsonian Institution, National Museum of American History,
     Division of Domestic Life (64.283)

197 WHISTLE RATTLE, c. 1700
Italy
Silver
The Marcia Hersey Collection (RC-12)

198 RATTLE, 20th century
Italy
Silver
The Marcia Hersey Collection (RC-14)

199 RATTLE, 1870
China
Silver
The Marcia Hersey Collection (RF-12)

200   **TEETHING RING RATTLE**, 1925-1930
France
Silver and ivory
The Marcia Hersey Collection (RE-28)

201   **TEETHING RING RATTLE**, 1925-1930
France
Silver and ivory
The Marcia Hersey Collection (RE-29)

202   **RATTLE PORTION OF TEETHING RING**, 1925-1930
France
Silver
The Marcia Hersey Collection (RE-30)

203   **RATTLE**, 1900-1910
France
Silver and ivory
The Marcia Hersey Collection (RI-5)

204   **RATTLE**, 1861-1865
USA
Wood with enclosed noisemaker
The Marcia Hersey Collection (RW-9)

205   **RATTLE**, 1860-1870
China (China trade item)
Silver and ivory
The Marcia Hersey Collection (RF-2)

206   **PACIFIER RATTLE**, 1800-1900
France
Silver and ivory
The Marcia Hersey Collection (RE-19)

207   **TEETHING RATTLE**, 1925-1930
France
Attributed to Ruhlmann
Wood and ivory
The Marcia Hersey Collection (RI-3)

208   **WHISTLE RATTLE**, 1797
France
Silver and coral
The Marcia Hersey Collection (RE-3)

209   **RATTLE**, 1905
Germany, Bavaria
Silver and ivory
The Marcia Hersey Collection (RC-9)

210   **RATTLE**, 1914-1920
Spain
Silver and ivory
The Marcia Hersey Collection (RC-21)

211   **RATTLE**, 1840-1888
British India
Painted ivory with enclosed noisemaker
The Marcia Hersey Collection (RI-15)

212   **RATTLE**, 1840
USA
Wood and rattan with enclosed noisemaker
The Marcia Hersey Collection (RM-3)

213   **TEETHING RATTLE**, 1900
USA
Ivory
The Marcia Hersey Collection (RI-6)

214   **WHISTLE RATTLE**, c. 1800
France
Silver
The Marcia Hersey Collection (RE-5)

215   **DRUM RATTLE**, early 19th century
Japan
Animal skin, wood, and metal
The Marcia Hersey Collection (RM-20)

216   **RATTLE**, 1880-1890
USA
Wood
The Marcia Hersey Collection (RW-8)

217   **WHISTLE RATTLE**, 1770
Eliza Tookey, maker
England
Silver and coral
The Marcia Hersey Collection (RB-7)

218   **WHISTLE RATTLE**, 1735
England
Silver and coral
The Marcia Hersey Collection (RB-8)

219   **RATTLE**, 17th-18th century
Spain
Silver
The Marcia Hersey Collection (RC-15)

220   **PACIFIER RATTLE**, 1900
Kate Greenaway, maker
England
Silver and ivory
The Marcia Hersey Collection (RB-40)

221   **TEETHING RATTLE**, 1907
England
Silver and ivory with enclosed noisemaker
The Marcia Hersey Collection (RB-39)

222   **RATTLE**, early 20th century
Philippine Islands
Cowrie shells and rope
Smithsonian Institution, National Museum of Natural History,
   Department of Anthropology (373190)

223   **RATTLE,** late 19th century
Africa, west coast area
Hemp and gourds
Smithsonian Institution, National Museum of Natural History,
   Department of Anthropology (165434)

224   **RATTLE**, 20th century
British Guiana (now Guyana)
Cane handle and gourd, filled with seeds
Smithsonian Institution, National Museum of Natural History,
   Department of Anthropology (397469)

225   **RATTLE**, 20th century
British Guiana (now Guyana)
Immature palm leaves, filled with seeds
Smithsonian Institution, National Museum of Natural History,
   Department of Anthropology (397468)

226   **DRUM RATTLE**, 20th century
USA
Painted metal
Collection of Rosalind Berman

227   **RATTLE**, 20th century
India
Carved ivory with enclosed noisemaker
Collection of Rosalind Berman

228   **RATTLE**, 20th century
USA
Carved wood and ivory with enclosed noisemaker
Collection of Rosalind Berman

Found in many parts of the world as a baby's first toy, rattles take advantage of infants' tendency to grasp objects, and of their first aimless movements. When babies find that these movements can produce sound—from bells or beads in the enclosure—they discover a way to amuse themselves. They also may learn implicitly how to soothe themselves, for rattles often include pacifiers, teething rings, and gum sticks.

Rattles have been made in a wide variety of materials, which provide information about cultural attitudes and economic conditions in different parts of the world. Some rattles here, for example, incorporate natural resources. Children whose first toys are crafted from rattan, gourds, shells, hemp, or cane become familiar at an early age with the appearance, feel, and smell of elements in the surrounding environment. Later they learn to appreciate the many practical applications of these natural resources, depending on them not only for basic needs, such as food, clothing, and shelter, but also for cherished, personal possessions.

Only well-to-do families in 18th and 19th century Europe and America could have afforded infant toys crafted from coral, pearl, or precious metals. Many of the finely worked silver rattles in the exhibit reflect popular decorative art styles of their time—a measure of the extent to which families sought to mirror their own socioeconomic status through infant items. These fanciful toys also include figures such as jesters, nursery-rhyme characters, animals, and instruments, illustrating parental attitudes about subject matter suitable for children.

Babies, delighted by the sounds and fanciful shapes of such toys, would not have known that rattles involved more than infant entertainment. Yet rattles have been used widely by adults to frighten away evil spirits, and baby rattles probably represent a vestige of this practice. Coral, for example, was a good luck symbol, and its presence on early infant toys was thought to promote health and welfare.

FEEDING

Unless otherwise indicated, the following feeders, detailed in cat. 241, are from the Smithsonian Institution's National Museum of American History, Division of Medical Sciences.

229   Probably Ancient Greece
Glazed terra cotta
Smithsonian Institution, National Museum of Natural History, Department
    of Anthropology (30B497.1)

230   USA, late 18th/early 19th century
Pewter (M 9637)

231   USA, late 19th century
Glass (M 13022)

232   USA, 18th century
Wood (M 4345)

233   USA, 19th century
Glass and pewter (M 4338)

234   USA, 20th century
Machine-produced glass bottle with marked measures (1984 0782 223)

235   USA, 20th century
Machine-produced glass bottle with marked measures (M 6707)

236   USA, 19th century
Hand-blown, etched glass; pewter (M 9580)

237   USA, 20th century
Machine-produced glass bottle with marked measures (M 6731)

238   USA, early 20th century
Glass with hard-rubber nipple (M 6681)

239   USA, 19th century
Glass (M 4342)

240   USA, 19th century
Glass and pewter (M 9581)

241   USA, 20th century
Glass with marked measures (8281305, 06, 07)

If you thought all baby bottles were made of tall plastic containers with throwaway pouches and specially sterilized nipples, then consider the examples in this exhibition. Bottles of every shape, size, and material have been used for at least 4,000 years by mothers who could not or chose not to breast-feed, and by caretakers other than the natural mother. Some glass and glazed terra cotta feeders—an example of the latter is included here—have been discovered by archeologists at Greek and Roman burial sites.

Before the 19th century, glass was a luxury item for most people. The wooden cylinder and pewter pieces here show how materials other than glass were crafted into infant feeders. Today we surmise that metal bottles and nipples, popular during the 17th and 18th centuries, may have contributed to the high infant mortality rate because their lead content induced poisoning.

In Western cultures, people living in the frontier or in remote, rural areas often made nursers from cattle horn, gourds, and other items readily available from the surrounding environment. Probably these people were unaware that babies in non-Western societies already had been fed for centuries from similar devices.

The late 18th- and early 19th-century glass nursers in the exhibit were hand-blown. Since glass cylinders were easier to clean than pottery, wood, or metal, they were especially popular in an age when health and hygiene dominated child care attitudes. Pasteurization and sterilization—introduced in the late 19th century—were outgrowths of this preoccupation, and played a significant role in reducing yet again the infant mortality rate. Bottles with vented ducts or tubes reaching into the bottom—designed to minimize the amount of air an infant would swallow—were developed with similar concerns in mind.

Widespread use of glass bottles began only after the 1903 invention of bottle-producing machines. Yet whatever was revolutionary about mass-produced feeders hardly rivaled the many innovations applied to the nipple. The flat feeders and some of the nippleless, earlier bottles in the exhibit originally were equipped with cloth swatches that could be sucked on. The texture of certain textiles was considered more appropriate for a baby's delicate mouth. Leather and sponge nipples followed. Eventually rubber emerged as a more desirable material because it was especially durable and relatively easy to clean.

242   **POSSET POT**, 1670-1730
Attributed to Niglet
England, London or Bristol
Polychrome, tin-glazed earthenware
Collections of the Wellcome Museum for the History of Medicine,
    The Science Museum, London (A 42356)

See cat. 247

243 **POSSET POT,** 1701-1750
Holland, Delft
Tin-glazed earthenware
Collections of the Wellcome Museum for the History of Medicine,
   The Science Museum, London (A 42351)

See cat. 247

244 **POSSET POT,** 1630-1730
England, London or Bristol
Polychrome, tin-glazed earthenware
Collections of the Wellcome Museum for the History of Medicine,
   The Science Museum, London (A 64409)

See cat. 247

245 **POSSET POT,** 1744
England, Liverpool
Tin-glazed earthenware
Collections of the Wellcome Museum for the History of Medicine,
   The Science Museum, London (A 102858)

See cat. 247

246 **FOOD WARMER,** 1801-1850
Wedgewood
England
Glazed creamware
Collections of the Wellcome Museum for the History of Medicine,
   The Science Museum, London (A 639871)

See cat. 247

247 **FOOD WARMER,** 1801-1850
England
Glazed pearlware
Collections of the Wellcome Museum for the History of Medicine,
   The Science Museum, London (A 639960)

Concern for aesthetic presentation and status partly was responsible for
the use in infant care of these elaborate feeders and food warmers. Here
appearance as a measure of the child's well-being often was as important
as functionalism and durability.

Originally these decorative containers were used for feeding invalids posset,
a drink composed of hot milk curdled with ale, wine, or other liquor, and
often flavored with sugar and spices. This liquid could be administered easily
by placing the pour spout directly in the mouth of the patient. Mothers and
nannies often used posset as a remedy for children's colds, and the vessels
also were popular for serving warm milk to infants. Despite their attractiveness, the spout of the posset pot often cloged, was difficult to clean, and
fostered infectious microrganisms that sometimes caused illnesses to the
babies who used them.

Nearly all of these examples are chipped, which is a measure of their
authenticity. Posset pots in more pristine condition usually are recent
creations, since a market still exists for the use of these containers as
decorative items.

248 *THŌB ABŪ QUTBEH* **DRESS,** c. 1925
Palestine, Jerusalem area
Palestinian people
Embroidered silk
International Folk Art Foundation Collections, Museum of International
   Folk Art, a unit of the Museum of New Mexico, Santa Fe (FA.72.25-11)

Child care is demanding. During waking hours, babies often require constant
attention. Infants cannot express to their caretakers what it is they might
want, but they can express displeasure readily, and crying often is a sign of
hunger. The sooner they are fed, the better, and nursing is one of the most
expeditious solutions. In cultures where babies are carried about with
their mothers from one daily task to another, the nursing mother's clothing
actually may be designed to afford the child easy access to the breast. This
handloomed, Syrian-silk dress, called "the stiched one" because it is pieced
together from different swatches of material, is an excellent example of
such specially designed wear. On either side of the embroidered chest
piece are slits that expose the breasts when an infant needs to be fed or
pacified. Western fashion has not yet popularized so practical a garment
for the nursing mother. Yet as Western women look to new conveniences
in child care, and as more of them return to breast feeding, designers may
find Palestinian dresses like this one helpful examples to follow.

249　FEEDER, 20th century
Kenya
Pokot people
Gourd, decorated with leather, fiber basketry, and beads
Smithsonian Institution, National Museum of Natural History,
　　Department of Anthropology (421402)

Pastoral Pokot babies feed on goat's milk from slender gourds like this one
if their mothers' supply becomes low. Children realize from an early age
that their nomadic lifestyle depends on the use of natural resources from
the surrounding environment. Gourds thus become handy bottles and
bowls, and at times are decorated with trade beads for aesthetic pleasure.

Eventually Pokot children will grow up to take over family herds of cattle,
camels, sheep, and goats, thus continuing an expert subsistence in a region
where arid conditions prevail nearly half the year. Since all welfare depends
on the herds, even orphaned animals may be kept alive by feedings from a
nursing gourd.

250　LACTATION BOTTLE, 19th century
Korea
Porcelain
Smithsonian Institution, National Museum of Natural History (401650)

See cat. 251

251 (a-c)　PAPBOATS, 19th century
Germany, Dresden
Porcelain; one with gilt edging
Smithsonian Institution, National Museum of American History,
　　Division of Medical Sciences (30838712, 308497.1, 308499)

Modern child care in many cultures emphasizes freshness and the nutritional value of baby foods. Some caretakers go to elaborate lengths to
prepare infant food from scratch, including only ingredients that are grown
naturally, easily digested, and rich in vitamins. Baby foods of the 18th and
19th century were different. Among the most popular—partly because it
was filling and partly because it was inexpensive and could be prepared
quickly—was pap, a milk-and-bread or flour-and-water substance that
sometimes resembled wallpaper paste. Papboats like those exhibited here
were designed especially to contain this food.

252　PUMPFEEDER, 19th century
USA
Glass
Smithsonian Institution, National Museum of American History,
　　Division of Medical Sciences (1978 0883 225)

See cat. 254

253　INFANT FEEDER, 19th century
USA, based on English design
Glazed earthenware
Smithsonian Institution, National Museum of American History,
　　Division of Medical Sciences (M 13848)

See cat. 254

254 (a-c)　INFANT FEEDERS, 18th century
England
Porcelain
Collection of Rosalind Berman

The long-stemmed pumpfeeder was designed with neatness in mind. Here
the intent was to keep as much distance as possible between baby and
food so as to prevent spilling. While the spout may have achieved that goal,
it also easily became clogged with mixtures of milk and cereal that spoiled,
thus harboring infectious microorganisms.

Food mixtures were poured into the holes on the tops of the flat, English-
style feeders. Pieces of cloth on which the baby could suck then were
stuffed into the more slender opening. The decorative appearance of such
nursers was as important as the ease of feeding they offered. They were
used widely until the 19th century, when issues of baby hygiene and the
ease with which feeders could be cleaned prompted an interest in glass
which could be sterilized.

REALITIES

Did they say you were born during hard times?

When there was famine, drought, war, disease?
When they had no wealth, no food, no medicines?

Did they say you arrived during good times?
In a world of calm and abundance?

Did they protect you?
Abandon you?
Embrace you?
Neglect you?
Cherish you beyond measure?

People in every age and place attempt through the newborn to ensure that their families and way of life might endure. Yet not every cultural and physical environment permits such continuity...

What might the next generation encounter?

HIROJI KUBOTA/
MAGNUM.
CHINA

HIROJI KUBOTA/
MAGNUM.
CHINA

This child may grow up with his parents, but it is unlikely that he will have a brother or sister. He is being raised in an era of reduced population growth. The over-population that strained the availability of food, medical services, and educational opportunities for generations past is being curbed by a Chinese policy regulating the size of families. Policymakers hope to demonstrate that fewer people in the next generation will mean greater resources for everyone.

With each handshake, Prince William learns to master the complex protocol required for ceremonial occasions. Since infancy, he has been smiling for photographers, attending formal functions, and learning about the weighty responsibilities of a future king. Perhaps this seems like an abnormal childhood. But every culture has its own ideas of social roles and its own ways of embedding those ideas in children. Just as Prince William is learning what is expected of him, so children in other places are learning to defend livestock from prowling animals, care for a younger sibling, or help their parents till the fields. Actions like these will determine how the next generation interprets interdependency and the value of shared human responsibility.

This Guatemalan mother must prepare yet another small grave within her village cemetery. Statistics show that 8.2 percent of the world's children will die in their first year of life. Most will perish from infections, parasitic diseases, diarrhea, and dehydration, made worse by malnutrition. Over half of these deaths could be prevented with vaccination programs, clean drinking water, and proper sanitation facilities, but much of the world remains without these basic needs. Making such resources available to the next generation will be costly and difficult, and is unlikely to happen on a wide scale. Safe-water sanitation projects alone, for example, would require at least $50 billion annually for the next decade—sums of money not easily or readily acquired.

Face-to-face with a new generation. This grandparent will see to it that new members of her lineage appreciate the Wodaabe proverb "A couple without children is like a tree without fruit, and will be alone until death." Wodaabe children are not only a link between past and present, they also are a resource for the future. As they grow they will learn to herd their fathers' camels, raise families of their own, care for their aged parents, and adjust to the demands of an ever-changing world.

This family has no way of knowing how radiation from Chernobyl will affect them. Concerned for the long-term well-being of their children and future generations, Germans have formed the most active anti-nuclear movement in Europe. Central to their protests is the placement of nuclear missiles, the danger of nuclear wastes, and the threat of malfunctions in nearby nuclear power plants.

This 15-year-old is a statistic: she is among 1 out of every 10 American teenagers who becomes pregnant. This is double the number of teen pregnancies in England, France, or Canada, and triple the number in Sweden. Adolescent pregnancies are on the rise. For teenagers, the responsibility of parenthood undermines educational and economic opportunities. In America, for example, only 50 percent of teen mothers will graduate from high school, and most will earn half the lifetime income of women who begin having children at a later age.

This child was to have been protected by the 1949 Universal Declaration of Human Rights, the Geneva Protocols of 1977, and the U.N. General Assembly. Yet the majority of victims in warfare today are children. Most child fatalities are the result of attacks on cities and villages, but increasingly there are reports of children being singled out for injury and death. The death of a child may rob a family or entire group of part of its future.

This child is a refugee. There are hundreds of thousands like him. The longer children remain unsettled, the more problems they have adjusting to a new home. In Southeast Asia, since the end of the IndoChinese War, an entire generation has come of age in refugee camps. Many are Cambodian children. Their worldview as adults will be shaped more by camp life than by the knowledge and traditions that might have been passed on to them through their families.

VICTOR ENGLEBERT.
ETHIOPIA

LUCINDA LEACH.
BANGLADESH

MARY ELLEN MARK/
ARCHIVE.
ETHIOPIA

KEVIN BUBRISKI.
BANGLADESH

For the last five years, 168 of every 1,000 Ethiopian infants have died before reaching their first birthday. Drought, accompanied by deforestation, has caused millions of people to migrate in search of food. Famine has been rampant, and the lack of adequate support services through which resources might have been distributed has taken its toll, especially on children. In this and other crises, political decisions often play as large a role as environmental factors in determining how many will survive. Death rates are declining. But whether or not the next generation will experience full recovery depends on peoples' access to reliable ground water supplies, reforestation programs, soil protection, and food assistance.

This child does not have enough to eat. Food production in Bangladesh has fallen behind population growth. Farmers lack seeds, capital, irrigation, and the means to control erosion. Yet here, as in many parts of the world, prices for food products are controlled to protect the urban middle class. The result in Bangladesh: three-quarters of all children suffer malnutrition. Changing this condition will not be easy. Until agricultural reforms and new water systems are made available, severe food shortages will continue to stunt the development of young bodies and minds.

ACKNOWLEDGMENTS

Generations is about birth and infancy, about tiny, utterly dependent human beings who inspire among people everywhere large and complex expectations and concerns. Commensurate with the magnitude of thoughts and feelings that surround a new arrival, *Generations* involved the minds and talents of hundreds of individuals.

Birth and beginnings, subjects well suited to an exhibition inaugurating the Smithsonian's International Gallery, were first suggested by Peggy Loar during her tenure as director of the Smithsonian's Traveling Exhibition Service (SITES). In the rituals and artifacts associated with creation accounts, fertility, and infancy, Loar recognized a unique opportunity to explore not only the rich diversity of life-cycle events around the world, but also the changing character of cultural traditions past and present. She brought her vision and enthusiasm for such an exhibition to her Smithsonian colleagues in charge of the International Center, John Reinhardt and Gretchen Ellsworth, who appreciated immediately the value of an inaugural program that combined multicultural perspectives with fundamental, universal human concerns.

Loar and Reinhardt envisioned an exhibition project that would tap not only the collections, but also the scholarly resources of the Smithsonian's many divisions in the arts, humanities, and social and natural sciences. They urged us to develop the curatorial content of *Generations* in consultation with Smithsonian curators of anthropology, art history, folklore, ethnography, and social and medical history. The expertise, insight, and sensitivity that these individuals, named earlier in this book on page 14, brought to the project—as well as the multidisciplinary, cooperative planning approach they provided—ensured that *Generations* fully represented the intricate mosaic of cultural life surrounding birth.

The Smithsonian is a rich repository of artifacts used in traditional birth rituals and early child-rearing. Yet locating and cataloging the best examples of these small-sized treasures from among collections numbering in the hundreds of thousands are formidable tasks. We are especially grateful to Valerie Fletcher, Douglas J. Robinson, and Phyllis Rosenzweig of the Hirshhorn Museum and Sculpture Garden; Andrea Nicolls, Louise

Trush, and Sylvia Williams of the National Museum of African Art; Eleanor Boyne, Chris Cameron, Mark Dreyfuss, Shelly Foote, Ann Golovin, Mike Harris, Ramunas Kondratas, Martha Morris, Stacey Otte, Nancy Ravanel, Rodris Roth, and Ellen Wells of the National Museum of American History; Kathleen Baxter, Sadie Boone, Joseph Brown, Susan Crawford, Catherine Creek, Linda Eisenhart, Paula Fleming, Natalie Firnhaber, Candace Greene, Margaret Greene, Jeanne Mahoney, Felicia Pickering, James Rubenstein, Margaret Santiago, Ruth Saunders, Vyrtis Thomas, Alice Thomson, Jane Walsh, and Deborah Wood of the National Museum of Natural History; and Richard Derbyshire, formerly of the Smithsonian's Office of Folklife Programs, for leading us to artifacts that would bring to life complicated concepts, and for attending to the myriad details required to make these objects available for public viewing.

Just as the Smithsonian takes pride in sharing its resources with others, so too do we benefit from collections and research scholarship elsewhere. Many hallmark examples of birth-related artifacts reside in private collections and museums throughout the world. Each of the lenders to *Generations* are cited on page 15 in this book. The generosity of these individuals and institutions has enriched the exhibition beyond measure, and in doing so has facilitated one of the largest international, historical surveys of imagery related to birth and infancy ever mounted.

Among the many people to whom we are indebted for participating in securing loans from collectors and museums are Belinda Kaye and Laurel Kendall of the American Museum of Natural History in New York; Terese Bartholomew and Jack Foss of the Asian Art Museum of San Francisco; Linda Altshuler of the B'nai B'rith Klutznick Museum in Washington, D.C.; Daniel Barrett, Ellen MacNamara, and Judith Swaddling of The British Museum in London; G.S.T. Cavanagh of the Trent Collection in the History of Medicine at the Duke University Medical Center Library; Ted Celenko of The Harrison Eiteljorg Collection in Indianapolis; Nancy Berman of the Hebrew Union College Skirball Museum in Los Angeles; Adriana Calinescu and Terry Harley-Wilson of the Indiana University Art Museum, Bloomington; Donna Elliott of the Library of Congress, Washington, D.C.; John

J. Hermann, Jr., of the Museum of Fine Arts in Boston; Charlene Cerny and Donna Pierce of the Museum of International Folk Art in Santa Fe; Dieter Eisleb, Gerd Hopfner, and Bruno Timm of the Museum für Völkerkunde in Berlin; Dorothy Hanks, Lucinda Keister, Elizabeth Tunis, and John Parascandola at the National Library of Medicine in Bethesda; Ha Hyo Kil of The National Museum of Korea in Seoul; Lucia LaVilla-Havelin of Pace Primitive in New York; Susan Bean and Lucy Butler of the Peabody Museum in Salem; Nancy Baxter of the Philadelphia Museum of Art; Lawrence R. Pizer of the Pilgrim Society in Plymouth; Charles E. Green and James Weinberger of the Princeton University Library; Tim Boon, Ghislaine M. Lawrence, and Andrew Mackay of The Wellcome Museum for the History of Medicine in London; Richard A. Born and John Carswell of The David and Alfred Smart Gallery at The University of Chicago; Judy E. Emerson, Lynne Poirier, Melissa Morgan Radthe, Deborah Smith, Mary Lynn Stevens-Heininger, and Patricia Tice of The Margaret Woodbury Strong Museum in Rochester; and Carol Bier, Stella Kao, Julie Link Haifley, and Anne Rowe of The Textile Museum in Washington, D.C. Special mention must be made of Nora Fisher, Curator of Textiles at Santa Fe's Museum of International Folk Art, Gordon E. Mestler of the State University of New York's Health Sciences Center in Brooklyn, and Lorraine Ward of London's Wellcome Museum for the History of Medicine, who worked tirelessly to provide research information and advice in selecting artifacts especially pertinent to our educational aims.

Birth and infancy are universal milestones. Yet, in every time and place, people welcome the newborn with celebrations and ritual practices that are culturally distinct. Repeatedly we found ourselves amazed by the enormous range and subtle nuances of cultural responses to new generations. In order to maintain the unique integrity of every culture examined in the exhibition—without losing sight of the human family's interrelatedness—we relied on careful analysis and feedback from selected scholars and educators. We are especially grateful to Judy U. Aaronson, Frederica Adelman, Catherine Allen, David and Linda Altshuler, Ann Anagnost, Joallyn Archambault, Clinton Bailey, Ann Bay, Gus van Beek, Dan Bosko, Alan Boyd, Marie Brown, Magali Carrera, Shirley Cherkasky, Jason Clay,

Angelo and Miriam Cohn, Harold Courlander, William Crocker, Claire Cuddy, Wilton Dillon, Christopher Donnan, James Early, Victoria Ebin, John C. Ewers, Rachel Field, William Fitzhugh, Margery Gordon, Chang-Su Houchins, Dorothea Houston, Harry Jackson, Brigitte Jordan, Adrienne Kaeppler, Natalie Kanten, Flora Kaplan, Trudi Kawami, Barbara Kirschenblatt-Gimblett, Jill Korbin, Carol Laderman, Robert M. Laughlin, David Maybury-Lewis, Carol MacCormack, Carol McClain, Laura McKie, Elizabeth Meggers, William Merrill, Jonathan Moreno, Paul Reisman, Kate and Ralph Rinzler, Alan Schapiro, Ruth O. Selig, Roy Sieber, Leon Siroto, and Susan Willens.

Generations includes nearly 300 artifacts from 90 different cultures. Every one of the objects, however small, holds a detailed history, purpose, and meaning. The task of illuminating these rich and varied stories was carried out with intelligence and dedication by 14 research scholars, cited on page 14 in this book. We extend our deepest thanks in particular to Leonard Bruno, Senior Science Specialist at the Library of Congress. The breadth and depth of Dr. Bruno's knowledge in matters that bridge culture and the natural sciences made him an invaluable resource for research and ideas.

Artifact research often led to obscure, yet important, information that generated yet further questions. Many gave generously of their time and expertise to help us find the answers. Here we would like to acknowledge Lisa Aronson, Laurie Baty, Neal Ben Ezra, Barry Brkic, Karen Calvert, Deborah Caro, Linda Castellanos-Russo, Margaret Coughlin, Spencer Crew, Peter David, Mary Kay Davies, John Flechner, Frances Fralin, Bela Ganguli, Ned Gilhooly, James Glenn, Susan Glenn, William Guth, David Haberstich, Wayland Hand, Marian Kaulaity Hansson, Sara Hernandez, Beth Howard, Marjorie Hunt, Zuhair Imadi, Lily Kecskes, Fred Lamp, Mary Lawrence, Judith Luskey, Margaret Ellen Mayo, James G. Mead, Caroline Morris, Sally Peterson, Enayetur Rahim, Didi Ratman, Richard S. Reed, Susan Rich, Betty Rodgers, Mary Sams, Ratik W.R. Soemarko, Gail Solomon, Sorena Sorensen, Janet Stanley, Frances Tally, Cem Tarhan, Dickran Tashjian, Betty Ann Twigg, and Roger Wieck.

Artifacts are only one form of cultural expression. Equally valuable information may be gleaned from a people's musical heritage and traditional lore. *Generations* includes poems, incantations, songs, and blessings that prescribe assurances for fertility and welcome the newborn into a community and way of life. The exhibition would not be richly endowed with such ethnographic materials were it not for the Archive of American Folk Medicine, the Archive of Folk Culture at the Library of Congress, Archives of Traditional Music in Bloomington, Indiana, Alan Boyd, the Center for the Study of Southern Culture at the University of Mississippi, Harold Courlander, Folkways, National Public Radio, and John Tyler of the Smithsonian Office of Telecommunications.

Generations needed to span time as well as space. Historical issues associated with birth and infancy could be explained effectively through artifacts and ethnographic music and writings. But the emotional character and contemporary, sociopolitical context of birth and child-rearing needed to be presented through photographs. Over a year of photographic research was carried out to arrive at the compelling images included in *Generations*. Initial research efforts were handled ably and admirably by Wanda Bubriski, and numerous photographic agencies and archives made materials available to us throughout the planning stages. We would like to thank especially Nancy S. DeVore at Anthro-Photo, Terry Barbero and Ann Schneider at Archive Pictures, L'Association des Amis de J.H. Lartigue, Michael Hersh and Yukiko Launois at Black Star, Carol Haggerty at Camera Press, the Center for Documentary Photography, Harry N. Abrams Publishers, International Center for Photography in New York, Life Picture Service, Elizabeth Gallen at Magnum, Barbara Shattuck at National Geographic Society, Sue Brisk at Sipa, *Stern* magazine, Stock Boston, Dallas Chang at Sygma, UNICEF, Cindy Meyer at Woodfin Camp and Associates (Washington, D.C.), Midge Keator at Woodfin Camp and Associates (New York), and Wide World Photos.

Individual photographers too came forth with generous offerings of time, technical assistance, and remarkable images. Suzanne Arms, Carol Beckwith, Thomas Bergman, Erna Beumers, Kevin Bubriski, Larry Clark, Mimi Cotter, Alexandra Dor-ner, Victor Englebert, Hella Hammid, Erik Hesmerg, Ken Heyman, N. Jay Jaffee, Camilla Jessel, Mary

Kalergis, Michael Katakis, Danny and Laurie Lehman, Arthur and Mimi Leipzig, Yan Morvan, Jim Richardson, Dave Sidaway, Vlastja Simončič and Suzanne Szasz gave *Generations* its human dimension, a lens through which our museum visitors would be able to see themselves in others. Jeffrey MacMillan deserves special mention for providing to the project not only his own work, but also much of the guidance that determined our photographic selections.

Generations involved pressing social concerns affecting populations now and into the future. Numerous individuals and institutions offered critical assistance in identifying and interpreting biological data, and statistics and international policy reports about the state of our world. Our deep appreciation goes to the American College of Nurse-Midwives, the Public Health Service Centers for Disease Control, the Children's Defense Fund, Cultural Survival, Judy Frater, the Fertility Center of Washington, Elizabeth Hudson, Johannes Linn, the March of Dimes, Cheryl D. Hayes and David Goslin at the National Academy of Sciences, the National Institute of Child Health and Human Development, the Population Crisis Committee, the Population Reference Bureau, Inc., Malcolm Potts, Susan Rich, Gideon Strassmann, Alan Trouson, UNICEF, Worldwatch Institute, and Xiangying Wang.

Words and images convey information, though not always in a way that entices people to learn. The desire to absorb and appreciate often is determined by the success of specially created environments or programs to stimulate and inspire. Chris White designed the *Generations* exhibition, Michael Baumbruck its audiovisual program, and Judy Kirpich, this book. Mark Gulezian and Alex Jamison did the studio photographs of artifacts that are interspersed with the essays on earlier pages. Each of these individuals is immensely talented, and the fruits of their respective tasks have enriched the visual and educational dynamic of this entire project.

The film programs that accompany the exhibition explore further the many expectations, fears, joys, and hopes that people everywhere have for new generations. Over 100 documentary films and videotapes were screened in order to select those that best illuminate the themes of *Generations*. Our deep appreciation goes to Jonathan Stack for his expertise and enthusiasm in guiding our research efforts and to the many filmmakers and agencies who made materials available to us during the planning stages. Special thanks goes also to Alicia Francis, Barbara Melosh, Deborah Rothberg, Wendy Shay, and Florence Stone for the many hours they contributed to planning these programs.

Our colleagues at the Smithsonian's Office of Exhibits Central provided an incalculable amount of technical assistance, including the delicate mount-making and art-handling needed to install the artifacts in *Generations*. We extend our sincere gratitude to Karen Fort, Bruce Hough, Rick Kilday, Marian Menzel, James Reuter, Paul Rhymer, Benjamin Snouffer, Walter Sorrell, and Rick Yamada. Equally crucial roles related to the production of *Generations* were fulfilled by individuals in the Smithsonian's Office of Design and Construction. Laura Hoing and William Thomas supervised all aspects of the design process, and Gary Brenner saw to it that a difficult, stringent production schedule went forth smoothly and carefully. George Bottner, superintendent for Associated Builders, Inc., orchestrated construction activities in the new International Gallery with his usual skill and efficiency. Laurie McCarriar of McCarriar Graphics ensured that exhibit text would be graceful and at the same time highly readable.

SITES is the machinery that fueled *Generations*. The sheer volume of details required to implement an international loan exhibition is too large, and the individual tasks too many to recount here. Linda Bell and her predecessor Antonio Diez, Martha Cappelletti, Kenneth Fenty, Claire Fronville, Laurie May, Eileen Rose, Myriam Springuel, and Allegra Wright participated at every stage of the *Generations* project.

The gathering of 300 artifacts from 45 lenders is an awesome task that involves clockwork organization to arrange for conservation, crate-building, packing, shipping, insurance, and the constant monitoring of fragile, valuable items. Fredric P. Williams supervised every one of these activities superbly in his capacity as Registrar for *Generations*. SITES' Head Registrar, Lee Williams, her predecessor Mary Jane Clark, and the SITES registrarial staff—Carol Farra, Linda Karsteter, Barbara Irwin, and Viki Possoff—handled innumerable details without a glitch.

Many aspects of public exhibitions involve work that public audiences in fact never see. Yet certain administrative components of museum programs—financial organization, contract negotiations, procurement procedures, to name but a few of the tasks—are fundamental to the success of the final product. *Generations* benefited enormously from diligent, astute financial analysis and monitoring carried out by Margaret Anderson at the Smithsonian. Contracting officers John Cobert and Robert Perkins handled complex negotiations on our behalf. Helen Donaldson and George Zumpf always gave unfailingly prompt attention to our myriad contract requests. Walter Dorritie handled the majority of purchase order transactions for *Generations*. Matters concerning gallery operations and public safety and security were ably managed by Jay Chambers, Frank Gilmore, Ronald Hawkins, William Lassiter, Robert Mealo, Bart Rinehardt, Michael Sofield, Andrew Wilson, and Robert Wilson. SITES' Public Relations Director, Dee Bennett, along with the Smithsonian's Office of Public Affairs' Ingrid Mendelsohn and Linda St. Thomas, prepared comprehensive media information. Richard Conroy, Brian LeMay, and Kennedy Schmertz saw to it that communication with foreign embassies and colleagues proceeded smoothly and expeditiously. Manjula Kumar, Jeffrey LaRiche, and Barbara Spraggins missed not a single detail in planning opening activities.

We created this book to capture the spirit of *Generations* by presenting contemporary and sometimes controversial interpretations of its themes within the context of artifacts and photographs on exhibition. During the early planning stages, Margaret Carlson, Carol Levine, and Ann Hulbert were especially helpful with advice that ultimately shaped our editorial objectives. We are equally grateful to the many writers who provided new articles, often with provocative viewpoints of birth and child-rearing. Publishers, agents, and authors of previously published materials, acknowledged on page 316, were generous with their suggestions, approvals, and administrative time. Wendy Wolf, Senior Editor at Pantheon Books, recognized early on the potential of an international audience for the images and ideas expressed in *Generations: A Universal Family Album*. We extend to her our deepest gratitude for ensuring that the content of our inaugural exhibition project would reach not only Smithsonian museum-goers, but also everyone interested in children and the larger human scheme into which they are born. ■

Generations Exhibition Staff
September 1987

NOTES

CURIOSITY AND MYSTERY

EXPLAINING THE MYSTERY OF CONCEPTION
1. Annette B. Weiner, *Women of Value, Men of Renown.* Austin: University of Texas Press, 1976.

2. Carol Laderman, *Wives and Mothers: Childbirth and Nutrition in Rural Malaysia.* Berkeley: University of California Press, 1983.

3. Mark Nichter and Mimi Nichter, "Cultural Notions of Fertility in South Asia and Their Impact on Sri Lankan Family Planning Practices." *Human Organization* 46, no. 1: pp. 18-28.

4. Yolanda Murphy and Robert F. Murphy, *Women of the Forest.* New York: Columbia University Press, 1974.

5. Ann W. Turner, *Rituals of Birth.* New York: David McKay Company, 1978.

6. Jane Richardson Hanks, *Maternity and Its Rituals in Bang Chan.* Ithaca, N.Y.: Cornell University Thailand Project, 1963.

7. Ashley Montagu, *Coming Into Being Among the Australian Aborigines.* London: Routledge and Kegan Paul, 1974.

CONCEPTION IN INDIA
1. Rajasthani folk song recorded by Dan Detha. Translated by Pria Devi.

INTENT

Old Wives' Tales, (pp. 72, 73, 90, and 91)
Archive of American Folk Medicine, Center for the Study of Comparative Folklore and Mythology. Los Angeles: University of California, Los Angeles.

THE CHILD IN INDIA
1. See D.D. Kosambi, *The Culture and Civilization of Ancient India in Historical Outline.* New Delhi: Vikas, 1970, p. 16.

2. *Adi Parva,* vol. 1 of *The Mahabharata.* Translated by M.M. Dutta. Calcutta: Oriental Publishing Co., n.d., pp. 107-8.

3. Ibid., p. 510.

4. Kālidāsa, *Raghuvamsha* 3: pp. 45-46. Translated by Sudhir Kakar.

5. See, for example, M. Cormack, *The Hindu Woman.* Bombay: Asia Publishing House, 1961, p. 11; S.C. Dube, *Indian Village.* New York: Harper and Row, 1967, pp. 148-49; T.N. Madan, *Family and Kinship.* Bombay: Asia Publishing House, 1965, p. 77; L. Minturn and J.T. Hitchcock, "The Rajputs of Khalapur, India," in B.B. Whiting, ed., *Six Cultures: Studies of Child-Rearing.* New York: John Wiley, 1963, p. 307-8. See also William J. Goode, *World Revolution and Family Patterns.* New York: The Free Press, 1963, pp. 235-36; D.G. Mandelbaum, *Society in India,* vol. 1. Berkeley:

University of California Press, 1970, p. 120. Cases of postpartum depression, for example, are much more commonly reported among mothers who give birth to a daughter than among those who have a son. See M.R. Gaitonde, "Cross-Cultural Study of the Psychiatric Syndromes in Out-Patient Clinics in Bombay, India, and Topeka, Kansas." *International Journal of Social Psychiatry* 4 (1958): p. 103.

6. Oscar Lewis, *Village Life in Northern India.* New York: Vintage Books, 1958, p. 195.

7. Irawati Karve, *Kinship Organization in India.* Bombay: Asia Publishing House, 1968, p. 206.

TRAVAIL

GRANDMA WAS A MIDWIFE
1. During the 19th century and a good part of the 20th, most Texas women— Native American, Hispanic, black, and anglo—delivered their babies with the help of midwives. Midwifery has always been, and still is, legal in Texas.

2. Mrs. Hunt: "Those people down there cooked bread, cooked that bread, and Grandma'd bring bread home and we was there to gobble it up. We loved it. We called it light bread. Now what the 'light' means, I don't know. They'd make [mash] this stuff up and set it, it would rise up easy and rise up and you make it down again and after awhile you put it in your pan and put it in the stove. That loaf bread was called light bread."

WELCOMINGS

Song Sung by a Woman While Giving Birth (p. 146)
Quoted in Willard R. Trask, *The Unwritten Song,* vol. 1. London: Jonathan Cape, 1969, p. 65.

Chants, Poems, and Lullabyes
p. 155: "It's my fat baby..." quoted in Trask, *The Unwritten Song,* p. 4.

p. 155: "The little girl will pick wild roses..." quoted in Jerome Rothberg, *Shaking the Pumpkin: Traditional Poetry of the Indian North Americas.* Garden City, N.Y.: Doubleday, 1972. p. 164.

p. 159: "So how shall we name you, little one?..." quoted in Trask, *The Unwritten Song,* p. 105.

p. 168: "Sleep my son,..." from *Lullabies of the World.* Washington, D.C.: Smithsonian Institution/Folkways Records, FE 4511. From liner notes.

p. 169: "Sleep, sleep..." from *Lullabies of the World.* Folkways Records, FE 4511.

p. 169: "I have made a baby board for you daughter…" quoted in Dorothea Leighton and Clyde Kluckhohn, *Children of the People.* New York: Octagon Books, 1969, p. 21.

p. 169: "You son of a clear-eyed mother…" quoted in Trask, *The Unwritten Song,* p. 77.

ROCK-A-BYE BABY…

1. Leslie Daiken, *The Lullaby Book.* London: Adlard and Son, 1959, p. 19.

2. Tran Quang Hai and Hoang Mong Thuy, *Musiques du Vietnam: Tradition du sud.* Paris: Societe Francaise de Productions (dist.), Anthology de la Musique Peuples, AMP 62903. From liner notes.

3. *Old Mother Hippletoe: Rural and Urban Children's Songs.* New York: The Recorded Anthology of American Music, Inc., New World Records, NW 291. From liner notes.

4. *Music of the Indians of Panama.* Translated by Diomedes Acosta. Washington, D.C.: Smithsonian Institution/Folkways Records, FE 4326. From liner notes.

5. Bess Lomax Hawes describes the use of these songs as lullabyes in "Folksongs and Function: Some Thoughts on the American Lullaby." *Journal of American Folklore* 87, pp. 140-48.

LIFELINES

CRADLES AND CRIBS

1. Robert B. Ekvall, *Fields on the Hoof.* New York: Holt, Rinehart and Winston, 1968, p. 86.

2. Quoted in Penelope Eames, *Furniture in England, France and the Netherlands from the 12th to the 15th Century.* London: The Furniture History Society, 1977.

3. Catholic University of America, *New Catholic Encyclopedia,* 4th ed. New York: McGraw-Hill, 1968, pp. 447-48.

4. Philippe Aries, *Centuries of Childhood.* New York: Knopf, 1962.

THE DIETA: POSTPARTUM SECLUSION IN THE ANDES OF ECUADOR

1. For a description of the dieta practiced by Amerindians in Imbabura Province, see E.C. Parsons, *Peguche: A Study of Andean Indians.* Chicago: University of Chicago Press, 1945.

2. Lauris McKee, "Los Cuerpos Tiernos: Simbolismo y Magia en las Practicas Post-Parto en Ecuador." *America Indigena* 62, no. 4 (1984): pp. 615-28.

3. G.F. Foster, "The Concept of 'Neutral' in Humoral Medical Systems." *Medical Anthropology* 8, no. 3 (1984): pp. 180-94; M. Logan, "Humoral Medicine in Guatemala and Peasant Acceptance of Modern Medicine," *in*

M.H. Logan and E.E. Hunt, eds., *Health and the Human Condition.* North Scituate, Ma.: Duxbury Press, 1978.

4. G.F. Foster, ibid.

5. Leviticus 12.

6. *The Penitential of Archbishop Theodore of Canterbury,* A.D. 668-90; J.T. McNeil and H.M. Gamer, *Medieval Handbooks of Penance.* New York, 1938, pp. 85-86; M. Douglas, *Purity and Danger.* Harmondsworth, Middlesex, England: Penguin Books, 1966, p. 76.

7. C. Ember and M. Ember, "Psychosexual Predictors of the Gender of Objective Nouns in French: An Exploratory Study." *Ethos* 7, no. 1: pp. 51-67.

8. Garcilaso de la Vega, *Royal Commentaries of the Incas and General History of Peru,* part 1. Translated by Harold Livermore. Austin: University of Texas Press, 1966, p. 213.

9. M. Richards and J. Bernal, "An Observational Study of Mother-Infant Interaction," *in* N. Blurton-Jones, ed., *Ethological Studies of Child Behavior.* Cambridge, England: Cambridge University Press, 1972, p. 176.

REALITIES

TEENAGE PREGNANCY: AN EPIDEMIC TAKES ITS TOLL

1. For teen pregnancy data by race, age, and state, see the following Children's Defense Fund publications: *Maternal and Child Health Care Data Book: The Health of America's Children* (1986), *Preventing Children Having Children: What You Can Do* (1985), and *Adolescent Pregnancy: Whose Problem Is It?* (1986).

2. Elise Jones et al., "Teenage Pregnancy in Developed Countries: Determinants and Policy Implications." *Family Planning Perspectives* 17, no. 2 (March-April 1985).

3. Among never-married black women age 18 to 24, the highest number of children ever born per 1,000 women, and the lowest percent childless, are in the South, where the smallest percent of the black population lives in central cities. U.S. Bureau of the Census, Current Population Report, series P-20, no. 401, "Fertility of American Women: June 1984," table 2 (Washington, D.C.: Government Printing Office, 1985). Older data show birthrates among black women aged 18 to 34 in nonmetropolitan areas at 1,689 births to date per 1,000 women, while the comparable rate in central cities was 1,535 births to date per 1,000 women. U.S. Bureau of the Census, Current Population Report, series P-20, no. 387, "Fertility of American Women: June 1982," table 2 (Washington, D.C.: Government Printing Office, 1984).

TEXT COPYRIGHT ACKNOWLEDGMENTS

GENERATIONS

Prepared by the
Smithsonian Institution Traveling
Exhibition Service

Andrea Price Stevens,
Publications Director

Text edited by
David B. Andrews, SITES

Designed by
Grafik Communications Ltd.,
Alexandria, Virginia:
Judy Kirpich,
Beth Brownlee Bathe,
and Pamela Page

Studio photography by
QuickSilver Photographers,
Alexandria, Virginia:
Mark Gulezian
and Alex Jamison

Calligraphy by
Julian Waters

Typeset in ITC Berkeley Book
by Type Studio, Ltd.,
Alexandria, Virginia

Printed on
Productolith Dullcoat
and Artemis Radiant Text
by Princeton Polychrome Press,
Princeton, New Jersey

Exhibition design by
Chris White
Design Associates,
Severna Park, Maryland

ANNA R. COHN is an art historian who is widely known for her expertise in developing exhibitions for museums in the United States and abroad, among them *The Precious Legacy* for the Smithsonian Institution Traveling Exhibition Service. She has published and lectured on art, museology, and material culture. She was director of the B'nai B'rith Klutznick Museum in Washington, D.C., where she has lived for 12 years. Ms. Cohn has a B.A. from the University of Minnesota and an M.A. from Williams College-Clark Art Institute Graduate Program in the History of Art.

LUCINDA A. LEACH is a museum consultant who specializes in anthropology, folklife, and photography. Her experience in exhibition research and museum education includes work at the Boston Children's Museum, Sculpture Placement in Washington, D.C., and the Smithsonian Institution. Ms. Leach has degrees in anthropology from Dartmouth College and George Washington University. She lives with her husband, photographer Jeffrey MacMillan, in Takoma Park, Maryland.

SHEILA KITZINGER is internationally recognized as a leading authority on pregnancy, childbirth, and women's health. Trained as a social anthropologist, Dr. Kitzinger lectures and writes extensively on these subjects. Among her books are *Experience of Childbirth, Birth at Home,* and *Birth Over 30.* Dr. Kitzinger is the mother of five and lives in England.